DECONSTRUCTING
THE BIBLE

This book represents the first attempt by a single author to place the great Spanish Jewish Hebrew Bible exegete, grammarian, philosopher, poet, astronomer, astrologer and scientist, Abraham ibn Ezra, (1089–1164) in his complete contextual environment. It charts his unusual travels and discusses changes and contradictions in his hermeneutic approach, analysing his vision of the future for the Jewish people in the Christian north of Europe, rather than Muslim Spain. It also examines his influence on subsequent Jewish thought, as well as his place in the wider hermeneutic debate.

The book contains a new translation of ibn Ezra's *Introduction to the Torah*, written in Lucca, northern Italy, together with a full commentary.

Irene Lancaster is Fellow in Jewish Studies at the Centre for Jewish Studies, Department of Religions and Theology, Manchester University, where she teaches Jewish political, social, religious and cultural history. She is particularly interested in the relationship between mediaeval Jewish philosophical and hermeneutic trends and contemporary literary textual approaches.

DECONSTRUCTING THE BIBLE

Abraham ibn Ezra's *Introduction to the Torah*

Irene Lancaster

RoutledgeCurzon
Taylor & Francis Group

First published in 2003
by RoutledgeCurzon
11 New Fetter Lane, London EC4P 4EE

Simultaneously published in the USA and Canada
by RoutledgeCurzon
29 West 35th Street, New York, NY 10001

RoutledgeCurzon is an imprint of the Taylor & Francis Group

© 2003 Irene Lancaster

Typeset in Sabon by LaserScript Ltd, Mitcham, Surrey

Printed and bound in Great Britain by
Antony Rowe Ltd, Chippenham, Wiltshire

British Library Cataloguing in Publication Data
A catalogue record of this book is available from the British Library

Library of Congress Cataloging in Publication Data
A catalog record for this book has been requested

ISBN 0–7007–1574–6

To my daughters, Kalela and Esther.

For more is not reserved
To man, with soul just nerved
To act to-morrow what he learns today
(Robert Browning, 'Rabbi Ben Ezra': XVIII)

CONTENTS

CONTENTS

ACKNOWLEDGEMENTS

There are many people without whom this book would not have seen the light of day. Firstly, I should like to thank Ruth Ghadiali, my marvellous neighbour in the Liverpool days, who kept open house for my younger daughter, Esther, when I started the research. I owe a great deal to Noel Boaden, who knew I had it in me. I must thank Roland Goetschel for introducing me so many years ago to Moshe Idel. It was Moshe who gave me the idea. Oliver Leaman was most encouraging. Emanuel Silver and Jonathan Broido read the translation and made many useful suggestions. In addition, Emanuel shared his expertise in manuscripts and editions, whereas Jonathan explained some of the mediaeval mathematics and science. Paul Marshall read through the typescript at an early stage and made pertinent comments about chapter lay-out. My father-in-law, Gabriel, made some helpful stylistic suggestions.

To my husband Les, I owe nearly thirty years of heated and lively debate. I have gained from his profound knowledge of the newish psychological fields of transpersonal and consciousness studies. Here he has blazed an ibn Ezra-like trail by being the first scientific psychologist to bring a thoroughly Jewish flavour to what was thought for so long to be a uniquely Buddhist domain.

However, the greatest debt of all I owe to my late parents: to my mother for giving me my love of languages; to my father for teaching me how to argue; and, most of all, to both for surviving the Holocaust.

A NOTE ON TERMINOLOGY

Torah

Stemming from a Hebrew word meaning 'teaching', Torah is the term most often used in Jewish traditional circles to refer to the Hebrew Bible, as well as to the process and result of studying it. In addition, Torah refers specifically to the first five books of the Hebrew Bible, known in non-Jewish circles as the Pentateuch. Gradually, the term came to include the study of the Hebrew Bible ('Written' Torah) by means of authorised interpretations, known as 'Oral Torah' (later written down). Such interpretations include the Mishnah, Talmud and midrash, which became the traditionally accepted commentaries on the 'Written Torah'. Eventually, 'Torah learning' implied the detailed knowledge of oral interpretations of scripture, rather than knowledge of scripture *per se*. Nowadays, the term 'Torah-true' refers to someone who acknowledges the authorised interpreters of scripture, rather than someone who knows the scriptural text.

Halakhah

Stemming from a Hebrew word meaning 'to go', halakhah is the theory and practice of Jewish law, based in biblical teachings as interpreted by the rabbinic authorities.

Tenakh

The Hebrew Bible itself is popularly called *Tenakh*. The word is an acronym from three Hebrew words, referring respectively to the Pentateuch, the Prophets and other 'Writings'. I sometimes also use the terms 'scripture' or 'biblical text', when referring to the Hebrew Bible as an organ of exegesis.

'Rabbis' and traditionalists

The general terms 'rabbis' and 'traditionalists' refer to those Jews who regard the Oral Torah as equivalent in sanctity and importance to the Written Torah. I use the term 'Orthodox' only when referring to a particular Jewish trend within modernity. It would be anachronistic, as well as misleading, to use modern terminology when referring to the classical and mediaeval periods. The term 'Rabbanites' refers to the traditionalist advocates of Oral Torah, who opposed sectarians, such as the Karaites. It is important to bear in mind that the 'traditionalists' were often radical and non-literal in both social and exegetical matters, whereas secessionists could be conservative.

'Islam', 'Muslim' and 'Arabic'

I use the term 'Arabic' to refer to a specific language. The terms 'Islam' and 'Muslim' thus refer not only to the religion of Allah, but also to a specific culture.

'Sephardi' and 'Ashkenazi'

These terms refer to the culture of the Jews living under the domains of Islam and Christianity respectively.

Dating

I use the traditionally accepted non-denominational terms CE (the Common Era) and BCE (before the Common Era).

Transliterations and translations

Transliteration in Arabic follow Fakhry 1983, without diacriticals. Hebrew transliterations follow general custom and usage. Unless otherwise stated, all translations from Hebrew, French, German and Spanish are my own.

The travels of Abraham ibn Ezra: an intellectual journey (1089–1164)

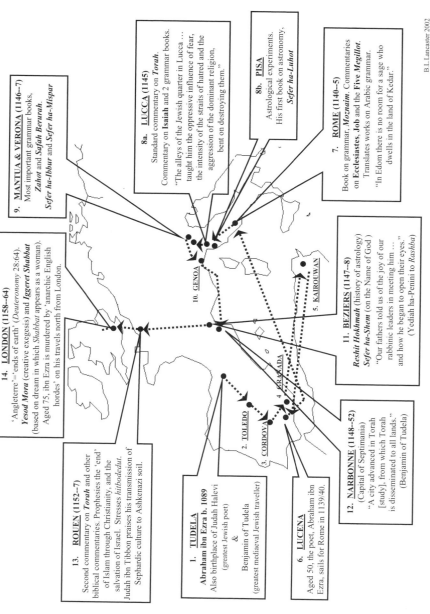

14. LONDON (1158–64)
'Angleterre'='ends of earth' (*Deuteronomy* 28:64).
Yesod Mora (creative exegesis) and *Iggeret Shabbat*
(based on dream in which *Shabbat* appears as a woman).
Aged 75, ibn Ezra is murdered by 'anarchic English
hordes' on his travels north from London.

9. MANTUA & VERONA (1146–7)
Most important grammar books,
Zahot and *Safah Berurah*.
Sefer ha-Ibbur and *Sefer ha-Mispar*

8a. LUCCA (1145)
Standard commentary on *Torah*.
Commentary on **Isaiah** and 2 grammar books.
"The alleys of the Jewish quarter in Lucca …
taught him the oppressive influence of fear,
the intensity of the straits of hatred and the
aggression of the dominant religion,
bent on destroying them."

8b. PISA
Astrological experiments.
His first book on astronomy,
Sefer ha-Luhot

7. ROME (1140–5)
Book on grammar, *Moznaim*. Commentaries
on **Ecclesiastes**, **Job** and the **Five Megillot**.
Translates works on Arabic grammar.
"In Edom there is no room for a sage who
dwells in the land of Kedar."

13. ROUEN (1152–7)
Second commentary on *Torah* and other
biblical commentaries. Prophesies the 'end'
of Islam through Christianity, and the
salvation of Israel. Stresses *hitbodedut*.
Judah ibn Tibbon praises his transmission of
Sephardic culture to Ashkenazi soil.

1. TUDELA
Abraham ibn Ezra b. 1089
Also birthplace of Judah Halevi
(greatest Jewish poet)
&
Benjamin of Tudela
(greatest mediaeval Jewish traveller)

6. LUCENA
Aged 50, the poet, Abraham ibn
Ezra, sails for Rome in 1139/40.

11. BEZIERS (1147–8)
Reshit Hokhmah (history of astrology)
Sefer ha-Shem (on the Name of God)
"Our fathers told us of the joy of our
rabbinic leaders in meeting him …
and how he began to open their eyes."
(Yediah ha-Penini to *Rashba*)

12. NARBONNE (1148–52)
(Capital of Septimania)
"A city advanced in Torah
[study], from which Torah
is disseminated to all lands."
(Benjamin of Tudela)

10. GENOA

5. KAIROUWAN

2. TOLEDO

3. CORDOVA

4 GRANADA

B.L. Lancaster 2002

INTRODUCTION

Ibn Ezra is one of the most complicated of the great Jewish exegetes whose commentaries on the Torah (as Pentateuch) have become part of the Jewish traditional canon. This book sets out to show that one of the difficulties faced by readers in elucidating ibn Ezra's views stems from his multifaceted approach. Ibn Ezra's biblical exegeses are also philosophical investigations, which display an expertise in sciences and mathematics never yet equalled in the genre. Then there is his particular penchant for 'grammar', a term that has also caused problems for all would-be interpreters of ibn Ezra. If we mix all these ingredients together, we end up with a concoction which I have termed 'philosophical grammar', a phrase first coined by the modern philosopher, Wittgenstein. Ibn Ezra's approach is thus neither purely linguistic, nor purely philosophical, nor yet traditional, but involves a heady mix of disciplines. It is impossible to examine his exegesis without also bearing in mind his philosophical views, and vice versa. Too many studies of ibn Ezra have adopted the stance most suited to the academic penchant of the analyst, resulting in an unacceptable one-sidedness in assessments of the man.

My book tries to remedy this lacuna, at least in respect of one of ibn Ezra's major creations, the *Introduction to the Commentary to the Torah*. For the sake of brevity, this title will be shortened to *Introduction to the Torah*, or simply *Introduction*. The book is divided into nine chapters.

The first chapter is a biographical outline of the last period of ibn Ezra's life, when ibn Ezra left his native Spain and travelled through Italy, Provence, northern France and England. The Jews in these countries, for whom ibn Ezra composed his many prose works, were Ashkenazim, most of whom had never encountered the heady mix of grammatically-based exegesis, philosophy and science which ibn Ezra offered them. I detail ibn Ezra's journeys and describe the major prose works he composed in each town he visited. I contrast and compare these different works, especially in relation to the *Introduction*, written relatively early on during his odyssey. I also trace the recurring themes, as well as the developments in ibn Ezra's thought, and record the responses to his work from the different Ashkenazi communities encountered.

The second chapter describes the fascinatingly diverse ways in which ibn Ezra has been received by his various readers. I start with the 'supercommentaries' on his own commentaries, continue with religious reaction, both positive and negative, and end with a short outline of the scholarly work on ibn Ezra. Emphasis is placed on the political context in which views on ibn Ezra have been aired. Assessments are always biased by current fads, which may, of course, lead to misunderstandings and exaggerations. In this chapter I also analyse some of ibn Ezra's terminology and highlight the philosophical side of his exegesis. I demonstrate how ibn Ezra studies have aided general Jewish studies research and helped to provide a platform for dialogue with non-Jewish exegetical and philosophical approaches.

In the third chapter I analyse Jewish approaches to biblical and post-biblical religious literature. In this chapter I also introduce some of the latest theories in hermeneutics. I assess their relevance to ibn Ezra and, more importantly, the relevance of ibn Ezra's approach today.

The fourth chapter constitutes an overview of early Christian approaches to the text, in the light of ibn Ezra's attack on Christianity in *Path Three* of his *Introduction*. I examine reasons for ibn Ezra's attack on Christian allegory at a time when this approach was decreasing in significance in Christian exegesis. This leads to an analysis of the nature of Christian anti-semitism, which ibn Ezra handles with brilliant linguistic panache. Simultaneously, I point out ibn Ezra's fears concerning the over-allegorising tendencies of his own Sephardi co-religionists, which threatened to divide the Jewish community.

The fifth chapter delineates some of the possible major influences on ibn Ezra from Muslim thinkers, mainly through intermediaries such as the Karaites and Ge'onim, which are the subject of the following two chapters. I analyse the extent to which Ezra's exegetical approach resembles Muslim hermeneutics, and how he uses these theories in order to demarcate a unique niche for himself. I also delve into some of the Muslim philosophical views which impacted on his own work. I examine Muslim ideas on 'plain' and 'figurative' interpretations of the sacred text, delineating parallel Jewish developments, and ibn Ezra's place in this scheme. I emphasise ibn Ezra's originality in equating Muslim mediaeval views on memory and the brain with Jewish views on tradition. Lastly, I illustrate ibn Ezra's multi-levelled approach.

The sixth and seventh chapters, which deal with the Karaites and Ge'onim respectively, relate to *Path Two* and *Path One* of the *Introduction*. I contrast ibn Ezra's negative attitude to both groups, as manifested in his *Introductions*, with his positive attitude to individual commentators from each group elsewhere in his oeuvre (mainly in his *Commentaries* on *Exodus*). I give detailed examples of such individual exegeses. I suggest reasons why ibn Ezra adopted such differing attitudes in the two types of literature. I also highlight similarities in style and exegesis between the Karaites and ibn Ezra, and similarities in philosophical and socio–political views between the Ge'onim and ibn Ezra.

The eighth chapter of this book comprises an original translation of the *Introduction* with a commentary following each translation. I hope that by providing the reader with an intellectual background to ibn Ezra's ideas, they will approach this chapter well prepared for some of the succinct, mysterious and sarcastic comments that ooze from every part of his five circular paths.

The fifth path is ibn Ezra's own, and in the ninth, concluding, chapter, I expand on what I mean by 'philosophical grammar'. This chapter looks to the future of hermeneutics, analyses the drawbacks of certain contemporary approaches and suggests the prime role that a revisited ibn Ezra might offer to today's exegetes. If the book has a moral, it must be that prejudice brings negativity in its wake. For too long, we have eschewed the 'objective', historical, rational, scientific and grammatically accurate. Now is perhaps the time to reintroduce some of these spurned approaches, in order to balance the 'sexier' 'midrashic' appeal of the subjective, open-ended, frivolous and circular. I conclude by suggesting that in ibn Ezra's *pshat* approach we have a strong hermeneutic contender for the twenty-first century.

1

THE BIOGRAPHY OF ABRAHAM IBN EZRA

Grow old along with me!
The best is yet to be,
The last of life, for which the first was made:
Our times are in His hand
Who saith "A whole I planned,
Youth shows but half; trust
God: see all nor be afraid"
(Robert Browning, 'Rabbi Ben Ezra': I)

Abraham ibn Ezra is one of the most highly regarded, yet misunderstood, of biblical exegetes. In Jewish tradition his *Commentary on the Torah* is regarded as second only to Rashi's[1] in popularity, and yet he is often underestimated as a mere 'grammarian', or advocate of the 'literal' meaning of the text. This book aims to demonstrate that far from being a 'literalist', ibn Ezra was interested in 'secret meanings'. He also espoused Aristotelianism, and was the first Jewish exegete to posit the conjunction of thinker, thinking and thought as the goal of man's desire to know God.[2] Most importantly, ibn Ezra's curious mix of disparate approaches, which he termed 'grammar', is of relevance in modern hermeneutic debates. This biography presents an overview of ibn Ezra's life, emphasising evidence linking his other writings to the *Introduction*.[3] Brief accounts of the political situation of each place he visited are also included wherever possible.

Abraham ibn Ezra was born in 1089 in Tudela in the northern Spanish province of Navarra.[4] His education was typical for a well-educated Spanish Jew of his time, being rounded and many-faceted. Ibn Ezra would have been immersed from an early age in the study of Jewish sources, including Torah, Hebrew poetry and linguistics, as well as Arabic poetry, linguistics, science and philosophy. It is important to note that ibn Ezra's native language was Arabic, not Hebrew. In 1115, when ibn Ezra was twenty-six years old, Tudela

1

was conquered by the Christians, which affected the status of its Jewish inhabitants.[5]

Very little is known of ibn Ezra's life in Spain, except that he travelled extensively in both Muslim and Christian areas, including Toledo (which had become a Christian stronghold in 1086, three years before his birth), Cordoba and Lucena. He also visited north Africa, a major centre of Jewish studies at this time, passing through Granada. Ibn Ezra was very close to the great poet, Judah Halevi, who was also born in Tudela and who often shared his travels. Other friends included the philosopher, Joseph ibn Zaddik and the poet, Moses ibn Ezra (no relation). During his travels, ibn Ezra encountered many Jewish communities, some harbouring refugees from the fighting between Christians and Muslims.

Much of ibn Ezra's poetic oeuvre was written during this early period, when his main domicile was the Iberian peninsula. Many poems were addressed to his benefactors in these communities, and often refer to the problems encountered by the Jews who found themselves in the midst of the two more powerful religions. It appears that ibn Ezra did not himself witness the Muslim Almohad invasion of the peninsula from North Africa, nor its effect on his older contemporaries, such as Moses ibn Ezra and Halevi. Nevertheless, he was fully aware of all the repercussions such tensions engendered.

In about 1140 we suddenly find ibn Ezra leaving Spain for Rome, and embarking on the 'second period' of his life.[6] He travelled widely through Christian Europe, until the year of his death, 1164. Various reasons have been given for his departure, including the Almohad threat, famine, poverty, marital difficulties, illness and betrayal. There may also have been pressure on ibn Ezra to convert to Islam, which led to his emigration to a Christian country, despite his negative feelings towards Christianity. Another possible reason was the inner urge to educate the Jews of Ashkenazi Europe, whose literary and analytical traditions were different from those of Sephardi Spain and North Africa.[7]

Ibn Ezra in Rome

Ibn Ezra was fifty when he left the Spanish town of Lucena as a well-known poet and philosopher.[8] From there he travelled to Rome 'in a troubled spirit',[9] alone and impoverished. As well as his 'strong pedagogical urge', his fears regarding the impending decline of Spanish Jewry and his desire to safeguard its cultural knowledge led him 'to take upon himself the role of planting her heritage on the living soil of the Jewish communities in Christian Europe.'[10] There, economic necessity forced him to tutor the sons of his wealthy benefactors. He wrote mainly for these students.

Ibn Ezra arrived in Rome shortly after the struggle of Pope Innocent II, with the 'antipope', Anacletus II (1130–8), who had been of Jewish origin. When greeted by a Jewish deputation on his entry into Rome, between 1138–9, Innocent had praised Judaism's 'Holy Law', but condemned the 'religious practice and ... faulty interpretation of the Jews,' not realising, perhaps, the link in Judaism between textual interpretation, Law and religious practice. In addition, the 'convocation of a great "ecumenical" council in 1139, the year after Anacletus' death', caused widespread consternation among the Jews of Europe. Although 'no anti-Jewish canons were adopted'[11] on this occasion, the atmosphere into which ibn Ezra immediately entered must have been extremely tense.

According to the famous Jewish traveller and fellow townsman of ibn Ezra, Benjamin of Tudela, Rome was the chief city of the 'kingdom of Edom', comprising about two hundred distinguished Jewish families, who did not even pay the usual special Jewish tax. Some of the Jews were actually in papal service. Two appeared to have had unlimited access to the papal household, including the contemporary head of the yeshivah (religious seminary).[12]

Despite earlier scholarly views to the contrary, Rome was a highly respected Talmudic centre.[13] This fact is relevant to the debate surrounding ibn Ezra's two *Torah Introductions*, written in Italy and northern France respectively. For instance, Nathan of Jehiel, who had been the head of the yeshivah before ibn Ezra's arrival in Rome, had written a lexicon of the Talmud and midrashim,[14] in which he had explained all the Talmudic terms, as well as their etymology. He had, in addition, been a fine linguist, having studied Aramaic, Latin, Greek, Arabic and Persian, as well as Hebrew.

Nathan had quoted from the Ge'onim[15] and other earlier, as well as contemporary, authorities, utilising the learning of the three chief Torah centres of the day: Babylon (Iraq), Kairouan (North Africa) and Mainz (Germany). However, Nathan had been unaware of the pioneering work of Arabic-speaking Hebrew scholars, such as Judah ibn Hayyuj, relating to Hebrew grammar.[16] It was, therefore, one of ibn Ezra's goals to educate the Jews of Italy in this field. Roth states nevertheless that Nathan's 'great talmudic dictionary ... bears testimony to the wide rabbinic learning and linguistic range of educated Roman Jewry at this time.'[17]

Levin describes the combination of wealth and yet foreboding that ibn Ezra encountered in the Jewish community of Rome, at a time when the Second Crusade was imminent. This feeling was aggravated by the sense of claustrophobia experienced in the narrow alleyways of the Jewish quarter of the town.[18] Nevertheless, ibn Ezra stayed in Rome for five or six years, making contact with noble Jewish families, and writing poems in their honour. His style of poetry was very different from that of the Italian Jews, being replete with the idiom and scientific accuracy of the Spanish School. Another of ibn Ezra's favourite devices was to pun on the name of the person to whom the poem was addressed, as in the case of Menahem,[19] one of his patrons. This device was also used in the *Introduction*.

It was here in Rome that ibn Ezra wrote *Moznaim*,[20] the first of several works on Hebrew grammar. He prefaced it with a detailed introduction, reviewing the work of previous grammarians.[21] Bacher calls it 'the oldest grammatical document in the history of grammar'.[22] Levin refers to its scientific methodology and precision. The aim of this work was not novelty. As with ibn Ezra's subsequent grammar books, it was rather a manual written 'to give to Jews who do not understand Arabic the knowledge and understanding of the system of grammar established one hundred years previously by Judah ibn Hayyuj and his followers....'[23]

In Rome, ibn Ezra translated three works on Arabic grammar by ibn Hayyuj and Judah ibn Gikatilla.[24] He also composed the first of his Bible commentaries, *Ecclesiastes*, in which he immersed himself in textual exegesis, insisting on precise interpretations and uncompromising reliance on grammatical rules. His excellent memory assisted him in quoting from the relevant sources, as he had been unable to carry books with him from Spain. Ibn Ezra also introduced philosophical and scientific ideas into his biblical exegesis. He endeavoured to unite all the various disciplines, in order to justify his view of the Bible as a self-contained unit. This was the approach ibn Ezra was to adopt in most of his biblical commentaries, including that on the Torah.

The *Commentary on Ecclesiastes* is critical of the poetic style of the early Palestinian religious poet, Eleazar ben Kallir,[25] who wielded great influence on the Italian school of Hebrew poetry.[26] In ibn Ezra's opinion, Kallir's *piyyutim* (liturgical poetry) contained inappropriate linguistic forms, an insensitive use of Talmudic language and words of foreign origin. Ibn Ezra found Kallir ungrammatical in his application of biblical words and insensitive to the rhymes and sounds of the Hebrew letters. Above all, he condemned Kallir's use of midrashic and aggadic idiom, which took the biblical sense beyond the *pshat*.[27] In contrast, ibn Ezra praised the Babylonian Gaon, Sa'adiah, for omitting such perceived errors from his poetry.[28]

Ibn Ezra also broke new ground in declaring that no sage, however ancient in origin, and therefore worthy of reverence and respect, is immune from criticism and re-evaluation.[29] Here ibn Ezra anticipates his stance in his *Introduction to the Torah*, where he states: 'I shall be no respecter of persons when I explore the Torah text, but shall thoroughly, and to the best of my ability, seek the grammatical [form] of every word'.

Ibn Ezra also anticipates his *Commentary on the Torah* by announcing at the opening of his *Commentary on Ecclesiastes* that 'a man cannot attain the rung of awe [of the Creator] until he ascends the ladder of wisdom and it is built and established on understanding.'[30] Ibn Ezra regards the means as being as important as the end. Only by 'ascending' the ladder, does one begin to 'build' it. In other words, only by leading a committed life does ones own life begin to take shape in the way one would desire. In the *Commentary on Ecclesiastes*, ibn Ezra hints that one needs to be knowledgeable in order to gain true understanding. He also recommends brevity in biblical exegesis. Both these themes are developed in the *Introduction to the Torah*.

Ibn Ezra's second biblical commentary was that on *Job*, which he introduced by reiterating his view that 'the majority of the commentaries of the early writers on this book are not [written] according to grammatical criteria.[31] Some, moreover, are [written] by the midrashic method'. Ibn Ezra's own approach involves defining each word, including technical difficulties, according to *pshat* interpretations and the most up-to-date laws of grammar. Only then does he explain 'the essence of the meaning.'[32] Nevertheless, despite his resolve, ibn Ezra himself occasionally succumbs to more detailed, long-winded explanations, a trait he abhors in others.

According to Fleischer, ibn Ezra completed his literary achievement in Rome with his *Commentary on the Five Megillot*.[33] The reaction of the Jewish scholars in Rome to the grammatical, yet philosophical and scientific, approach of ibn Ezra was one of astonishment. Ibn Ezra had introduced them to a totally novel approach, embracing many different disciplines under the title of 'exegesis', whilst demanding precision and self-discipline in poetry. In one of his own poems, ibn Ezra was to say generally of his stay in Italy that 'in Edom there is no room for a sage who dwells in the land of Kedar'. His meaning is that the Jews of Christian Europe did not wish to accommodate the new ideas of the Muslim-influenced Jews from Spain.[34]

Ibn Ezra was aware of the general accusations of heresy aimed by Jews in Christian lands at the Spanish Jewish scholars. These must have increased his sense of geographical and cultural isolation and alienation. In addition he was totally dependant on his hosts for financial support. He had obviously reached an impasse in Rome and, immediately after completing the *Commentary on the Five Megillot*, he left to continue his life of perpetual travel. It may not be too far-fetched to suggest that ibn Ezra's emphasis on 'paths' and 'movement' in the search for God, not to mention the 'circle' imagery of the *Introductions*, is a reflection of his own wanderings.

Ibn Ezra in Lucca

In 1145 ibn Ezra travelled north to Lucca, a six-day journey from Rome. It is possible that, in addition to the negative reasons for this move, ibn Ezra may, whilst still in Rome, have received an invitation from Jewish scholars residing in Lucca. Alternatively, he may just have thought that he might find much-needed financial and emotional support there.[35]

Before 1000 CE an important Jewish community had existed in Lucca.[36] It is even possible that, as early as the ninth century, a Talmudic academy had been founded there by the prestigious Kalonymus family. Lucca's Talmudic fame was such that it had influenced the academies of France and Germany, which were the Ashkenazi heart-lands of the time. This environment stimulated ibn Ezra in his scientific endeavours,[37] whilst he, in turn, enhanced the town's reputation. In the mid twelfth century there were around forty Jewish families in Lucca, consisting of some two hundred people. Nevertheless, it could not compare in stature with the much bigger Jewish centre in Rome.[38]

It was in Lucca that ibn Ezra wrote the *Commentary on the Torah*, including its *Introduction*, which is the subject of this book. Although the later, French, version was longer, this earlier composition is regarded as the standard version. It is more complete and accessible to the general reader, being included in the authoritative interpretative canon, *Mikra'ot Gedolot*.[39]

Levin compares ibn Ezra's approach in his *Commentary on the Torah* to his earlier comments on *Ecclesiastes*. Once again ibn Ezra emphasises the importance of grammatical accuracy in revealing the true, i.e., *pshat*, meaning of a word or phrase. He is devoted to disciplined and succinct language. However, he is also prone to digress on matters of philosophic or scientific interest, refusing to accept that any subject or opinion is exempt from debate. We shall see that this tendency does not prevent him from criticising others for the same trait. Occasionally, ibn Ezra appears to engage in what we would now call 'biblical criticism'.[40] In such cases, however, ibn Ezra's language is veiled and allusive, rather than direct. This could be out of reverence for the holy writings, fear of his Italian patrons, or because he genuinely believed that only the 'wise' would be capable of understanding such truths.

Although a detailed dissection of the *Introduction* occupies us later on in the book, an overview will be given here, in order to set it in its chronological and geographical context. Ibn Ezra discusses five alternative approaches or paths to God, Who is designated as the centre of a circle. As we have seen with the *Commentary on Ecclesiastes*, no authority is exempt from criticism or fresh examination, as ibn Ezra commences his analysis of these paths.

The Ge'onim, representatives of the first approach, are criticised for wordiness and deviations from the text. The Karaites of the second path are the butt of ibn Ezra's biting sarcasm, for they did not adhere to the traditional teachings laid down in the Oral Torah, the lynch-pin of the traditional form of Judaism espoused by ibn Ezra. The Christians, depicted in the third path, are attacked for treating biblical passages as allegories, even when perfectly reasonable simple explanations are called for. Ibn Ezra certainly does not dismiss the mystical approach, but contends that words can have both a straightforward and mystical meaning simultaneously. He thus implies that a multi-levelled approach to the text is possible, and sometimes to be welcomed. The fourth, midrashic, path is espoused by the majority of Ashkenazi thinkers of the day. Ibn Ezra concedes that these rabbis must be respected, but proceeds to ridicule aspects of the midrashic approach which are plainly contradicted by science and common sense.

The fifth path is ibn Ezra's own, the direct path to God. This path demands a knowledge of grammar, science and all contemporary secular subjects, as well as insight into Written and Oral Torah. For ibn Ezra, such comprehensive knowledge is essential if a seeker wishes to fathom the depths of the hidden meanings embedded in the biblical texts.

In Lucca ibn Ezra decided to write a commentary on all the biblical books.[41] He obviously regarded each commentary as part of a whole, because he refrained from discussing points he had already made in earlier commentaries, or which he intended to make in later commentaries.[42]

Levin characterises ibn Ezra's next commentary, that on *Isaiah*,[43] as fearless, and its allusions as less veiled that those to be found in the *Commentary on the Torah*. Here, ibn Ezra discusses the subject of prophecy, reading into the prophetic utterances the roots of his own philosophic and scientific system. Ibn Ezra's view of prophecy has links with the mediaeval Aristotelianism which was popular among Muslim, as well as Sephardi Jewish thinkers, including Rambam, who may well have been influenced by ibn Ezra. Ibn Ezra believed that the prophetic capacity is endowed by nature, but is implemented only when the endowed individual also has a prophetic mission. Naturally the prophetic gift brings the prophet nearer to God. Nevertheless, ibn Ezra did not claim that God could be known in Himself, but only through His works, a view taken up and expanded by Rambam.[44]

Levin also suggests that ibn Ezra's sympathy for the negative historical reality depicted in the book of *Isaiah*, aspects of which he had already discussed in his *Commentary on the Torah*,[45] was influenced, at least partially, by his own experience of the repressed existence of the Jewish community:

> [T]he alleys of the Jewish quarter in Lucca ... taught him the oppressive influence of fear, the intensity of the straits of hatred and the aggression of the dominant religion, bent on destroying them.[46]

Ibn Ezra also polemicised against christological interpretations of *Isaiah*,[47] as well as questioning those popular Jewish interpretations of the book which he regarded as historically inaccurate.[48]

In Lucca, ibn Ezra also wrote *Sefer ha-Yesod*, the second of his grammar books. It was ibn Ezra's custom to write books for his pupils, which he then gave to them without retaining a copy. When someone else in a different town requested a book on the same subject, he was thus compelled to write another. His intention was not to write anything new in his later grammar books, but to amass all the grammatical rulings which had been transmitted in Arabic to as large an Ashkenazi readership as possible. Nevertheless, new ideas do appear in each of his grammatical works.[49]

In a poem which may have introduced the work, ibn Ezra states that 'Sefer ha-Yesod [The Book of Roots] will reveal to you every secret [sod] of the language of the Hebrews'. This rhyme is reminiscent of the pun-filled prayer with which he begins his Introduction to the Torah. It provides evidence that ibn Ezra did indeed believe that the 'secret' of the Hebrew language was embedded in its philological 'roots', which could be revealed only by an expert such as himself.

It is probable that another work of grammar, Sfat Yeter, was written at the end of ibn Ezra's stay in Lucca. Unlike Sefer ha-Yesod, however, this work was later mentioned in the supercommentaries on ibn Ezra's works by Tov Elem, Motot and Profiat Duran. It disappeared shortly after the beginning of the fifteenth century, but was rediscovered in the nineteenth century. This book is sometimes also known as The Defence of Sa'adiah Gaon.[50]

In the book's Introduction, ibn Ezra states that trying to understand the biblical text without being an expert in grammar is like 'banging your head against a brick wall'.[51] He uses a similar expression in Path Three, when depicting the Christian, allegorical, approach to the text,[52] although, in the present case he is attacking the poet, Menahem ibn Saruq, a contemporary of ibn Labrat.

In Sfat Yeter ibn Ezra also opposes those who think, like ibn Saruq, that a biblical text can be interpreted in many different ways, when in fact there is only one true meaning. He concedes that the ancient rabbis added or 'drew out' meanings, sometimes by use of asmakhta (biblical support) and sometimes by drash interpretations. He reminds the reader, however, that for these same rabbis a central axiom was that 'no text can be deprived of its pshat'.[53] He cites the early Aramaic commentator, Onkelos, as one of those who knew the grammatical rules better than contemporary Jews, and is therefore permitted to add midrashic meanings when he deems it necessary. From these examples it can be seen that Sfat Yeter contains similar ideas and phraseology to the Introduction.[54]

It is probable that at this date ibn Ezra succeeded in carrying out some astrological experiments and also wrote his first book on astronomy, Sefer ha-Luhot.[55] A second version of this book, composed some years later in Provence, enhanced the reputation of ibn Ezra as a major player in the history of astronomy. As with his books on grammar, ibn Ezra was able to educate the Jewish communities in Christian Europe about a subject which until then had been available only to Arabic speakers. The same urge to educate which had encouraged ibn Ezra to migrate to Italy in the first place persisted in his desire to introduce different examples of the spiritual and cultural heritage of Muslim Spain to his varied and attentive audiences.

The inhabitants of northern Italy must have been astonished at this biblical exegete, philosopher, grammarian and poet, who also displayed expertise in scientific subjects. In contrast to the hostility he attracted in Rome by the novelty of his approach, in the Lucca area ibn Ezra appears to have been ably supported by one or more admirers, and was able to complete one of his great masterpieces, the *Commentary on the Torah*.[56]

Ibn Ezra's remaining sojourn in Italy

Ibn Ezra moved north-east to Mantua in 1146, where he wrote his most important grammatical work, *Sefer Zahot*, which crystallised everything he had written previously on the subject. He added a section on the quantitative metres of Spanish Hebrew poetry, giving examples and explaining their Arabic origin.[57] He was to write another grammar book, *Safah Berurah*, in Verona, between 1146 and 1147, because one of his students, Solomon, asked him to do so. In *Safah Berurah* he listed the place of origin of all his previous grammar books. At this time ibn Ezra wrote *Sefer ha-Ibbur*, which discussed the fixing of the Jewish calendar,[58] and *Sefer ha-Mispar*, a book on arithmetic, which included *excursi* on grammar.[59]

After residing for seven or eight years in Italy, in 1147 ibn Ezra decided to leave. By this time he had gained an insight into the mentality of the Italian Jews and had taught them as much as he could of Sephardi culture. Nevertheless, he had also experienced disappointment, alienation and poverty on his travels, and could not think of any one place as his permanent home.

Levin describes his stays in various places as stop-gaps between the essential task, that of travel. Ibn Ezra had a restless personality, as well as being in constant need of financial support. He was also proud, and resented the disrespect occasionally shown to him by people he regarded as ignorant. There was a great difference between the small Italian communities and the large, dynamic cities of Spain. Although he was uncertain of how successful he had been in Italy, ibn Ezra influenced it permanently. Sometimes, however, his physical and spiritual turmoil prevented him from thinking clearly and impeded his capacity for creativity.

As well as these personal problems, we should also take into account the external factor of the Second Crusade, which had already affected the communities of Germany and France. The fact that the seat of the Church was in Italy may have contributed to ibn Ezra's decision to leave, although the Italian Jews were, ironically, spared the fate of their co-religionists in France. Although the terror bred from far-off rumours caused great anxiety, ibn Ezra was now to move to some of the very lands in which the Crusade had already wreaked havoc, so that he might complete many of his masterpieces.[60]

Ibn Ezra in Béziers (Provence)

Fleischer[61] discusses the various routes that ibn Ezra could have taken on his journey to Provence. He thinks that ibn Ezra travelled by boat, either from Venice, which would have entailed a long journey around Italy or, more likely, from Genoa, on the west. Ibn Ezra probably reached the Provençal town of Narbonne and travelled on from there to Béziers, arriving in 1148. Ibn Ezra had already been in contact with the Jews of this region whilst residing in Spain or Italy.[62]

According to Benjamin of Tudela, who visited a few years later, there were a number of Jewish scholars residing in Béziers. Ibn Ezra wrote *Sefer ha-Shem* for two such scholars and an astronomical text-book, probably *Reshit Hokhmah*, for a third.[63] The sympathetic and liberal intellectual atmosphere prevalent among the Jews of Provence may have contributed to the success of the scientific, mathematical, astronomical and astrological works he wrote in this area.

Jews are known to have lived in Béziers from before the tenth century. The synagogue was built at about the same time as ibn Ezra's arrival in the town. Jews lived in both parts of the city, which was divided between the count and the bishop. Béziers is infamous for its organised onslaughts against the Jewish population during the Easter period, which included the stoning of the Jewish Quarter.[64] The town was known as 'the little Jerusalem' and its fame increased as a result of ibn Ezra's residence.

The first book ibn Ezra wrote in Béziers was probably *Reshit Hokhmah*, which is divided into ten chapters. It contains a detailed description of every aspect of contemporary astrological science,

11

including references to earlier work gathered from Babylonian, Persian, Indian and Greek sources, starting with Ptolemy. At that time astrology was regarded as a branch of astronomy and formed an important part of the scientific Muslim Spanish cultural heritage, which Ibn Ezra desired to transmit to the Jews of Provence.

As with his other works, *Reshit Hokhmah* was written in an organised and systematic fashion. It demonstrated expertise in both astronomy and astrology. Although he completed this book in record time, ibn Ezra immediately set to writing a further six books on astronomy, containing his own, fresh, ideas. This creative spurt may have been motivated by the curiosity of the people of Béziers, his own enthusiasm, or both. He caused consternation in his readers because, in line with his custom, he wrote everything from memory.[65]

Ibn Ezra's next work, *Sefer ha-Shem*, dealt primarily with the ineffable four-letter name of God. In Jewish tradition this name consists of the Hebrew letters *yod*, *heh*, *vav* and *heh*, the correct pronunciation of which is unknown. *Shem* means 'name'. It is used in specific circumstances as a circumlocution for the name of God Himself. In addition, the book's eight chapters also discussed outstanding grammatical problems, as well as testifying to ibn Ezra's mathematical, philosophical, astronomical and astrological skills. As always, he endeavoured to unify these disciplines, in order to depict a holistic world-view, corresponding to the 'oneness' of God.[66]

Ibn Ezra in Narbonne (Provence)

Narbonne is about sixteen miles from Béziers, and ibn Ezra stayed there for a short time until 1152. It was the capital of mediaeval Septimania and has the earliest written evidence of Jewish residence in France, dating from 471. The town was taken from Muslim hands in 759. According to legend, its Jewish residents helped the Christians in the eviction of the Muslims. As a reward they were granted the right to elect a 'Jewish king'. There was a princely Jewish dynasty in Narbonne, which dated from the eleventh and twelfth centuries. Between 1134 and 1143, however, political clashes took place between Narbonne and Toulouse, resulting in Jewish emigration from Narbonne.

According to the *Sefer Kabbalah*, a historiography by ibn Ezra's younger Spanish contemporary, Abraham ibn Daud, in 1143 there were two thousand Jews resident in Narbonne. Benjamin of Tudela records the existence of three hundred Jewish families, or about one thousand five hundred inhabitants. In 1163 the Jewish population was attacked by Spanish crusaders, but was protected by both the religious and secular Provençal authorities. Benjamin calls Narbonne 'a city advanced in Torah [study], from which Torah is disseminated to all lands'.[67] Benjamin mentions that a scion of the Kalonymous family was the leader of the community, and also names the head of the yeshivah. Ibn Ezra had therefore reached a town with a proud, though oppressed, Jewish history, famous for its learning. Here ibn Ezra probably wrote his astronomical work, *Ta'amei-ha-Luhot*.

Ibn Ezra's stay in Provence proved to be one of the most fruitful periods of his life. The scholars in this area were much more understanding of Spanish culture than the Italians, as there had already been considerable intellectual interchange between Spain and Provence. In Italy ibn Ezra had felt the necessity for psychological self-sufficiency. Here he found true friendship.

In fact, two generations after his death, the poet, Yediah ha-Penini ben R. Abraham of Béziers, extolled ibn Ezra by name in the famous 'Letter of Apology' sent to Rabbi Solomon ben Adret, the Rashba. This important rabbi had been angered by the study of so-called 'external wisdom', or philosophy, by the Jews of Provence. Yediah demonstrated that in every generation Jewish sages had studied these sciences. Of ibn Ezra specifically he states: 'our fathers told us of the joy of our rabbinic leaders in meeting him as he passed through, and how he began to open their eyes.'[68]

Why then did ibn Ezra leave for northern France? One of his reasons may have been rumours about the Almohad destruction of the Jewish communities of Spain, together with their culture. He may have felt an increasing urgency to implant all the seeds of this culture in as many Ashkenazi lands as possible. This might also explain his emphasis on different aspects of this culture in different areas. Ibn Ezra now found himself in the Kingdom of Anjou, which at that time embraced the whole of the northern part of France, from the Pyrenees to Normandy. He reached 'Rodus' in 1152.

Ibn Ezra in 'Rodus'

For a long time there was considerable debate about exactly which town in Normandy constituted 'Rodus', but the majority opinion has opted for Rouen.[69] Jews had lived in Rouen from at least the early eleventh century. It was one of only two French towns whose Jewish inhabitants were forced to accept baptism or death during the time of the First Crusade. After that date Normandy belonged to England, whose ruler, William Rufus, treated these forced converts well. During the twelfth century the Jews of Rouen, unlike other Norman Jews, were placed under the authority of a local bailiff. A number of London Jews owned houses in the Jewish Quarter of Rouen, whilst some Jews of Rouen had debtors in England. It is thus easy to understand why ibn Ezra eventually left Rouen for London.

Ibn Ezra was very ill when he arrived in northern France, where he was tended by Rabbi Moses ben Meir. He vowed that if he recuperated he would write a second *Commentary on the Torah*.[70] The only parts extant are a few fragments on *Genesis*, together with the *Introduction* and the entire *Commentary on Exodus*. This *Second Introduction* mentions ibn Ezra's sick-bed vow and describes the same five exegetical methods already discussed in the Lucca *Commentary*. However, in Rouen ibn Ezra changes both order and emphasis, reversing the position of the Ge'onic and Christian paths. He starts with a detailed negative exposé regarding Christian allegorical exegesis, but downplays his criticisms of the Ge'onim. No doubt context played a large part in ibn Ezra's change of emphasis.

The *Second Commentary* on *Genesis* also differs from the earlier version. It contains a preface on fine points of grammar and etymology, followed first by a grammatical and then by an exegetical commentary. The earlier version did not make this sharp differentiation.[71]

The *Second (Standard) Commentary* on *Exodus* is longer than that on all the other four books of the Pentateuch put together. Although it often agrees with statements made in the *First Commentary*, there are occasional contradictions between the two.[72] In this second commentary, ibn Ezra emphasises that the mysteries of the soul cannot be comprehended before one fully understands the workings of the body and the practice of the mitzvot.[73] His stress on the activity known as *hitbodedut* has led to speculation that ibn Ezra practised a form of meditation.[74] The commentary also discusses Israel's role in the astrological framework. It expresses the view that, in exceptional circumstances, the power of prayer is capable of moving God to overturn Israel's 'fate'.

Ibn Ezra was more fearful of the 'Arabic Galut' (forced diaspora) than that of Christendom, because he thought that the destruction of Jewish culture in Spain would hasten the 'end' in the Messianic sense. At this time he was subject to apocalyptic astrological visions regarding the destruction of 'the Kingdom of Ishmael', through the defeat of the Almohads by their Christian enemies. He also prophesied that 'light' would finally come to the Land of Israel.[75] He refers to this 'light' towards the end of *Path Four* of his *First Introduction*.

Ibn Ezra's next work, the *Second Commentary on Daniel*, was written in October 1155, immediately after his own visionary experiences.[76] He describes this commentary as 'succinct, with riddles and ... mystical meanings', comprehensible only to those who 'understand the roots'.[77] Nevertheless, he also declares that his commentary will be written 'according to grammatical criteria'. It is the juxtaposition of the grammatical and the mystical that makes ibn Ezra such a unique writer, as we will see below. This commentary is also consistent with his other works in its rational treatment of miracles, together with philosophical asides.[78] Ibn Ezra's descriptions of redemption may be connected with his apocalyptic visions of the contemporary political situation.

An important view expressed in this commentary, and which relates to the *Introduction to the Torah*, is that the appointed Jewish festivals, the *mo'adim*, had been fixed in the past by dependence on early prophecies. All the future *mo'adim* had been determined in exact detail[79] and written down many years before, but after Daniel's time. This approach to the *mo'adim* may explain the anger expressed by ibn Ezra towards the Karaites in *Path Two*, for daring to interpret the festivals according to their own calculations, which do not follow Oral Torah.[80]

Another unusual feature is that, unlike most previous commentaries on *Daniel*, the 'fourth kingdom' is interpreted as referring to the present time and not to Daniel's age, and is identified as the kingdom of Islam rather than Rome/Christianity. It is obvious that ibn Ezra's own visions of Judaism's redemption through Christendom played a part in this interpretation, and is further proof of his belief that the Messianic Age was nigh. It is even possible that he identified himself as a modern-day Daniel, come to liberate his people from their cultural servitude.

It is probable that the *Second Commentary on Esther* was written immediately after the *Commentary on Daniel*.[81] It provided ibn Ezra with an appropriate biblical context, the first recorded attempt of mass genocide of the Jews, from which to expound on his own ideas on the imminent spiritual destruction of the Jewish people.

Ibn Ezra had already written a *Commentary on the Song of Songs* in Italy. The *Second Commentary*, produced in Rouen, consists of three sections. These can be described as grammatical, literary and allegorical.[82] In the third section ibn Ezra responds positively to the midrashic and aggadic stories of the rabbis, in order to depict the higher aspirations of the *Song*. This unusual stance contrasts sharply with his customary view of midrashic interpretations, but can perhaps be explained by the exceptional history of *Song of Song* exegesis in Jewish tradition.

In Rouen ibn Ezra also wrote a *Second Commentary on Psalms*. It was written very quickly, although it is the most detailed of all his commentaries. In it he expounds his scientific and philosophical opinions at length, relating his theory of the cosmos both to divine miracles and also to the soul's efforts to return to her source. In this commentary ibn Ezra relies on ideas expressed in some of his earlier works, but refrains from allusions and produces writing of great lucidity. He identifies closely with the poetry of the *Psalms* and emphasises the book's ethical message. Once again, ibn Ezra provides much aggadic detail, as well as grammatical explanations.

The *Standard Commentary on the Minor Prophets* was completed soon after the *Commentary on Psalms*.[83] It was probably the last of ibn Ezra's works to be written in Rouen, and is extremely succinct. Ibn Ezra briefly discusses each prophet and tackles the text from a grammatical point of view. As in the previous commentary, he devotes some space to the subject of ethics. For instance in his comments on *Hosea* 6:3, he uses his favourite metaphor of the 'ladder of wisdom' to describe the soul's ascent to God.[84]

Ibn Ezra was highly respected by those Jews in northern France whom he encountered during his five-year stay. As we have seen, during his sojourn in Rouen he wrote a second, and often longer, version of his Bible commentaries, in contrast to the astronomical and astrological works composed in Provence. Nevertheless, the commentaries incorporate the fruits of all his scientific research. In addition, they were influenced by his own visions and fears for the future of Judaism in an antagonistic world.

How was ibn Ezra accepted by French Jewish scholars? We know that he was admired by Rabbenu Jacob Tam (1100–71), Rashi's grandson, considered 'the greatest [Talmudic] scholar of the generation'. The two exchanged letters, although we have no proof that they actually met. They both wrote works entitled *Sefer-ha-Yashar*, the title ibn Ezra gave to his own *Standard Commentary*. It is recorded that ibn Ezra asked Rabbenu Tam a halakhic question regarding the dating of Pesach.[85]

There is controversy as to whether ibn Ezra met Rabbenu Tam's elder brother, Shmuel ben Meir, the Rashbam (1080/5–1158/71),[86] to whom he wrote poems of praise, whilst strongly disagreeing with aspects of his biblical exegesis.[87] Ibn Ezra feared that Rashbam's approach to *pshat* interpretation might lead to infringements of the halakhah. Ibn Ezra regarded the safeguarding of the halakhah at all times as the lynch-pin of Jewish interpretation, whereas those biblical exegetes who were also, like Rashbam, Talmudic experts, were willing to 'experiment' a little more with the biblical text.[88]

To assess the impact of ibn Ezra's achievement in France, we only have to study the tribute paid to him by the translator, Judah ibn Tibbon,[89] a few days after ibn Ezra left the country for England. As a translator himself, ibn Tibbon was particularly impressed by ibn Ezra's role as the first Hebrew populariser of grammar books written in Arabic. Rashi and Rashbam, on the other hand, relied on the inaccurate earlier works of ibn Saruq and ibn Labrat. Now, because of ibn Ezra's translations, French Jews were able to utilise the linguistic advances made by the Sephardi Jews.[90]

Ibn Ezra in England

One of the most puzzling questions in Jewish intellectual history is why ibn Ezra should have come to England? The answer may well lie in the contemporary cultural and financial links between the Jews of Normandy and England, described above. However, other reasons may have been equally important for ibn Ezra. In many ways England could be considered as prime virgin territory for the implanting of Sephardic cultural seeds at the end of one man's very long life. In those days 'Angleterre' was regarded as being at the 'edge of the earth',[91] and was therefore of great interest to someone of ibn Ezra's evangelical and messianic mentality.

Ibn Ezra arrived in 1158, having crossed the Channel by boat with a group of companions. He quickly found himself pupils in London. Most London Jews had arrived in England from Rouen with William the Conqueror. Henry I encouraged them to stay by granting them a charter through which they had freedom of movement, without having to pay tolls or customs. They had permission to be tried in their own law courts and swear the oath on a Torah scroll. However, the anarchy which ensued during the subsequent reign of Stephen (1135–54) harmed the Jewish community. It was during this period that the 1144 Norwich blood libel occurred, the first such defamation in European history.[92] Nevertheless, Stephen protected the Jewish community throughout the Second Crusade.

When ibn Ezra arrived in England, Henry II (1154–89), the first of the Angevin kings, was on the throne, ruling both England and large parts of northern France. By this time Jews had been barred from guilds and forbidden to hold land. They now became authorised money-lenders, under total control of the king. Their welfare depended on his stability and his need for their financial support.[93] At this time the community attracted many settlers from both Europe and North Africa.[94]

Ibn Ezra composed various works for the Jews of England, including *Yesod Mora*,[95] written for Joseph ben Jacob. It was completed in only four weeks. Like the *Introduction to the Torah*, this work examines approaches to the biblical text. However, in *Yesod Mora*, the emphasis is on the mitzvot. Ibn Ezra states that if one correctly understands and practises the mitzvot, his soul may eventually reach the divine realm.

According to ibn Ezra, the correct use of secular subjects, such as philosophy, science and astrology, is essential for a true understanding and correct practice of Jewish law. Ibn Ezra found justification for all these areas of study in the biblical text itself. Using his favourite metaphor of wisdom as the ladder ascending to God, he argues that those who do not understand the mitzvot should obey them nevertheless, if necessary in a child-like fashion.

It is particularly interesting to compare *Yesod Mora*'s descriptions of the four kinds of one-sided researchers with those discussed in the two earlier *Introductions to the Torah*. In *Yesod Mora* ibn Ezra starts by criticising the massoretes for their emphasis on preservation of text, rather than creativity in analysis. In his *Introduction*, on the other hand, the massoretes are criticised for their adherence to midrashic rather than common-sense explanations.

In contrast to the two earlier works, ibn Ezra also criticises the grammarians for non-creativity. This volte-face is astonishing in the light of ibn Ezra's earlier championing of the grammatical approach. It may be that towards the end of his life he realised that most people did not understand 'grammar' in his original esoteric way, and was hoping to set the record straight by pointing out the drawbacks of the every-day grammatical approach.

In *Yesod Mora* ibn Ezra's criticises the Karaites in more measured tones than in the *Introductions*.[96] He also praises Talmudic scholars for their legal expertise and general secular knowledge, but condemns their use of midrashic explanations. He also criticises experts in the law of torts, whose 'knowledge has no intrinsic spiritual significance.'

It can therefore be seen that in England ibn Ezra once again altered his emphasis towards various approaches to the biblical text. In his first *Introduction*, he had been sarcastic and polemical in attack, whilst praising his own 'grammatical' method, which he attributed to the ancient sages. In the *Second Introduction* he changed the order of attack, starting with the dangers of Christian allegory and ending on an innovative note, by offering to teach the present-day sages the rules of grammar. He thus admitted that most of the Ashkenazi rabbis were uneducated in this method.

In *Yesod Mora*, he imitates the *Second Introduction* by placing his categories in ascending order of worthiness, commencing now with the massoretes and ending with the Talmudic scholars. However, in *Yesod Mora*, ibn Ezra's attitude to the various exegetical approaches is also much more balanced than earlier in his life. He accentuates creativity rather than the mere acquisition of exegetical tools. This emphasis was already apparent in his earlier works, but is spelled out in much more detail here. It could be argued that each of his three attempts to define a perfect textual approach represents a development in his thought.

On the other hand, it is possible that, at the end of his life, ibn Ezra decided to accentuate the transcendent power of creative imagination over grammatical accuracy, in order to pinpoint the way in which he felt that textual exegesis should be carried on after his death. This shift in emphasis is especially highlighted in his fifth path, which aims at self-perfection through knowledge of God's mitzvot and understanding of His deeds. In the two *Introductions* this path had consisted of adjuring the reader to obey the perfect *Bet Din*, rather than their own interpretations. It could, therefore, be argued that by the time ibn Ezra wrote *Yesod Mora*, he had internalised his concept of the *Bet Din*.

Ibn Ezra's last major work was *Iggeret Shabbat*, written in 1159. It was composed in the form of a letter, starting with a poem, purporting to be written by Shabbat (the Jewish Sabbath) herself, personified as a woman. Ibn Ezra describes himself as having received this 'letter' in a dream. 'Shabbat' admonishes him for having in his possession an exegetical work whose contents encourage her desecration. Ibn Ezra states that he wakes from his dream on Shabbat and realises that the damaging work belongs to a pupil who has left it with him. This work includes a commentary on *Genesis* 1:5 which could lead to a definition of the word 'day' which is totally opposed to the halakhic definition. Angrily he tears up the book, even though this act itself constitutes a desecration of Shabbat![97]

Simon contrasts ibn Ezra's real anger towards the book's author, the Rashbam, with his frequent sarcastic sallies against 'heretics', such as Hivi al-Balkhi, Karaites such as Anan,[98] and those he really wishes to protect, such as ibn Janah, Sa'adiah Gaon, ibn Labrat, and, occasionally, even himself.[99] Ibn Ezra's concern that the term 'day' should be properly interpreted is already made clear from his *Introduction to the Torah*, *Path Four*, and constitutes a large part of his determination to define calendrical dates correctly.

No doubt ibn Ezra was particularly infuriated by the Rashbam's interpretation, because he was a leading Ashkenazi rabbinic authority who, like ibn Ezra himself, espoused the *pshat* approach to the text. Unlike the Rashbam, however, ibn Ezra wished to subsume both halakhah and Oral Torah under his definition of *pshat*.[100] Ibn Ezra may have feared that, on reading this book, the average person might be tempted to celebrate Shabbat at the 'wrong' time. Rashbam was quite happy to separate biblical from legal exegesis, as was pointed out above.

It is somewhat ironic that ibn Ezra's final work is a quasi-poetic dream interpretation, resulting in a major difference of opinion with the leading French legal and biblical scholar of the day. This stance, however, sums up the man: lonely, without female company (note his personification of Shabbat), fiercely protective of the divinity of textual interpretation and eerily prophetic as to the future of exegesis, together with his own mythological status as the archetypal 'Wandering Jew'.

Mystery surrounds the exact place of ibn Ezra's death.[101] In the nineteenth century Graetz took a 'midrashic' approach to ibn Ezra's life. In his opinion, ibn Ezra retraced his steps in a most complicated manner just before the end of his life. There are traditions that he died in Rome, Tudela, Calahorra, or even Palestine. However, Fleischer, ibn Ezra's most respected biographer, thinks that he was fatally attacked by 'anarchic English hordes' in a forest north of London, whilst conducting yet another journey to pastures new.

Common sense, or a *pshat* approach, including documentary evidence, would favour Fleischer's view. An old man, aged seventy-five, who had never retraced his steps before, would be more likely to stay in his country of residence, rather than embark on a dangerous sea journey. Moreover, fifty years after his death, Rabbi Moshe ben Hisdai reported that the Jews of England had informed him that ibn Ezra had died there. If so, ibn Ezra died as he had lived, on the road, or as the Hebrew word '*derekh*' expresses it, on the straight path towards God.[102]

2

A HISTORY OF THE
SCHOLARLY WORK ON IBN EZRA

Now, who shall arbitrate?
Ten men love what I hate,
Shun what I follow, slight what I receive;
Ten, who in ears and eyes
Match me: we all surmise,
They this thing, and I that:
Whom shall my soul believe?
(Robert Browning, 'Rabbi Ben Ezra': XXII)

Because ibn Ezra is so difficult to decipher, it might be useful at this juncture to offer an appraisal of how he has been received through the ages. The history of ibn Ezra's reception is almost as fascinating as ibn Ezra's own work. Perhaps more than any other exegete, ibn Ezra has been turned into an idol, either to be worshipped or execrated, as the case may be. To recount his fate at the hands of those following him is to gain insight into the intellectual battles within Judaism which have contributed so much to our present understanding of ibn Ezra.

There are three main categories of writing on ibn Ezra. The first and earliest category are the supercommentaries, i.e., commentaries on his commentaries. Supercommentaries purport to elucidate ibn Ezra, but, instead, they often provide a hook for the author's own views and often contradict each other. The second category of writing on ibn Ezra, dating from the seventeenth century, can be termed 'religious reaction'. The third category, dating from the nineteenth century, is scholarly work, although from our vantage point it is easy to question the scholarly contribution of some of these attempts.

Supercommentaries

According to Simon, supercommentaries on commentaries on the Torah differ from the original commentaries in that the later author is dealing with a product of the human mind, rather than what is regarded as a divine entity, the biblical text.[1] Because ibn Ezra is so difficult to understand, it is not surprising that supercommentaries on his work were already being written in his own lifetime. However, this proliferation of texts only aggravated the situation.

One of the earliest 'bibliographies' of the supercommentaries appeared in the supercommentary of Judah ibn Mosconi of Bulgaria, written in 1362.[2] He reports that the first supercommentary on ibn Ezra's work was that of Abishai of Sagori, also from Bulgaria, reputedly dated 1170, six years after ibn Ezra's death. However, this has now been shown to be incorrect. The second supercommentary mentioned is that of the thirteenth-century Moses ibn Tibbon.[3] Nearly thirty further supercommentaries, all written in the fourteenth century, are also mentioned by Mosconi. Steinschneider's more scholarly appraisal lists thirty-six named, and twenty anonymous, authors of supercommentaries.

Supercommentaries were often written on the Bible commentaries of more than one author, in order to elucidate the 'true' meaning of the scriptural text through a process of comparison. Both Ramban and Joseph ibn Kaspi (1279– after 1332) advocated comparing the commentaries of Rashi and ibn Ezra. David Kimhi, the Radak (ca. 1160–1235), wrote an earlier commentary on *Genesis* 1–3, utilising ibn Ezra's own *Commentary*, which he occasionally compared with Rashi's. This cannot be truly regarded as a supercommentary.

Ibn Tibbon influenced the greatest of all supercommentators, Joseph ben Eliezer, 'the Spaniard' (also known as Bonfils Tov Elem), through the work of ibn Yaish. This is no longer extant. A supercommentary which was not mentioned by Mosconi, but which paralleled much of ibn Tibbon's thought, was written by the latter's contemporary, Eleazar b. Mattiya. Both supercommentaries were written towards the end of the thirteenth century. Simon concludes therefore that both oral interpretations of, and written supercommentaries on, ibn Ezra existed from the middle of the thirteenth century.

The most important surviving supercommentary is that of the early fourteenth-century ibn Kaspi, which is preserved in manuscript. One of the reasons for the revived interest in ibn Ezra in the second half of that century was the growing fascination for, and the desire to reconcile, a combination of seemingly disparate subjects, including astrology, Rambam and Kabbalah. Thirteen supercommentaries have been discovered from that period. Simon states that two groups, philosophers and exegetes, were particularly interested in ibn Ezra's *Commentary on the Torah*. They wrote supercommentaries reflecting their respective interests, because in those days it was easier to write commentaries than engage in scientific research.

Many of the philosophical commentators were intent on placing 'R. Abraham Ibn Ezra, "the perfect scholar," on a par with Maimonides.'[4] One such was Joseph ibn Wakker of Toledo, who died in about 1360. He influenced as least five fourteenth-century supercommentators, including Moses Narboni, Samuel ibn Zarza, Solomon Franco and Samuel ibn Motot. Of the four remaining philosophical supercommentators, two were indirectly influenced by ibn Wakker: Ezra Gatigno (also known as En Solomon Astruc of Barcelona) and Shem-Tov ibn Mayor. Despite much disagreement among these supercommentators, they generally agreed about the correctness of their philosophical approach. They therefore criticised those supercommentators who rejected philosophy, interpreted ibn Ezra according to whim, or accused ibn Ezra of heresy.

On the other hand, the six most important Spanish super-commentaries which relate to ibn Ezra's exegetical approach are those by Solomon ibn Yaish the younger, Mosconi, the anonymous author of the 1382 manuscript (British Library 195), Joseph b. Eliezer the Spaniard, Haim of Briviesca and Isaac Profiat Duran (also known as Efodi, or Isaac ben Moses Levi). The most important of these is Joseph ben Eliezer's, known as *Zafenat-Pa'aneakh*. Together with the supercommentaries of ibn Motot and ibn Zarza, it comprises the edition printed in Amsterdam in 1772, known as *Margoliot Tovah*. In addition to these, Asher Crescas of Provence wrote a supercommentary at the beginning of the fifteenth century.

Simon concludes that the exegetical method used by these commentators interpreted ibn Ezra's text more clearly than the philosophical method employed by their contemporaries. The supercommentaries of Mosconi and Joseph ben Eliezer are regarded as particularly successful because of their exegetical emphasis. Although it is unlikely that the two men ever met, they were both of the opinion that one could not fully understand ibn Ezra's *Commentary* without a knowledge of contemporary sciences. Moreover, Joseph was fully aware that ibn Ezra's concise style impeded a correct understanding of his allusions. This resulted in diverse interpretations by different commentators, which often contradicted the actual sense of ibn Ezra's words. Simon usefully summarises 'the supercommentator's double obligation – avoiding over-exegesis on the one hand and under-exegesis on the other'.[5]

Later supercommentaries were written by the sixteenth-century Moses Almosnino of Salonika, Yom Tov Lipmann Heller of Moravia and Vienna, and the eighteenth-century Pole, Solomon Maimon. Modern supercommentaries include those by Moses Crémieux, Judah Leib Krinsky, Isaack Meijler, Leopold Fleischer and Solomon Zalman Netter.[6]

Religious and philosophical reaction to ibn Ezra

I now turn to the second category of writing on ibn Ezra: religious reaction. The great Dutch Marrano philosopher, Spinoza (1632–77), was the first thinker in early modern times to make use of ibn Ezra's *Commentary* in order to support his own views on the non-divinity of the Bible. Although Spinoza exaggerated the import of ibn Ezra's apparently 'heretical' words, his interpretation of ibn Ezra was crucial in defining the latter's 'modern' image among biblical critics and seventeenth-century deists alike.

Such approaches to ibn Ezra may be seen as heavily ironic, when we recall that his actual aim was to effect the harmonisation of Written and Oral Torah, or of *pshat* and *drash* interpretations, in order to safeguard Jewish tradition, and thence the Jewish community, from internal and external inroads. However, he was regarded by the reformers as the chief exponent of the redefined *pshat* approach, in which rabbinic tradition became irrelevant, and even harmful. It could therefore be argued that ibn Ezra was being used in a way which was antithetical to Jewish tradition, and one which denied the authority of the traditional community to define itself.[7]

This may be one of the reasons why the far-sighted ibn Ezra was so worried about the exegetical approach represented in his own day by the Rashbam, as discussed previously in Chapter One. Ibn Ezra must have foreseen that in divorcing the text from its connection with the living tradition of the contemporary Jewish community, Rashbam's approach might lead to Spinoza.

The second major Jewish thinker to use ibn Ezra in corroboration of his own arguments was Moses Mendelssohn (1729–86), the pioneer of modern Jewish Bible commentary and translation, whose philosophical and hermeneutic views have much in common with ibn Ezra. Like ibn Ezra, Mendelssohn also wrote an

Introduction to the Torah, in which he argued for the 'inherent multivalence' of language and 'the legitimacy of rabbinic exegeses that go beyond the plain meaning of the biblical text.' Like ibn Ezra, Mendelssohn contended that:

> the rabbis ... were masters of the methods needed to discern the intended secondary meanings of specific words and phrases. Their interpretations ... are to be accepted as the unveiling of a level of *intended* significance that goes unrecognized by those whose understanding of language is faulty and/or whose methods of exegesis are superficial.

Moreover, Mendelssohn was not only devoted to revealing this broadly defined *pshat* interpretation, but relied on ibn Ezra heavily in the process.[8]

Mendelssohn's views are described by Harris as 'too idiosyncratic' for the majority of western Jewish intellectuals. These preferred the anti-Talmudic approach and also regarded ibn Ezra as their perfect prototype. Examples were the eighteenth-century Michael Creizenach, who regarded ibn Ezra as 'a pioneer of Reform living in an age that was not yet ready to hear him', and Abraham Geiger, a leader of the incipient nineteenth-century Reform movement.[9] Although he was aware that previous commentators had interpreted ibn Ezra, not always correctly, in a way which suited their purposes, Geiger himself succumbed to this temptation, using ibn Ezra as a support for his own anti-Talmudic, pro-*pshat* stance.

However, the one way in which ibn Ezra differed from the reformers and modernisers was in his desire, clearly emphasised in the *Introductions to the Torah*, to uphold, not destroy, religious tradition. The refusal of the 'reformers' to recognise this fact and their very inclination to overlook it altogether, verges on dishonesty and places them in a most precarious position with respect to their enthusiasm for his work. In later life, Geiger revised his emphasis and saw ibn Ezra as the epitome of the 'wandering Jew', whose inability to convey his exegetical genius to his contemporaries led to his life of travel and interest in astrology.

In summary, there has been a strong tendency for religious 'reformers' since Spinoza to use ibn Ezra in order to justify a new definition of *pshat*, which denigrated *drash* and hence, Jewish tradition. Only Mendelssohn attempted to harmonise both these exegetical approaches. Ironically, this enthusiasm on the part of the

Jewish 'reformers' towards ibn Ezra led to his popularity among some non-Jewish adherents of a type of exegesis which was, and still often is, unsympathetic, or even hostile to 'Judaism'.[10]

In contrast to the 'reformers', a number of nineteenth-century German and Lithuanian Orthodox Bible and Talmud commentators implicitly rejected ibn Ezra's approach, whilst the Hungarian School did so explicitly. They all disagreed with what they took to be his interpretation of *pshat*, resenting his popularity among the leaders of the 'reforming' movement. This rejection did not, however, prevent individual Orthodox commentators from using him when it served their exegetical purposes. Indeed, a close investigation into the actual words of the major nineteenth-century traditional commentators will show that ibn Ezra was closer to their approach than has been realised.

The problem is primarily that of the definition of the terms *pshat* and *drash*. Ibn Ezra's definition of these terms followed the pioneering work of the Babylonian Ge'onim. *Drash* was not so much discarded by them, as redefined. In his own day ibn Ezra endeavoured to bridge the exegetical gap between *pshat* and *drash*. Similarly, the nineteenth-century traditionalists felt the need to go one step further in the war against 'reform', and to redefine *pshat* either by completely submerging *drash* within it, or by completely suppressing *pshat* in favour of *drash*.

A contemporary of Mendelssohn, but typical of the mainstream traditional rabbi, the Gaon of Vilna (1720–97) was more attached to *pshat* in exegesis than his predecessors, despite advocating adherence to *drash* in practice. Like ibn Ezra, he 'lumped together' Bible and Talmud in his exegetical approach. However, he also advocated the 'authority of rabbinic derash to deviate from scriptural peshat, to harness and manipulate the authorial intention of the biblical text.'[11] Later exegetes were to reject the Gaon's division between these two interpretative modes.

For instance, Harris states that Naftali Herz Wessely (1725–1805) initiated the attempt 'to identify rabbinic midrash with *'omeq ha-peshat*", the 'deep' sense of the *pshat*. This approach was continued by Mecklenburg, Hirsch, Hoffmann and Malbim, all of whom are discussed below. Harris contrasts their approach with that of Rashbam, to whom *pshat* signified 'the plain meaning of the text, stripped of all midrashic accretions'. As I have already stated, ibn Ezra aimed to integrate rabbinic *drash* with the *pshat* of the text, in order to uphold rabbinic supremacy against the enemies of Oral Torah.

Apart from the ultra-Orthodox Hungarian School, both radical and traditional nineteenth-century exegetes wished to elevate *pshat* exegesis, although for diametrically opposed reasons. Mecklenburg's (1785–1865) commentary on the Torah 'sought to demonstrate the conformity between the oral tradition and the written law'. It could be argued that ibn Ezra's aim was identical, and that Mecklenburg's antagonism towards the religious reforms of his own day was paralleled by ibn Ezra's attitude to the Karaites. Mecklenburg described the difference between *pshat* and *drash* as being:

> like the difference between the inside and the outside of a vessel. The outside (corresponding to peshat) could be seen with one look, everything revealed, open and spread out. The inside (derash) may be concealed in the first look, but a second look will reveal what is hidden there.

He also distinguished the types of *drash* which are used as mnemonic devices, *asmakhtot*, from those inherent in the text itself which:

> ... penetrate the depth of the roots of the language and the hiddenness of the style of Torah, so that from the language of the Torah itself one can understand the countless laws and their offspring found in the Talmud, to the extent that almost all of the oral law is revealed and explained in the books of Moses, with the result that the oral law is fully united with the written law.

There are striking similarities in both form and content between ibn Ezra and Mecklenburg in three areas: the need to elucidate the 'true' meaning of the text; the differentiation between *asmakhtot* and deep inherent meanings; and the link between Written and Oral Torah.[12]

Samuel David Luzzatto (1800–65) was an Italian exegete whose main aim was to 'protect' Jewish thought and tradition from both Protestant biblical criticism and 'evolutionary historical relativism', although he approved of philological research. However he condemned the use of philosophy as an exegetical tool (blaming it for the mystical reaction) and particularly ibn Ezra's own role in this context. Luzzatto's approach was actually not dissimilar from that of ibn Ezra. This is particularly evident when he condemns ibn Ezra for introducing irrelevant scientific material into his exegesis, a trait which, paradoxically, ibn Ezra himself condemned in others.[13]

Meir Leibush Malbim (1809–79) is best known for his fearless stance against the Reform movement, for which he was imprisoned. His commentary on the Torah resulted from this negative view of Reform, which he regarded as undermining the very foundation of Judaism. In order to safeguard traditional Judaism, he used the same tools as those used by ibn Ezra against the Karaites and allegorists, namely exegesis based on knowledge of Hebrew and the search for the 'plain' meaning of the text. He aimed to demonstrate that the Oral Torah was 'implicit in the plain meaning of the verse and in the profundity of the language and that the interpretation is only the plain meaning based upon accurate, linguistic rules'. He stated, furthermore, that the sages had 'important principles and fixed rules for the grammatical forms and the foundations of the language and logic' which had subsequently been forgotten.[14] These are ibn Ezra's arguments exactly.

In many ways Samson Raphael Hirsch (1808–88), the 'father' of modern neo-Orthodoxy, differed from his traditional contemporaries in advocating political emancipation for the Jews, as well as the necessity of secular studies. He was at first a very close friend of the Reform leader, Geiger, but ended by opposing him vehemently, because of their religious differences. Hirsch's method of reducing *drash* to *pshat* is described by Harris as the employment of 'etymological contrivances'.[15]

Naftali Zvi Yehudah Berlin (1816–92) was influenced in his own approach to *pshat* by the Babylonian Ge'onim, who had themselves influenced ibn Ezra. Like Malbim, Berlin attempted to prove that the Talmudic interpretation of the Torah did not contradict either the plain meaning of the text, or the rules of Hebrew grammar and syntax. Weiss Halivni considers that the attitude of Malbim and Berlin constitutes 'a clear change in interpretative state of mind', in that 'their devotion to peshat was complete and consuming', whereas even the most fervent mediaeval *peshatist*, Rashbam, did not completely exclude *drash*.

At first glance it would appear that ibn Ezra's approach is very different to that of Berlin, but, in fact, ibn Ezra was also trying to prove that Hebrew grammar and rabbinic interpretations were not mutually exclusive. It could be argued that ibn Ezra's use of the term *sod*, usually designating the 'secret' or mystical meaning of a text, is comparable to the inherent type of *drash* described by Mecklenburg. If this assumption is correct, then ibn Ezra is closer to the nineteenth-century Orthodox exegetes than may have been supposed.

David Zvi Hoffmann (1843–1941) was regarded as the greatest German halakhic authority of his day. In his fight against reform movements he wrote responsa against all those who criticised Oral Torah: non-Jews, whether anti-semitic or not, apostates and biblical critics, without offering an alternative approach. However, he was also interested in secular subjects, such as philosophy and mathematics. Like Malbim and Berlin, he advocated the unity of Written and Oral Torah, often quoting ibn Ezra on specific details, despite rejecting the positive reception of him by the 'reformers'.[16]

In contrast to the above traditionalist approaches, three ultra-Orthodox Hungarian rabbis rejected both the *pshat* approach and ibn Ezra for his espousal of it.[17] In Pressburg, Moses Sofer (1762–1839) founded the largest yeshivah since Babylonian times, as part of his struggle against the Reform movement. He was totally opposed to the maskilim (adherents of 'Enlightenment' values) and followers of Mendelssohn, although he was not against 'secular' study as an aid to Torah learning, or as a means of livelihood. He re-interpreted a Mishnaic phrase to coin the adage: *'hadash asur min ha-torah'* ('the Torah forbids innovation'). He was convinced that the smallest breach in Orthodoxy would result in inexorable changes, and that any acknowledgement of secularity for its own sake would result in the destruction of traditional Judaism. He was particularly alarmed by Mendelssohn's pioneering translation work from Hebrew into German, as well as his philosophical understanding of Judaism, which he regarded as hostile to polysemic interpretation. These factors also coloured his view of ibn Ezra, even though the latter had been a pioneer of Hebrew exegesis and also had a multi-faceted view of language.[18]

Moses Schick (1807–79) continued Sofer's fight against the Reform movement, derogatorily and sarcastically referring to the rabbis who convened the 1844 Reform Conference held in Brunswick, Germany, as 'Karaites'. It is ironic that he also rejected ibn Ezra's approach, calling *pshat* 'a mere corridor' to the real truth. Instead, Schick utilised aggadic and kabbalistic arguments. Ibn Ezra would not have been totally unsympathetic to this approach, which he recognised as practised by those who were close to the truth, even though he preferred a non-aggadic approach, if at all possible. A third Hungarian rabbi with similar views, Akiva Joseph Schlesinger (1837–1922), continued Schick's attack on innovation, and also espoused complete separation from reform movements.

It can therefore be seen that ibn Ezra was exploited, often for political ends, by traditionalists as well as reformers, most of whom took no real account of ibn Ezra's unique, complex approach to the text. It is perhaps unsurprising, therefore, that the stance taken towards him by most contemporary religious commentators continues to be influenced by internal Jewish political factors. The Reform and Conservative movements claim him as a radical non-fundamentalist. The ultra-Orthodox continue the antagonism expressed by their spiritual forefathers, and tend to ignore him unless he is mediated through the commentaries of Ramban. The more mystical Orthodox movements regard him as a spiritual forerunner of Kabbalah. The modern Orthodox respect him, somewhat from afar.

Scholarly work on ibn Ezra

The third category of writing on ibn Ezra is based on a more 'objective' approach than the first two. It should be remembered however, that 'objective research' may itself be based on a prejudice: i.e., that by an 'objective' attitude to the author, or their works, one can find the 'truth' of what they meant. Finding the 'truth' is not exactly easy. Subjective, even unconscious, prejudices can often colour attitudes and conclusions, as is evident from research into earlier periods of 'scientific analysis'.[19]

The first major biographical study of ibn Ezra was that included by Graetz (1817–91) in his *Geschichte der Juden von den ältesten Zeiten bis zur Gegenwart*, which is regarded as 'the first comprehensive attempt to write the history of the Jews as a living people and from a Jewish point of view.' Graetz' work contributed to the field of historiography, using many literary sources for the first time, despite the lack of archival material. Graetz focused on leading Jewish personalities, neglecting social, economic and even political sources. A typical product of his age, he emphasised rationalism at the expense of traditional Jewish interests such as the Talmud, Kabbalah and mysticism, but was, nevertheless, not averse to accepting stories about ibn Ezra which were grounded in folklore, as we saw in Chapter One.[20]

A more scholarly approach to the study of Jewish culture was that of Steinschneider, one of the founders of modern Jewish bibliography and scholarship. Steinschneider's main interest was in the relationship between Jewish and general culture, especially in the Middle Ages. His serious and thorough recording of all the available printed and manuscript materials led to Hebrew bibliography being established on a firm scholarly basis.

The major English biographer of ibn Ezra was Friedlaender, author of *Essays on the Writings of Abraham ibn Ezra*, although many of his findings have now been superseded. Arguably the greatest contributor to ibn Ezra biography in the first half of the twentieth century was J. L. Fleischer, whose scholarly articles on ibn Ezra, often refuting the work of his predecessors, appeared in various Hebrew language journals from 1912.[21]

The first two major grammatical studies on ibn Ezra were Bacher's *Abraham Ibn Esras Einleitung zu Seinem Pentateuch-Kommentar* and *Abraham ibn Esra als Grammatiker*. However, Bacher had not read the *Second Introduction*, written in France. From his reading of the standard Italian *Introduction*, he concluded that ibn Ezra's 'paths' comprised a chronological approach to the history of exegesis, rather than a carefully nuanced set of hermeneutic critiques, based on political, social, cultural and economic, as well as literary, factors.[22]

The major studies of ibn Ezra's astronomical and astrological oeuvre are those of Cantera, ben Menahem, Halberstam, Millás Vallicrosa,[23] Sirat and Langermann.[24] Ibn Ezra's contribution to poetry has been discussed by Rosin, Egers, Kahana, Schirmann[25] and Levin.

A major feature of ibn Ezra's philosophy is his number symbolism, first discussed by Olitzky in 'Die Zahlensymbolik des Abraham Ibn Ezra'.[26] Olitzky outlines Greek and Jewish antecedents to ibn Ezra's approach, emphasising the great influence on him of the early Hebrew mystical text, *Sefer Yetzirah*.[27] He argues that ibn Ezra was also influenced by neo-pythagorean and neoplatonic philosophy, as mediated through contemporary Muslim currents. He also recognises the importance of ibn Ezra's definition of time, and therefore of creation, as relating to the movement of the spheres. This idea derives from Aristotle and is a crucial component of ibn Ezra's *Introduction to the Torah*.

The subject of creation leads Olitzky to an analysis of ibn Ezra's definition of the number two, anticipating Greive in his discussion of the exact meaning of the Hebrew term, '*etzem*'. Olitzky outlines ibn Ezra's comparison between the relationship of God to the intelligible world and that of the centre of a sphere to a line. In ibn Ezra's *Path One*, truth is compared to the centre of a circle, whilst proponents of differing hermeneutic approaches are described as standing at various distances from this centre, depending on the veracity of their method. Olitzky also discusses ibn Ezra's identification of the philosophical 'forms' or 'genera' with the eternal statutes of Jewish law.

Three nineteenth-century authors, Krochmal, Jastrow and Rosin, tried to create a coherent philosophical picture from ibn Ezra's unsystematic approach.[28] Krochmal was influenced by the contemporary German idealist philosophy of Hegel and Schelling, but also emphasised the importance of religious knowledge, arguing that philosophy could be used as a tool in understanding 'the Absolute Spirit'. He regarded this approach as identical with the mediaeval Jewish philosophical view that the Torah and philosophy are entirely compatible and complementary. Harris sees Krochmal's approach as 'essentially exegetical ... dedicated to locating the concepts of German philosophy in Jewish thought'. He also regards it as 'a response to the most interesting and serious philosophical critique of Judaism the nineteenth century produced', in which Christianity was extolled at the expense of Judaism.[29]

Krochmal tried to link contemporary nineteenth-century German secular philosophy with the ideas of Jewish mediaeval thinkers, including ibn Ezra and Rambam. Denying Luzzatto's claim that these two thinkers had exchanged Jewish ideals for Greek philosophy, he asserted that Muslim-influenced Sephardi thinkers were the very epitome of Jewish religious thinking. He deemed them especially relevant as part of the drive, shared by many contemporary German Jewish intellectuals, to demonstrate the compatibility of Jewish and German culture, and thence the acceptability of Jews within German society. Krochmal's interpretation is 'one of the more creative exegetical feats of the nineteenth century Wissenschaft movement', in which 'once again, Ibn Ezra is turned into a proto-modern figure', anticipating the philosophical discoveries of the Christian idealists.[30]

Krochmal attempts to interpret ibn Ezra's use of the term *etzem*. The Hebrew word connotes 'substance', 'matter', or 'essence', and it is often difficult to decide which of these three meanings ibn Ezra intends. It appears that Krochmal was unaware that ibn Ezra occasionally followed ibn Gabirol in defining *etzem* as 'spiritual matter', in the Aristotelian sense of substratum or substance. However, Krochmal shared ibn Ezra's view that God was both the cause and totality of the world, a position made possible by the concept of *etzem* as both essence and substratum.[31]

Oral Torah also played a significant role in Krochmal's system. Krochmal describes halakhic midrash as either 'determin[ing] the principles implicit in the laws of the Torah', or 'deduc[ing] the consequences of the biblical commandments', thereby 'reveal[ing] what had been concealed, but was present all the time'. Accordingly, 'the Oral Law does not stand alongside the written Torah, but is included within it by way of logical implication'. In *Second Path Four*, ibn Ezra implies a similar view of midrash. If we cannot comprehend a biblical or midrashic passage by linguistic or rational means, we are advised to admit that its sense is 'hidden from us', because our intellect is weaker than that of our predecessors. Like ibn Ezra, Krochmal interpreted aggadic statements as metaphors adapted to the understanding of the masses, rather than as the literal truth.[32]

Rosin was 'part of the "Breslau school" of Jewish philosophical research, which was committed to asserting the place of Jewish philosophy within the larger framework of Western thought.'[33] For Langermann, Rosin's is 'to this day ... still the best, perhaps, in truth, the only, comprehensive and detailed study of the thought of Ibn Ezra'.[34] Unlike Krochmal, Rosin was aware of, and acknowledged, ibn Ezra's debt to ibn Gabirol. He does not, however, adequately acknowledge the influence on ibn Ezra of Muslim neoplatonic writers, such as ibn Sina, maybe due to the lack of availability of the relevant sources in the nineteenth century.[35]

In the twentieth century, ibn Ezra continued to be discussed, albeit within tighter parameters, by the majority of philosophical analysts. Ground-breaking work was, however, done by H. A. Wolfson and Altmann, who both regarded ibn Ezra as a major thinker. More recently, Sirat has emphasised ibn Ezra's astrological oeuvre and the importance of context in interpretation. Idel and E. Wolfson have accentuated his influence on mystical thought, a subject which was practically ignored in the nineteenth and early twentieth centuries.

The differing approaches outlined in this chapter demonstrate the importance of the context within which ibn Ezra is appraised. To the first supercommentators he represented a reconciliation of astrology, Rambam and Kabbalah. To Spinoza, ibn Ezra represented a fearless example of the first biblical critic. Mendelssohn relied on him in order to extend the interpretation of *pshat*. To the reform movements he was hailed as a pioneer, although at least one of their adherents also saw him as the epitome of the 'Wandering Jew', misunderstood by his contemporaries. Most of the nineteenth-century Orthodox thinkers dismissed ibn Ezra simply for being an icon to the reformers, although some used his exegesis when it suited their purposes.

Scholarly approaches have also been biased by current interests, whether in the German Jewish scientific Wissenschaft movement, idealist philosophy, or Muslim thought. Contemporary interest in astrology and mysticism have brought us full circle. It may be that the twenty-first century will repeat the mediaeval view of ibn Ezra as a curious amalgam of astrologer and mystic, spiced with the dash of Maimonidean rationalism which in many ways he anticipated.

3

CLASSICAL AND MEDIAEVAL JEWISH APPROACHES TO TEXT

Rather I prize the doubt
Low kinds exist without,
Finished and finite clods, untroubled by a spark....
Rejoice we are allied
To That which doth provide
And not partake, effect and not receive!
A spark disturbs our clod;
Nearer we hold of God
Who gives, than of His tribes that take, I must believe.
(Robert Browning, 'Rabbi ben Ezra': III and V)

From Bible to Mishnah

In the previous chapter I stated that, in order fully to understand his hermeneutics, it is essential to place ibn Ezra in context. In this and subsequent chapters I shall trace the history of classical and mediaeval hermeneutics, as mediated through Judaism, Christianity and Islam, and evaluate their possible influences on ibn Ezra's approach in his two *Introductions to the Torah*.

As well as being influenced by Jewish antecedents, ibn Ezra was also influenced, negatively or positively, by the Christian and Muslim traditions. The Muslim tradition had considerable influence on the Karaite and Ge'onic approaches. The Karaites constituted a group within the Jewish community which repudiated the divinity of the Oral Tradition, known as Oral Torah. They had an ongoing feud, both literary and political, with the main upholders of this Oral Tradition, the Babylonian Ge'onim. Ibn Ezra was influenced by both groups.

Ibn Ezra's *Introduction* is written in the form of a rhymed critique of four paths to God and a fifth, the 'grammatical' path, which is his own. One aim of this book is to elucidate what ibn

Ezra meant by 'grammar'. Ignorance of his definition of this term has been a major stumbling block in his acceptance by a major part of the traditional Jewish establishment, as well as by postmodern midrashists.

A surface reading of ibn Ezra's 'path' analysis would probably depict it in the following terms. The first path deals with the Ge'onim, whom ibn Ezra accuses of being too rationalistic and philosophically oriented. The second path criticises the Karaites for repudiating the Oral Tradition and for resorting exclusively to scripture, in order to explain law and exegesis. The third path attacks Christian allegory for holding the spiritual to be superior to the physical. The fourth path criticises the tendency to interpret midrash literally, rather than rhetorically, or figuratively. The fifth path extols 'grammar' and rebukes the traditionalists for failing to comprehend the philosophical significance of many midrashic explanations.

In order to understand his arguments, it is necessary to delineate the four-fold interpretative model used by later Jewish exegetes, which is anticipated by ibn Ezra, and to compare it with the Christian equivalent. The Jewish model, known by its acronym, *pardes*, consisted of four levels of interpretation: *pshat*, *drash*, *remez* and *sod*. Although these terms underwent extensive reinterpretation, they are commonly thought to represent the 'plain' sense, rabbinic herme-neutic, philosophical allegory and 'secret' meaning respectively.

The Christian four-fold model is sub-divided into the literal, allegorical, moral or tropological and anagogical levels of inter-pretation. However, Talmage has shown that these terms do not correspond exactly to the Jewish model. *Pshat* does not always mean 'literal'; *remez* is different from Christian allegory, or typology; *drash* is not exclusively a moral category and *sod* is not anagogy. It may even be more accurate to define ibn Ezra's model as a four-tiered unit, rather than as four different levels of interpretation. This may constitute as important a distinction between the Christian and Jewish models as the difference in definitions of individual terms. In a now famous passage, Talmage uses ibn Ezra as the model for this distinction:

> The question of the development of the four-fold system needs further investigation. For the present, one might be inclined to go along with the coy, jocularly serious or earnestly humorous Abraham Ibn Ezra ...who likened the four senses of Scripture to the four functions of the nose – to

ventilate the brain, to drain it of mucus, to smell, and to improve one's appearance.

Talmage has also suggested that the Christian scheme may actually derive from the Aristotelian four causes, whereas the Jewish model has closer affinities with the Muslim model. This is a pertinent point, as it is generally thought that the Christian tradition was responsible for the development of *pardes* (which is actually a product of early rabbinic thought). In reality, however, Muslim currents, influenced by Greek philosophy, had a far greater influence on the milieu in which ibn Ezra lived.[1]

In this book I analyse the development of the concepts *pshat* and *drash*, as well as a variety of approaches to allegory. I link *sod* to ibn Ezra's fifth, 'grammatical' path, based as it is in *pshat*. I endeavour to demonstrate that, using the nose analogy, ibn Ezra elaborated a system whereby the four modes of interpretation are all contained within the *pshat* and that this constitutes the 'secret' of his grammatical approach.

There is another factor which plays a key role in any hermeneutic analysis: the relationship between text, reader and meaning. This relationship has been well documented in the literature. There are however, specific requirements in the interpretation of religious texts. Once a book has been 'completed', even its author may admit to ignorance of all its possible meanings. This is especially the case when a collection of texts, such as the Hebrew Bible, is canonised and thus becomes a source for praxis as well as theory. Whereas some may argue that interpretation is open-ended, canonical status demands an authorised interpretation.

Authority occurs once the collection of texts has become 'fixed' into one 'text'. A specific group, which has been successful in deciding on the form the 'text' should hold, thenceforth has the authority to interpret. Usually this group has the political leverage to brand viewpoints very different from its own as 'schismatic', or 'sectarian', if not 'heretical'. The politically dominant group thus defines itself as the sole arbiter of authoritative commentary. This phenomenon is very obvious in the development of the Christian Church. However, it also played a large role in the development of Judaism. Punishments for 'heresy' were not as grave in the Jewish communities as among Christians, because Jews did not usually have the political status with which to carry out such punishments. Moreover, a certain amount of intellectual leeway was actually allowed, or even encouraged. This will be described below.

Often, when the authoritative approach is challenged by sectarians, a re-appraisal is deemed necessary by the official interpreters. However, in cases where outside, non-sectarian, forces question not only the interpretation and the interpreters, but the very legitimacy of the religion and its practitioners, then further factors are added to the necessity for constant hermeneutic re-appraisals.

The authorised version of Hebrew biblical writings was known as 'Written Torah', and the authorised commentaries as 'Oral Torah'. It has been demonstrated that both the 'Written' and 'Oral' Torot were edited even before assuming their very earliest unitary forms. Both the process and the result of rabbinic interpretations of Written Torah are known as midrash. Midrashic writings, together with the Mishnah and Talmud, constitute part of Oral Torah.

Central to rabbinic interpretation was the fact that the rabbis regarded the five books of Moses (one of the definitions of Torah) as a text that had been communicated by God, and thus, by definition, as completely unified and consistent. However, it was a text that the human mind could not decipher in its entirety all at once. In order for this to become possible, it was necessary to devise certain principles of interpretation, known as *middot*, 'measures' or 'norms'.[2] These tools of interpretation were influenced by the 'Hellenistic civilisation then dominating the entire Mediterranean world.'[3] Rabbinic tradition maintained that Scripture had to be 'interpreted' (*drash*) and that this idea had been transmitted through a long chain of commentators, commencing with Moses.

In fact, the key biblical passage encouraging rabbinic interpretation was taken to be *Nehemiah* 8:8. In the fifth century BCE, after the return of the children of Israel from exile in Babylon, Ezra the scribe stands in the newly built Second Temple in Jerusalem, together with all the people, men and women alike, and reads from the Hebrew Bible, interpreting it to them. The implication is that only interpretation enables the people to carry out Jewish laws fittingly, and is thus seen as the blue-print for Jewish existence in the future.

The early rabbis believed that the Oral Torah (interpretation) had been given to Moses at Sinai, simultaneously with the Written Torah (text), and that Ezra was merely resuming the practice of interpretating after some years of delay in exile. By the mediaeval era, both the text and its interpretation(s) had become canonised and a further level of interpretative activity had been instigated.

The more modern 'objective' approach to the biblical text has been outlined in the previous chapter. One of its drawbacks is that it does not recognise the claims of the people and norms of the society for which the 'text' is also a holy book and source of practice. The 'objective' approach regards every single artefact, including the Bible, as a historical document, a human product of its age, without relevance to contemporary communities. As 'document', it is considered to relate purely to the specific past, whose communities are dead and buried.[4]

This 'objective' (one is tempted to say 'object-centred') approach fails to appreciate that writing may, at the very least, contain inner contradictions, not to mention a multiplicity of possible interpretations. The early rabbis obviously recognised this problem, as, otherwise, they would not have been compelled to introduce norms of interpretation.

We now know that the interplay of text, reader and meaning is a very subtle one, which needs to be delicately balanced. An exclusively text-oriented approach may overemphasise the impersonal. An exclusively reader-oriented approach may overemphasise the subjective. However, an exclusively meaning-oriented approach may diminish the impact of living a religious life. This third approach may be seen as the primary failing of postmodern exponents of midrashic hermeneutics. All three approaches must be delicately balanced in any attempt at biblical exegesis.

One of the trickiest problems is to define the main rabbinic modes of interpretation, *pshat* and *drash*. Although *pshat* is generally defined as the 'plain' sense, Loewe argues that *pshat* was:

> ... not necessarily the natural meaning of the biblical text, but rather the meaning *traditionally accepted as authoritative or at any rate familiar,* however far from the primary sense of the words it might be.[5]

Occasionally, therefore, a *drash* interpretation could actually become the *pshat* of a phrase or word, depending on the traditionally accepted understanding. Loewe stresses the authority of the teacher, together with the willingness of the community to accept his authority, as the hallmark of a *pshat* interpretation. Thus, even the most far-fetched interpretation could be regarded as *pshat*, as long as it was accepted by a teacher respected in the community.

In this context the amoraic phrase: *ain mikra yotsei midai pshuto* ('no text can be deprived of its *pshat*') seems most apposite. Ibn Ezra uses this phrase in *Path Four*, when criticising the contemporary literalistic approach to midrash. For Loewe, however, the phrase means 'that the student should assimilate his teacher's meaning before employing his own ratiocinative powers'. Here it is authority which is underlined, the problem being legal rather than literary. Loewe concludes that, because of subjective factors, no distinction can be made between *pshat* and *drash*. He proceeds to link the two, or subsume one to the other, rendering any contrast psychological rather than semantic:

> The real distinction between them ... seems to be that *derash* is exegesis naturally, or even experimentally propounded without secondary considerations; if it is popularly received, and transmitted into the body of conventional or 'orthodox' opinion, it crystallises into *peshat*.[6]

These 'secondary considerations' were of prime importance to ibn Ezra. He regarded the keeping of the Jewish law, epitomised by the mitzvot (commandments), as paramount, and directed his exegesis to this end, allegorising where necessary. In contrast, exegetes such as his contemporary, Rashbam, were quite happy to separate biblical exegesis from Talmudic interpretation, as long as the populace still observed Jewish law. Ibn Ezra, however, feared that this separation in interpretation might actually lead to the breaking of Jewish law.

As with other near-eastern texts, the earliest Hebrew scribes copied and accepted lists of 'classical' or 'canonical' writings, emphasising continuity of tradition. The written word was copied, checked and preserved for future generations. In Hebrew, truth and justice were regarded as eternal verities, represented by the terms *emet* and *mashar* respectively. Two biblical books refer to the lost *Book of Yashar*, meaning 'straight' or just.'[7]

Ibn Ezra follows this early tradition when he starts his *Introduction* with a prayer in which he describes his own *Commentary* as *Sefer ha-Yashar*. However, he uses the term *emet* to refer not only to God and holy writings, but also to the upholders of Jewish law, together with their legal and exegetical interpretations. For him, therefore, the term 'truth' covers 'the ancients', their words as God's emissaries and their path(s) to God. It would seem therefore that, in ibn Ezra's case, 'truth' was not a static concept, but involved correct authorised behaviour, as promulgated in different times and contexts.

As well as internal shifts in Jewish definitions of terminology, which affect practice, there are also differing attitudes to the written word in the various non-Jewish exegetical traditions. Handelman compares Greek and Jewish thought. In her view Greek thought had greater influence on the origins of Christianity, which aimed at a 'silent ontology', where the need for words would ultimately disappear. On the other hand, the 'letter' (despised in the New Testament) was all-important to the rabbis, leading them to a:

> highly sophisticated system of interpretation based on uncovering and expanding the primary concrete meaning, and yet drawing a variety of logical inferences from these meanings without the abstracting, idealizing movement of Western thought.[8]

Although Handelman regards this approach as demonstrating the supremacy of rabbinic *drash* over Christian hermeneutics, her definition is actually close to the definitions of *pshat* given above. By driving a wedge between Greek and Jewish thought, Handelman fails to take account of the evidence that the rabbis were in fact influenced by near-eastern and hellenistic ideas in their very methods of interpretation. Fishbane is probably nearer to the truth when he suggests that the ancient Israelites already possessed their own interpretative methods, which they found within the text itself, although later rabbis undoubtedly made additional use of the surrounding hermeneutic tools.

Another advocate of a purely *drash* type of interpretation is Rawidowicz:

> There is no creation which is not at the same time interpretative. Still further, not only a thought but even our sense experience is deeply steeped in interpretations ... as soon as we become aware of our sensory impressions, still more so the instant we begin to conceptualize our sense data, while applying certain laws and forms to them, we are already involved in a process of *interpretatio*.[9]

Rawidowicz contrasts *interpretatio* positively with the more passive activities he terms *explicatio* and *commentatio*. These latter types of interpretation merely 'uncover' and explain the text from the aspect of its form, content, language and historical background. *Interpretatio*, on the other hand, seeks the 'real' meaning of the text. Here we see a typical modern exegetical approach which rejects the nineteenth-century type of biblical exegesis. However, Rawidowicz continues:

> The men of *interpretatio* ... have preserved Israel's thought from "Karaization," from being stifled through limiting literalism and fear-filled *peshatism*. It is they who ... expanded Israel's Sinai, Sinai for Israel, and thus strengthened Israel's capacity and will for survival.[10]

Here, Karaite thought is equated with *pshat* interpretation as the enemy of true 'Judaism', which can only be saved by midrash. As we have seen, however, and will see in subsequent chapters, the truth is far more complicated than this. According to Rawidowicz' definition, it would appear that exegetes espousing the *pshat* approach, such as ibn Ezra, could not be the enemy of Karaism (itself a more complex entity than appears in the anti-Karaite literature). It appears that ibn Ezra has often simply been left out of the equation in the present pro-midrash intellectual climate.

Boyarin recognises the problem of defining *pshat* in the light of contemporary 'midrashic' hermeneutics. He cites Kermode's dictum that:

> Midrash is a reading of the "plain sense of things", but only if we recognize that the plain sense grows and changes throughout history and that this is the Bible's underlying meaning.[11]

Boyarin introduces the concept of intertextuality, the idea that texts are constituted of conscious and unconscious citation of earlier discourse and are dialogical, whilst cultural codes both constrain and allow the production (not creation) of new texts within the culture.

Fishbane also discusses the inner workings of the Hebrew Bible, maintaining that it is itself the product and source of many re-interpretations, carried out because of contemporary political needs. He further suggests that tradition needs constant re-appraisal through transmission, which also helps sustain the religious community. Fishbane replaces the terms 'text' and 'commentary' by *traditum* and *traditio*, thus underlining the symbiotic relationship between the two. He is convinced that all post-biblical commentary on the Hebrew Bible can already be found within the biblical text. He acknowledges the negative, as well as the positive aspects of the *traditio*, which 'culturally revitalizes the *traditum*, and gives new strength to the original revelation' whilst 'it also potentially undermines it.'[12] He gives three reasons for the need for a *traditio*: historical determinants, inner-textual problems and the way the 'tradents' perceived the issues. In this he agrees with Boyarin.

Faur goes more deeply into the status of 'written' and 'oral'. Some texts could be 'read', but not 'written' and vice versa. The Tanna (formulator or transmitter) transmitted the 'rigidly controlled text.' Eventually, 'writing' was regarded by the 'people of the Book' as an 'insane game':

> Rather than play "the insane game of Writing" they heeded the advice of King Solomon – the traditional author of *Ecclesiastes* – "that of making many books there is no end" (12:12). The canonization of Hebrew Scriptures (ca. 100) is the formal acknowledgement of this advice. Henceforth, writing would be a surrogate for the spoken word. It would belong to the "oral Law", which is the "commentary" of the written Law.[13]

'Commentary', or 'oral Law' (Oral Torah), would have two important characteristics. It would be 'unwritable', i.e., incapable of being interpreted in terms of biblical exegesis or *drash*. It would be explained in terms of itself. In addition, unlike the Written Torah which was consonantal only, Oral Torah would be vocalised. The point of contact between the two Torot is *kri'ah*, the vocal version transmitted by the oral tradition of 'reading'. It is the reader who 'mentally supplies the vowels to the consonantal text.'

As this activity 'involves interaction between the reader and the text ... the consonantal text acquires meaning'. According to Faur, there are therefore two aspects of Written Torah: the written but unreadable, and the vocal but unwritable. This is not the same distinction as that between Written and Oral Torah, but rather constitutes written and oral texts of the Written Torah, known as *ktiv* and *kri'ah*. One can 'read' Torah, i.e., recite the unvocalised text according to vocal tradition, from a scroll which is *pasul* (liturgically invalid). 'Writing', on the other hand, is the copying of the scriptural text.[14] According to Fishbane, the process of canonisation started early in the history of ancient Israel, and thus the Hebrew Bible is full of passages that began as Oral Torah and ended as Written.

The rise of Christianity and the threat from its sacred writings, the New Testament, which often appealed to the same texts, made precise definition of the Jewish Canon, on its own, an insufficient safeguard for preserving the Jewish religion. The conflict thus extended into the field of the interpretation of the scriptures which the two communities had in common. This will be seen as one of the influences on ibn Ezra's own hermeneutic approach. It has even been argued that *Targum Onkelos*, one of the earliest translations/ interpretations of the Hebrew Bible, which itself soon became part of the Jewish 'canon':

> may well have been a part of the general attempt in Judaism from the second century A.D. [*sic.*] onward to provide authoritative translations as a safeguard against Christian interpretations of scripture based on LXX.[15]

Certainly, anti-Christian polemic, as well as great respect for *Targum Onkelos*, feature prominently in ibn Ezra's *Introduction*.

There were also Jewish sects which predated the rise of Christianity, such as the Samaritans, Alexandrians and inhabitants of Qumran. It is generally held that the Samaritans were more 'conservative' in interpretation than the group whose views were later to become the norm for the early rabbis, i.e., the Pharisees, although both Fishbane and Weiss Halivni have challenged this view.

The custodians of the *traditum*, or interpretative tradition, were the scribes. Fishbane suggests that, out of respect for the authority of the biblical manuscript, the scribes would deliberately copy textual errors, or at least retain them with their own amendments. He suggests that there are 'internal *textual* criteria for the identification of glosses' and that it is a misnomer to look for the 'original' or 'authentic' text.

The one mediaeval thinker whom Fishbane singles out as being aware of scribal textual annotations is ibn Ezra, specifically with reference to his comment on the phrase *be-yasdo* ('*when it was founded*') in *Ezra* 3:12. Contrary to the traditional interpretation of this phrase, ibn Ezra's historical and common sense persuade him that it refers to the Second and not the First Temple (which had been built about five hundred years earlier). Fishbane thus sees ibn Ezra as a pioneer in the field of historical interpretations, based on the work of the ancient scribes.

In addition to annotations, there were also scribal corrections, which were made not only for textual and lexical reasons, but increasingly for theological reasons, for example, to remove 'pagan' elements from the text. Ibn Ezra is again singled out as a commentator who interpreted the phrase '*bnei-Israel*' in *Deuteronomy* 32:8 as referring to angels, or divine beings, rather than to the more straightforward '*children of Israel*'. Fishbane interprets this unusual reading as proof of ibn Ezra's awareness of an even older reading than that found in the massoretic text, which has been confirmed by the LXX and Qumran versions. Here the phrase '*bnei-el*', '*children of God*' or '*angelic beings*' is used instead of '*bnei-Israel*, '*children of Israel*'.[16] It could be argued that in his interpretation of this phrase, ibn Ezra, the arch-*peshatist*, is not simply practising clarification or *explicatio*, but also *interpretatio*, creative interpretation. Ibn Ezra appears to anticipate the modern approach of combining a comparison of different texts with a qualitative judgment, based on sophisticated theological considerations.

For Vermes, only one factor, canonisation, distinguishes biblical from post-biblical midrash (interpretation). There are various factors involved in interpretation: linguistic problems, or contradictions, 'gaps' in the text, evolutions of ideas and custom. For instance, by the beginning of the Christian era, Jewish exegesis was more than elucidation of Torah. It was now used to support traditions arising from the Pharisaic movement, which itself was regarded as the continuation of the scribal traditions. For Vermes, exegesis inhering in the text itself is 'pure', whereas extra-biblical exegesis is 'applied'. For him: 'scripture as it were engendered midrash, and midrash in its turn ensured that scripture remained an active and living force in Israel'.[17]

In the early part of the post-exilic age, a largely hereditary class of priestly and Levitical scribes had been responsible for the transmission and exposition of scripture. The Pharisees, however, came from the progressive branch of the traditional Jewish laity and could not cite hereditary status in defence of their interpretations. They were therefore obliged, where their doctrine departed from the norm, to use arguments solidly backed by scripture. Out of this arose the technique of exegesis conforming to the *middot*, outlined at the beginning of this chapter. Vermes emphasises the importance of 'applied' exegesis in doctrinal controversies determining sectarian claims, for instance concerning Sadducean literalness. He points out, following Loewe, that 'modern' solutions to scriptural difficulties are often anticipated by this classical approach:

> scholars not misled by the analytical tendency of the literary-critical school will fully appreciate the importance of primitive midrash to a proper understanding of the spirit in which scripture was compiled.[18]

Those who transmitted the scribal, or 'soferic' tradition, together with the 'pairs', or *zugot* (the most famous of whom were Hillel and Shammai, who lived at about the time of Jesus), were later called 'the wise men' (*hakhamim*), 'early wise men' (*hakhamim ha-rishonim*), or 'elders' (*zekenim*). Ibn Ezra may be referring to these groups when he recommends following the 'authorities' when all other attempts at exegesis have failed to unite text and doctrine. It is possible that ibn Ezra regarded the endeavours of these groups as similar to his own attempt to protect interpretation from 'scripturalists', or 'Sadduceans'. Just as he attacked the Karaites for ignoring Oral Torah, so had the Pharisaic tradition attacked conservatives, such as the Sadducees, for sticking rigidly to 'scripture' and divorcing text from life.

Mishnah to Talmud

It has been demonstrated that regard for Oral Torah was already present during the redaction of the Hebrew Bible. When we reach the era of the Tannaim, those rabbis traditionally thought to have redacted the Mishnah, rules for life (halakhot) appear to have become divorced from their scriptural source. There was now a differentiation between halakhah, a collection of rabbinic decisions about the practical application of Written Torah, and aggadah, a means, often rhetorical and fanciful, of inspiring and encouraging individuals to accept and follow those decisions. The first method appealed to reason, the second to the emotions.[19]

The aggadic element gradually attracted ridicule, at first from Christianity and later from Islam and sectarian Jewish groups, such as the Karaites. It was therefore necessary that a change in rabbinic emphasis take place. The Babylonian Ge'onim particularly, influenced as they were by the emphasis on rational thought encouraged in their Muslim environment, downgraded aggadah, conflating it with *drash*, whilst redefining *pshat* as the 'plain' meaning of the text. This factor helps to explain ibn Ezra's own position within the Muslim-influenced Spanish tradition to which he belonged. By his time, moreover, midrashic explanations were often being re-interpreted philosophically.[20]

Ibn Ezra suggests at the beginning of *Path Four* that in his time it was mainly rabbis from lands dominated by the Byzantine Church who supported midrash literally. He singles out examples of midrashim which, in his view, should be regarded as mere light relief after a difficult Talmudic argument. He also variously regards midrash as a support (*asmakhta*) for *pshat*, an example of metaphor, or a philosophical idea.

According to Faur, the difference between halakhah and aggadah is not only one of content, but also of authority and form. Whilst halakhah represents precise, authoritative formulations, aggadah represents those lacking in authority. Halakhah emphasises verbatim transmission; aggadah stresses ideas conveyed by one's own words. Faur even states that 'the object of halakha is to hand down the text, not the sense of the text',[21] adding that occasionally the transmitter himself did not know its sense.

Faur describes three levels of halakhic study. The first is *girsa*, or memorisation, a term stemming from the Arabic 'to fix permanently'. *Girsa* was regarded as a most strenuous activity, which demanded relaxation between bouts of study. An allusion to this practice is found in ibn Ezra's reference to light relief during complex halakhic discussion. The next state is *gamir*, or 'textual analysis'. The final state is *savir*, attainable only after full mastery of the first two states.

As the distinction between text and interpretation became blurred by the halakhic tradition, often held to be more important than the text itself, the rabbis asked why, if the whole Oral Torah had been given at Sinai, some laws were regarded with the strictness of biblical precepts and others as lesser rabbinic injunctions. The answer given was that God taught Moses the principal rules only, and that the authorised teachers of later times were therefore needed to explain the details, thus providing a rationale for traditional rabbinic authority.

The rabbis also argued that there had been times when both Torot had been forgotten, for example during the exile in Babylon in the sixth century BCE and at the destruction of the Second Temple in the first century CE. Certain customs had survived, whilst others had fallen into disuse. Those customs which enjoyed neither textual support, nor logical basis, but which were obviously of ancient origin, were also designated as having been transmitted to Moses at Sinai.[22] We can see, therefore, that the status of Oral Torah soon resembled the canonical status of Written Torah. Weiss Halivni sums up the situation thus:

> The difference in severity between a biblical injunction and a rabbinic ordinance most likely emerged during the tannaitic period. A great many laws previously considered biblical (with prooftexts) now became rabbinic.[23]

The problem facing the mediaeval period was how to explain the anomaly that a rabbinic law could be accompanied by a biblical prooftext and yet remain rabbinically ordained. The answer is that 'by the eleventh century the notion of *asmakhta* [support] had come to mean any biblical exposition that did not live up to current standards of exegesis'.

Weiss Halivni relates this argument to the work of ibn Ezra, and especially to his *Second Introduction*. In contrast to the other great mediaeval *peshatist*, Rashbam, with whom, it will be remembered from Chapter One, ibn Ezra had a major exegetical disagreement, ibn Ezra's main aim was to preserve halakhah, if necessary at the expense of *pshat*:

> Ibn Ezra is ready to compromise peshat (as we understand it) when it contradicts a practical halakha and assume that the rabbis of the Talmud must have known better what constitutes the true peshat. Ibn Ezra insists that we must trust them. Such was Ibn Ezra's commitment to the ultimate value of peshat that he could not conceive of the rabbis having violated it.[24]

We have seen above however, how Fishbane has demonstrated that ibn Ezra occasionally took readings from non-massoretic texts when they seemed to fit the context better. This implies that ibn Ezra regarded the scribes as having contributed to the final redaction of the scriptural text. However, he did not always agree with these redactions, especially those of a non-halakhic nature. Boyarin gives two examples of ibn Ezra's approach: one as literalist, the other as non-literalist.[25] It is in this latter sense that ibn Ezra can be depicted as being influenced by the text itself, searching for all its possible meanings. He strives to interpret 'according to the path of philological structure, which primordial Adam engraved'. In other words, he 'lets the language speak for itself', but only within a grammatical framework which he himself defines!

Talmud

According to Wolfson, the Tannaitic interpretation of the Bible, which we have just considered, together with the later Amoraic interpretation of the Mishnah and the subsequent interpretation of the Talmud can be compared in approach to:

> that of the jurist toward the external phrasing of statutes and laws, and perhaps also, in some respect ... that of ... historical and literary criticism which applies the method of psycho-analysis to the study of texts.[26]

Wolfson also states that the text as a whole is more important for what it implies than for what it actually says. Wolfson makes another comparison: that of a scientist studying nature, who assumes a uniformity and continuity in human reasoning.[27] Jacobs has demonstrated how this comparison between the 'unity of Torah' and the 'unity of nature' can be specifically applied to one of the *middot*, *binyan av*. This method is used 'not as a derivation but as a means of 'discovering' a support in the Torah for the law already known.'[28]

It may be that Weiss Halivni's definition of *drash* is comparable to Jacob's definition of *binyan av*. Weiss Halivni cites two kinds of reaction to this kind of 'reading in'. Firstly, *drash*, or 'applied meaning', can be defined as 'simple meaning' in depth, a concept discussed in Chapter Two. Secondly, as ibn Ezra intimates, *drash* does not imply the discarding of *pshat*.

Like Wolfson, ibn Ezra appeals to nature to justify uniformity and continuity in the biblical text. Just as the nose and tongue have more than one function, so words and phrases have more than one interpretation, which can all be held simultaneously, as discussed at the beginning of this chapter. Ibn Ezra criticises Christian allegorists who retain the spiritual meaning of a text, at the expense of the obvious, contextual and physical. To ibn Ezra this is akin to rejecting half of life, and is thus intellectually dishonest.

According to ibn Ezra of course, especially given the Muslim environment into which he was born, not only the senses, but also reason, is essential to discovering the truth of a text. To emphasise the point, he compares intelligence to 'the angel [i.e. messenger] between Adam and his God.'[29] He concedes that Christians are aware of the significance of reason, but regrets that they do not make use of this faculty, grounded in the senses. One reason for this omission might be their ignorance of the Talmudic rule that two contradictory biblical statements need a third to reconcile them. Ibn Ezra does not directly state that he is using the *middot* in his arguments, but his careful use of examples to illustrate his points reflects the view, pervading his *Introductions*, that Oral Torah is the key to understanding Written Torah. The fact that Christianity rejects this aspect of Torah condemns it to stand forever outside the 'circle' of knowledge, as we shall see.

Another example of ibn Ezra's use of the *middot* in exegesis appears in *Path Five*, where he dismisses the massoretic and midrashic explanations for variations in spellings of the same word in different parts of the Bible. By offering a common-sense explanation of the historical time-lag between two appearances of the same word, he is using the Talmudic precedent of *gezerah shevah*, scriptural analogy.

In the same path, however, he appears to contradict himself by praising *Targum Onkelos* for adding midrashic meanings to a specific text, because 'even the uneducated could understand its *pshat* interpretation'. In this case, according to ibn Ezra, the *pshat* interpretation is so obvious, that Onkelos, who 'knew the root [meanings] better than we', is justified in delving beneath the surface meaning of the text. Here we see a superb mix of ibn Ezra's intellectual arrogance, combined with his attempt to defend the 'ancients' at all costs. Seeing the contradiction in this approach, and maybe in order to keep all his options open, ibn Ezra adds that Onkelos' *pshat* interpretation 'does not deviate ... on account of *drash*.' This is a legal, as well as literary, point. Onkelos cannot help being correct, therefore his *apparent* use of *drash* is not a rabbinic deviation, but part of the authorised tradition.

Jacobs uses the key Talmudic term, *sabara*, to describe this 'common-sense', or reasoned type of argument.[30] A law arrived at by this process required no scriptural warrant, but enjoyed full scriptural authority. As we have seen, ibn Ezra sometimes starts by arguing from common sense, but then inserts a rabbinic hermeneutic device, based on logic, to support his claim. The use of the senses and reason in interpretation was thus enjoined by internal Jewish, as well as external hermeneutic, factors.

In many ways the Talmud came to be regarded as canonical. However, disagreement arose. Was the Talmud solely a source for study, or a legally-binding structure?[31] Weiss Halivni describes the difficulties which arose between scriptural and rabbinic interpretation, especially with regard to practice. Very few exegetes (Rashbam being an exception) regarded their activity as purely exegetical. Ibn Ezra's avowed aim in the *Introductions* is to uphold the legitimacy of the authorised interpreters of Oral Torah (the *Batei Din*), even beyond finding the correct linguistic approach to the text. However, his linguistic integrity prevents him from accepting that *drash*, the preferred rabbinic hermeneutic tool, is necessarily the correct way to understand the text. His solution is to suggest that, unlike the original rabbis, contemporary commentators do not understand the original *drash* interpretations, and are therefore prone to interpret it literally.

For Faur, as for Rawidowicz, there are two classes of reading: the passive kind whose function is 'to unveil the meaning of the text as intended by the author' and 'a crisis of choice', i.e., creative interpretation, which 'excludes intertextuality'. 'Interpretation processes multiple meanings and transforms them into a single significant text.' However, Joseph ibn Megas, an exact contemporary of ibn Ezra, defined formal grounds of distinction between written Scripture and the Talmud. According to Megas, since the Talmud is a commentary, it can never be identical to the 'true Torah'. The 'static' reading of the Bible was made possible by lack of vowels. It was 'unreadable' and thus needed interpreting.[32] Despite this formal lack of canonical status, in practice:

> in the Middle Ages ... rabbinic teaching was indeed the basis of all Jewish religious life. "Judaism" was rabbinic Judaism; the other ancient forms of this once-varied tradition had disappeared. Talmudic literature was now public property; not that everyone studied it, but everyone accepted its authority. Talmudic law was more than material for study, it now really was the law of the community. As such, it demanded clarification and application in all sorts of novel situations.[33]

If Talmudic literature now became 'public property' and was generally accepted as 'the law of the community', then it might also have become canonical, like the Written Torah. Instead, it became 'the official *pirush* 'commentary' of the *Tora*',[34] by dint of its different style and function as an interpretative tool of Torah. However, in practice, it was often regarded as identical in status to the Written Torah.

If Rawidowicz replaced the terms *pshat* and *drash* by *explicatio* and *interpretatio*, Faur uses the terms 'semiotic' and 'semantic'. However, we have seen how Loewe has demonstrated that this distinction is not necessarily defensible, Moreover, Weiss Halivni has argued that one cannot use midrash as 'a kind of salvage operation.'[35] For instance, one has to take into account the Talmudic dictum: 'no text can be deprived of its *pshat*', mentioned above. This phrase is used by ibn Ezra in *Path Four* to demonstrate that the true meaning of a text should be decipherable by *pshat*, with *drash* simply acting as a rhetorical device.

It would be helpful at this juncture if one could define exactly what ibn Ezra understood as *pshat*. Weiss Halivni's discussion of the historical development of its definition actually highlights the problems involved. He shows that in two of the three occasions when the word is used in the Talmud, it signifies 'context'. In the third case, however, it:

is not only against the simple, literal meaning of the verse, a deviation which the rabbis of the Talmud would have tolerated, but is also against the context.[36]

He says that *pshat* only meant 'plain, simple meaning' to the mediaeval thinkers. However, by the time of ibn Ezra, the balance was being restored, as we see below.

In mediaeval times the *drash* interpretation came to be associated with the Muslim concept, '*ta'wil*', or figurative meaning.[37] By ibn Ezra's day, the definition of aggadah and midrash had altered considerably among Jews living in this environment. *Pshat* came to be regarded as the 'original intended meaning'. Ibn Ezra tries to adapt his interpretations to one of the many definitions outlined in this chapter. If all else fails, he introduces the concept of the 'secret' meaning, which he claims is directly attainable through proper understanding of *pshat*, and is not divorced from it, as in so many other cases of Jewish – and, of course – Christian interpretation.

This chapter has aimed to show how the Mishnah, itself the authorised commentary on the Hebrew Bible, needed to be interpreted in its turn. The result was the compilation of the Talmud. Certain rules of argument were established, some of which were expanded by the later Ge'onim and then adapted by ibn Ezra. The status of Bible and commentary were supposed to be differentiated, but in practice Oral Torah often took on canonical dimensions. There is an element of scholarly disagreement about the exact meaning of the hermeneutic terms used in textual exegesis. However, it is clear that the threat from outside religions, as well as internal schisms, encouraged a revised approach to the terms *pshat* and *drash*. By the end of the Talmudic period, it appears that interpretations were regarded more as 'textual implications' than as 'readings in'.

One of the major problems faced by ibn Ezra was that of explaining away authorised usages of *drash*, which he would otherwise dismiss as rhetoric or embellishment. I shall be elaborating this point in subsequent chapters. Now, however, let us turn to an analysis of Christian and Muslim exegesis, which may provide an answer to this thorny problem.

4

EARLY CHRISTIAN
HERMENEUTICS

Let us not always say
'Spite of this flesh to-day
I strove, made head, gained ground upon the whole!'
As the bird wings and sings,
Let us cry 'All good things
Are ours, nor soul helps flesh more, now, than flesh helps soul!'
(Robert Browning, 'Rabbi Ben Ezra': XII)

In order to understand ibn Ezra's attack on Christianity in *Path Three*, as well as his attitude to allegory as a whole, it is essential to analyse the development of Christian exegesis from its earliest beginnings up to ibn Ezra's time. Although most of the following ideas were mediated only indirectly to ibn Ezra, they are, nevertheless, relevant to his hermeneutic work.

In the last chapter I already mentioned ibn Ezra's attack on the Christians for their supposed spiritualised allegorical approach, which appeared to discard the text. This chapter demonstrates however that, in reality, Christian commentators faced similar problems to those encountered by Jewish exegetes, even though their emphases were different.

For the Jews, as we have seen, the main hermeneutic problem was the dichotomy between *pshat* and *drash*, with allegory playing a comparatively minor role, at least in the early stages. For the Christian commentators, allegory was of primary importance, literal and rhetorical interpretations taking second place. However, from the outset Christian exegesis appeared uneasy about a purely allegorical approach, and attempts were constantly made to understand the 'letter' of the text.

However, the Christians failed to understand that the Jews were not 'scripturalists', but emphasised rabbinic commentaries (interpretation) rather than Bible (text), the Oral, rather than the Written Torah. It was primarily the Christian refusal to countenance the

Jewish right to self-determination in interpretation, rather than the Christian allegorical approach, which lead to ibn Ezra's virulent attack on them in *Path Three*. In fact, the allegorical approach had been largely superseded in Christian exegesis by ibn Ezra's day. Ibn Ezra had to face the reality that many Jews were now tending to allegorise difficult passages, a danger he did not hesitate to address.

Fishbane has demonstrated how allegorical typology actually played a part in the inner structure of the Hebrew Bible itself, thus anticipating the typological material extant in the New Testament and its development in the Early Church. In modern times some commentators continue to promote their brand of Christian typology, at the expense of both biblical criticism and Jewish types of typology! On the other hand, there are those who prefer to use critical criteria, in order to downgrade the rabbinic approach. Lampe, for example, accentuates the historical and contextual approach, together with the author's original intentions. He incorrectly regards this approach as alien to the early rabbis. For him, therefore, both *drash* and especially allegory constitute a method which 'cuts away the roots of sound exegesis'. This phrase is reminiscent, in a very different context, of ibn Ezra's endorsement of Onkelos, discussed above. In contrast, Smalley demonstrates that Christian *drash*-like rhetorical methods actually played a part in reviving mediaeval Christian interest in the Hebrew text.[1]

Woollcombe introduces the concept of 'signs' into the concept of typology. He is more sympathetic than Lampe towards the rabbinic approach:

> the Rabbis ... did not discard the text, once they had found the undersense, as one discards the shell of a nut, having found the kernel. ... The object of Alexandrian exegesis was to free the spirit of the text from the shell of words in which it was encased, whereas the object of Palestinian exegesis was to use the actual text to describe the activity of God.[2]

This 'rejection of the text' is, in a nutshell, ibn Ezra's main criticism of the allegorists in *Path Three*. He himself uses allegory only as a last resort and without discarding the text, as he wishes to 'conjoin' (the Hebrew root *hbr* also denotes 'friendship') the obvious and the not so obvious.

Talmage enters the fray by separating the distinction between philosophical allegory and symbol from that between allegory and typology. The first is a mediaeval distinction, the second is modern Christian apologetics. Allegory:

> with its roots in Philo and Origen is seen as discarding the literal or historical sense; the latter, with its purpose of establishing the link between one historical reality and another, is seen as preserving it. Typology is then, 'a legitimate extension of the literal sense, while word allegory is something entirely alien: the former is in truth exegesis, the latter is not.'[3]

Ibn Ezra attacks 'Christian' allegory at a time when total disregard of the obvious meaning was no longer the norm in Christian exegesis. It is indeed possible that his attack includes a veiled warning against the contemporary growth in Jewish philosophical allegorisation, which threatened to undermine religious observance.

The Church Fathers till Jerome

The previous chapter discussed canonical status in the Jewish tradition. The Christian Canon was formulated by common consent. Rabbinic hermeneutics defined at least three kinds of interpretation: authoritative (*pshat*), playful/rhetorical (*drash*, which itself could, with time, be subsumed under *pshat*) and allegory, which was already part of the biblical structure itself.

Very early on, Christian exegesis occupied itself with the role of Jewish Law, Oral Torah. The new religion decided that the biblical ceremonial precepts were to be interpreted allegorically rather than literally. For instance, gentile Christians did not need to undergo circumcision, even though the source of this commandment, the Pentateuch (the Jewish Torah) was regarded by Christians as inspired. In *Path Three*, ibn Ezra scathingly attacks the Christian view of circumcision. For Jews it was a physical 'sign' of God's covenant with His people, not a concept to be allegorised. The phrase *brit milah* can be translated as 'covenant of the mouth', as well as circumcision, thus adding to the connection between the spiritual and physical in Jewish tradition.[4]

According to Lampe, in Christian thought, on the other hand:

> allegory was ... a temptingly useful weapon both in apologetic against contemporary Jewish literalism [sic] (the rabbis came to discourage the use of allegory because of the

advantages which Christian propaganda derived from it), and against Marcion's rejection of the Old Testament [sic].[5]

Lampe does not define what he means by 'Jewish literalism'. Although Christian allegorising was indeed a problem for Jewish exegesis, this was for socio–political, as much as for religious or literary reasons. Christians erroneously translated such New Testament Greek concepts as *gramma*, depicting the Jewish approach, by 'letter', rather than 'writing', or 'written code'.[6] Jews could thus be seen as literalistic, legalistic, stiff-necked and thus worthy of persecution, simply because of an 'incorrect' approach to the text, which Christians felt that they had now superseded. Even those who refrained from injuring Jews physically were ardent in their literary battles against 'Judaism', the religion.

The Church Father, Origen, accused by Lampe of being one of the originators of unacceptable allegorising, actually divided the senses of Scripture into three, the literal, moral and spiritual. He also introduced textual criticism and contemporary Jewish insights into his analysis of linguistic and historical textual problems. The Antiochenes came even closer to 'Jewish' exegesis, by extending the plain meaning to include metaphors and other forms of symbolism. They also made a distinction between *theoria* and 'the mere grammatical construction of words'. In all these tendencies they appear to anticipate the method of ibn Ezra, although they had apparently little influence on mainstream Christian thought.[7]

Patristic hermeneutic approaches to the Hebrew text

I now turn to the limitations of Christian hermeneutics, even when emphasis was laid on the Hebrew text. This was due to both theologico–political prejudice and scant linguistic knowledge. I shall describe the corrections and redaction of the Christian scriptural texts, the growth of the Christian four-fold hermeneutic model and the gradual acceptance of the authority of the Church Fathers as authorised interpreters of the holy text. I have already pointed out that the emphasis on the spiritual interpretation and dichotomy between 'letter' and 'spirit' in Christian thought may be based on a mistranslation of the former word from the Greek. After Jerome, many corrections were made to the Latin texts, by using either the Hebrew Bible, or contemporary Jewish (mainly convert) expertise. However, the main goal of the exercise was to use this new-found knowledge to support the exegesis of the Fathers.

Like Origen, Jerome posited three modes of biblical interpretation, relating to body, soul and spirit, which he reduced to two, the literal and the spiritual, with metaphor vacillating between them. Jerome used the anagogical (mystical) approach as a method of 'ascent' from the literal to the allegorical, but insisted that the spiritual develops naturally out of the literal. However, tropology (the moral path):

> is free and is limited only by these laws, that it must be a pious meaning keeping close to the language of the context and must not violently conjoin really disparate matters.[8]

After learning the rudiments of Hebrew, Jerome began to pay more attention to the 'literal' interpretation of the text, defining the function of the exegete as that of elucidating difficult passages. Jerome came to realise that the Greek translation of the Hebrew Bible, the LXX, was full of errors and re-editings. He therefore decided to revise the Latin translation and subsequently made a new and original translation of the Hebrew text, helped by the oral assistance of Jewish teachers, 'reflected in the occasional agreement of his version with the Targum',[9] and Greek versions. This endeavour culminated in the Latin work which eventually became known as the *Vulgate*.

It is interesting that the Hebrew manuscripts used by Jerome were regarded by him as 'the Hebrew truth',[10] whereas they too, of course, had been subject to editing, as discussed above. The phenomenon of admiring Jewish scholarship, and even requesting assistance from contemporary Jews, whilst retaining a contempt for the Jewish people themselves and their Oral Torah, remained a dichotomy up to and including the period of ibn Ezra. Sensitive Jews must have been aware of this prejudice. It is undoubtedly one of the factors behind ibn Ezra's harsh invective against Christians and their ideas.

Loewe compares the habit amongst early mediaeval Christian teachers of using whichever of the Latin texts best suited their 'missionary activity' to 'the rabbinic device of revocalizing a word in the Hebrew text.'[11] This was a common midrashic practice, and one that is frowned upon by ibn Ezra in *Path Four*.

Jerome's translation helped acquaint Christians with the Hebrew Bible, an achievement continued by the eighth-century Alcuin. From this time, the authorised Christian commentaries were invested with nearly as much authority as Scripture itself, thus paralleling the attitude displayed towards the Talmud by the Babylonian Ge'onim, which will be discussed below. By the eleventh century, just before ibn Ezra's era, the Latin texts of the Bible and its commentaries were being corrected with general church approval. Nevertheless, all changes were aimed at elucidating the earliest church exegesis, just as Jewish exegesis aimed at better understanding of the early rabbis. In the latter case, of course, faulty translations were not the issue.

Loewe makes it clear, however, that 'textual conservatism' in Christian exegesis lasted until the twelfth century, when Abelard and others exposed 'inconsistencies found within the Fathers themselves.'[12] At this point there was renewed interest in Hebrew scholarship, especially in the field of exegesis. In 1109, the third abbot of Citeaux, Stephen Harding, 'erased such passages of the Old Testament as were not to be found in the Hebrew', with the assistance of a Jewish convert who spoke French. It is possible that encounters such as these particularly annoyed ibn Ezra. He may well have regarded converts to Christianity as traitors, who betrayed their people twice, firstly by converting and secondly by helping the 'enemy' gain inroads into the 'betrayed' religion.[13]

Augustine

The great commentator, Augustine, took a middle path 'between literal and allegorical exposition' and 'gave the 'letter' a concrete chronological reality which it never had before.' He maintained that one must first believe a fact and only subsequently seek its spiritual meaning. Like the Antiochenes, he subsumed metaphor under 'literal' interpretation, and regarded textual difficulties as 'part of the divine plan for disciplining the rebellious human mind.'[14] In addition, Augustine recognised the importance of community in interpretation. He would therefore appear in many ways to be encouraging a hermeneutic similar to the Jewish one, but he has had a mixed reception among Jewish analysts.[15] It is probably fair to say that his view that the 'letter' leads to a higher spiritual 'truth' differed in emphasis from the mainstream rabbinic view that the 'letter', properly understood, itself encapsulated the 'truth'.

Christian exegesis from Augustine to Bede

Gradually, Christian exegetes grew uneasy with allegorical interpretations. In at least one case, described below, lack of life experience is cited as the reason for often interpreting scripture against its plain sense. However, as with Jewish exegesis, there were times when non-allegorical approaches could lead to unsophisticated rhetoric, unlikely to aid greater textual understanding.

The Bible began to be regarded as 'an encyclopaedia which contained all knowledge useful to man, both sacred and profane'. Methods used in the deciphering of contemporary classical literature were introduced into biblical interpretation, leading to a 'piecemeal' approach, based on the 'accumulation of curious and marvellous facts'.[16] Ibn Ezra seems aware of the danger of this approach when criticising the Ge'onim for introducing 'alien wisdom', without understanding methodology.

Gregory expanded Augustine's teaching that all knowledge was contained in the Bible, encouraging a personal approach to the text. Gregory understood that his audience needed digressions and asides in order to retain interest in the subject. This approach, similar to midrashic rhetoric, is dismissed by ibn Ezra as being useful only for the unintelligent and immature. He expected more of his readers.

The patristic tradition ended with the Venerable Bede who, in contrast to Gregory, was well versed in contemporary science and sparing in his use of allegory. However, he was of the opinion that:

if we seek to follow the letter of Scripture only, in the Jewish way, what shall we find to correct our sins, to console or instruct us, when we open the book of the blessed Samuel and read that Elcana had two wives, we especially, who are celibate ecclesiastics, if we do not know how to draw out the allegorical meaning of sayings like these, which revives us inwardly, correcting, teaching, consoling?

Statements such as these, in which approval of celibacy is linked to both moral rectitude and allegorical interpretation, were bound to trigger an adverse reaction in ibn Ezra, even though, in his own day, Christian exegesis was becoming far more attentive to the actual text.[17]

Christian exegesis from Bede to the Victorines

This period witnessed the further canonisation of the authorised Christian tradition, as expounded by the Church Fathers. Jerome's

Vulgate was revised and anthologies were formed to make the patristic tradition more accessible. The formation of the new compilations is not dissimilar to the description of the development of Talmudic learning in Chapter Three:

> Instead of taking their quotations from the original patristic writers, they were apt to enlarge existing sets of extracts, or their memories of oral teaching derived from the Fathers, or to employ pupils to collect extracts for them.[18]

Just as Jewish readers had to find methods to deal with contradictions in the Bible and Talmud, so Christian exegetes had to reconcile conflicts between different, and sometimes unequal, writers. The solutions found by these Christian exegetes were similar to those faced by Jewish exegetes:

> One alternative was to give both explanations, leaving no doubt as to his real preference by a turn of phrase; another was to reconcile the two, showing that fundamentally there was no disagreement; the boldest course was to discuss and select, admitting that as human authorities the Fathers stood below the divine authority of Scripture.[19]

There was one major difference between these Christian methods and those used by the Jews: 'the divine authority of Scripture' was not a phrase which appealed to the rabbis. So keen were they to stress the exclusivity and divine sanction of their own oral tradition, that they branded so-called Jewish 'scripturalists', those who did not follow Oral Torah, as 'heretics'. One could argue that for the rabbis, the Talmud became more, not less authoritative, than Scripture.

Gradually, Christian compilations gave way to commentaries, which led to an acceptance of differing views and the raising and answering of questions. Variant readings were discussed, including comparisons with the Hebrew text. One very important development was the attempt to define 'letter' and 'spirit', and to decide, yet again, where to subsume metaphor. Questioning patristic authorities and studying Hebrew were the two main achievements of this period, leading to the achievements of mediaeval exegesis. A similar trend appeared among Babylonian Jews in post-Talmudic times. Just as the Christians studied the Hebrew sources more closely, so the Ge'onim were influenced by Muslim advances in linguistics and philosophy, utilising them in all their intellectual activities. From the tenth until the middle of the eleventh century there was a sudden shift away in Christian interest from compilations and commentaries to liturgy and secular studies. Once again, we can see how ibn Ezra deals with this dichotomy in his own tradition. He extols the virtues of 'arts or sciences', but only as an aid to better understanding of the biblical text, which, he feels, leads to a greater awareness and practice of Jewish tradition. The Christian 'alogical' period was followed by a growing expertise in dialectic:

> Rhetoric ... could be used as an aid to Bible study without any danger to the student's faith; the only risk was frivolity. Dialectic could be turned against Christian doctrine, and grammar in the hands of a trained logician could raise complicated problems.... When original written exegesis began again towards the middle of the eleventh century, it had gained by the long preparation. Commentators brought to their studies a fresh awareness of difficulties, with a new and more forceful technique.[20]

Ibn Ezra's own dichotomy consists of balancing midrash, theology and grammar. This leads him to a redefinition of midrash as philosophical truth.

In conclusion, by the time of ibn Ezra, Christian exegetical emphasis had altered to include textual analysis and acceptance of rhetoric as a religio–politically relevant hermeneutic device. The type of Christian exegete ridiculed in *Path Three* no longer represented reality. Ibn Ezra's attack is thus not exclusively an anti-Christian polemic, but is also aimed at two types of Jewish exegete. Firstly there are those, like the Christians, who do not accept Oral Torah and whose grammatical approach is 'scripturalist'. Secondly, there are those, like the Christians, who threaten to undermine the keeping of the mitzvot, by espousing philosophical allegory. The first group is encapsulated for ibn Ezra by the Karaites and the second by the Ge'onim. In ibn Ezra's view, these two disparate groups threaten to undermine the unity of the Jewish community and its reciprocal relationship with authorised interpretation.

5

MUSLIM HERMENEUTICS

Earth changes, but thy soul and God stand sure
(Robert Browning, 'Rabbi Ben Ezra': XXVII)

This chapter discusses the main factors in Muslim hermeneutics and philosophy which formed the basis of ibn Ezra's approach. The extent of Muslim influence on ibn Ezra's hermeneutics has not always been appreciated in traditional Jewish circles, although it has been recognised in scholarly circles. It is, however, difficult to assess the extent of direct influence on ibn Ezra. There is no doubt that ibn Ezra was heavily influenced by ibn Sina,[1] known in western circles as Avicenna. Ibn Ezra was also influenced by his Jewish forbears, the Karaites and the Ge'onim, who themselves were directly influenced by Muslim hermeneutics and philosophy. Muslims and Jews residing in Muslim lands used similar methods to overcome hermeneutic problems. Inevitably, the definitions and comparative importance of the concepts *pshat* and *drash* changed in the process.

The Muslim scholastic interpretative tradition was known as *kalam*. It was not philosophy *per se*, but arose to buttress Muslim beliefs by logic and defend Islam from attack. In the same way, certain principles of logic had been established in the Jewish tradition, as discussed above. Gradually, *pshat*, the contextual approach, joined logic and the senses in acting as a bulwark to buttress the Jewish tradition, especially against Karaism.

One of the main branches of the *kalam* was known as the Mu'tazilite school. The Mu'tazilites emphasised reason and therefore explained anthropomorphic passages in the Qur'an allegorically. By the eighth century various translations of Greek philosophy into Arabic were underway, introducing practical subjects, such as science and medicine, to the ever-growing Muslim empire. Among the major translations were the main works of Aristotle and Plato, as well as the neoplatonic *Enneads*, by Plotinus (204–70), wrongly attributed to Aristotle, and *Liber de Causis*, by

Proclus (420–85), the last important Greek philosopher. These translations greatly influenced the development of Muslim philosophy, which in turn influenced Jewish thought.

The first philosopher to write in Arabic was al-Kindi, a Muslim who was completely ignorant of Syriac and Greek. He became a patron of the translations movement and was also a precursor of the Mu'tazilite school. He attempted to find a balance between theology and philosophy.

As well as adherents of *kalam* and neoplatonism, two other Muslim groups influenced subsequent Jewish ideas: the Shi'ites and the Kharijites. The former arose after a quarrel between the followers of the fourth Muslim caliph and Muhammad's son-in-law, Ali. The caliph's followers were known as Sunnites; the secessionists Shi'ites. This group posited the idea of an 'ideal' caliph, stemming from the direct line of Muhammad and who was therefore designated for office rather than elected.

The Shi'ites branched off into three groups, all of which influenced subsequent Jewish thought: the Messianists, Isma'ilis and 'Twelvers'. Many Shi'ites contributed to Mu'tazilite thought. They esteemed the independent judgment of qualified jurists above rulers. However their intellectual elitism would not have appealed to the majority of Jewish traditionalists, known at this time as Rabbanites. For these, the traditions of the Jewish community were of paramount importance. The Kharijites questioned the basis and limits of political authority, and advocated the Qur'an as a last source of appeal. Their approach can be compared to that of the Karaites.

Thus, by the ninth century, three or four main currents of Muslim thought had arisen, aided by the translation of Greek classical and neoplatonic texts. Nevertheless, many of the tensions necessitating such a development were already present within Islam, as they had been in Judaism and Christianity.

Al-Kindi (ca. 790–866)

Al-Kindi's influence on ibn Ezra was probably indirect, being mediated through the work of the Jewish philosophers, Isaac Israeli and Sa'adiah Gaon. There are nevertheless, four main areas in which al-Kindi may be compared to ibn Ezra. He attempted to explain scripture through philosophy; he believed in the 'chain of tradition'; he regarded sense experience and reason as the foundation of knowledge; he was long-winded. Despite being the first Muslim writer to attempt the harmonisation of philosophy and theology, he nevertheless 'departed from the teaching of Aristotle on a number of major issues and remained thoroughly imbued with the spirit of Islamic dogma.'[2]

Al-Kindi's description of the relationship between motion and time (based on Aristotle) is similar to that of ibn Ezra. For al-Kindi, the creation of the universe is a form of change, or motion. However, unlike Aristotle – and in tangent with monotheistic religion – he regarded motion, time and the universe as finite. Like the Mu'tazilites, al-Kindi regarded God as having a special unity, which transcended matter and form. In similar fashion, ibn Ezra states that God is 'One, whilst creation is dual, of matter and form, or two worlds'. Al-Kindi regards human creation as passive, in the sense that humanity acts merely as God's 'agents'. He nevertheless concurs with the Aristotelian 'great causal chain of being', thus avoiding the total passivity which might denigrate God's total power over creation. Ibn Ezra appears to share this compromise position. He regards planets, angels, human intelligence and even the rabbinic judges as divine 'agents', whilst allowing the latter two a certain amount of independence. Both thinkers use the term 'wisdom' to denote these agents.

Al-Kindi was also influenced by Aristotle in his view that causation and truth were the goals of knowledge. For ibn Ezra, this truth is embodied in the early authorised interpreters of the sacred text. Already, Aristotle had claimed that the 'forefathers' embody truth. As Al-Kindi states:

> dedicated to the quest of truth, we ought to begin by setting forth the views of our predecessors as readily and as clearly as possible, supplementing them where necessary "according to the norms of our own language and times". We should avoid prolixity in discourse, which has allowed false seekers after truth to misinterpret and repudiate the study of philosophy in the name of religion, of which they are devoid, and which they merely exploit for their personal aims and ambitions.[3]

This passage is very similar both in content and language to views later held by ibn Ezra. He discusses the importance of linguistic norms and customs when criticising both the Karaites and the massoretes. He condemns prolixity in the Ge'onim, but in support of religious tradition rather than philosophy. He condemns prolixity in midrashists, in order to support philosophy rather than religious tradition! He uses the term *reyq*, 'devoid', when accusing the Karaites of being ignorant of Hebrew, and therefore incapable of discussing biblical grammar points. He also accuses the Karaites of vacillating according to their whim, just as al-Kindi accuses theologians of exploiting religion for personal gain.

Al-Kindi defined philosophy as 'the knowledge of the reality of things according to human capacity',[4] dividing 'knowledge' into the sensory and the rational. Ibn Ezra considers it a duty to stretch ones capacity to the utmost for the sake of truth. Possibly basing himself on Sa'adiah, he also states that if reason, common sense and tradition contradict each other, we must, as a last resort, interpret according to our utmost 'capacity'.

Another area of similarity between al-Kindi and ibn Ezra concerns the relationship between the soul and the process of cognition. Al-Kindi alluded to the relationship between imagination and prophecy, a theme later developed by al-Farabi and others. Ibn Ezra discusses the link between prophecy and reason, divorced from sense perception:

> There are passages in the Torah which contradict others, such as '*Man does not see Me and live*' [*Exodus* 33:20], which [does] however [convey] the truth through the balance[d use] of reason. Another passage [states]: '*And they saw the God of Israel*' [*Exodus* 24:10], which is confirmed by reason.[5]

Al-Kindi regarded himself as following the Aristotelian view of reason in which 'in the act of cognition, the distinction between Reason and its object disappears completely'. As I stated at the beginning of Chapter One, ibn Ezra was the first Jewish thinker to posit the goal of union between the person thinking, the act of thinking and the thought.

Al-Kindi aimed to use philosophical ideas to support religious tradition.[6] Ibn Ezra wishes to strike a similar balance. He criticises the Ge'onim for using philosophy as a goal rather than a tool, whilst at the same time occasionally succumbing to their methods. Like al-Kindi, ibn Ezra hints at the possibility of a very rare type of prophetic knowledge, situated beyond the capacity of the senses and reason. According to al-Kindi:

> ... it is not excluded that such knowledge might be possible at the superhuman, or divine level. Such ... is the case with prophetic knowledge, reserved by God for his chosen

emissaries or apostles, who can dispense altogether with the human process of rationalization and partake directly of a supernatural light, which God imparts to whomsoever he pleases.[7]

The description of such knowledge is remarkably similar to ibn Ezra's description of his grammatical approach, *pshat*, or 'the straight path'. To reach the goal of *pshat* in ibn Ezra's system, one would have to assimilate all available types of scientific, as well as religious, knowledge. One would also have to perfect his religious practice, and thereby prove to be a suitable channel for the expression of God's truth. For ibn Ezra, this type of knowledge is mediated through the *Bet Din*, the spiritual descendants of those to whom God spoke through prophecy and who, in his view, combine within themselves all necessary tools for knowledge of the highest wisdom. Ibn Ezra even hints at the possibility of divinity in the ancient rabbis by equating them with 'truth'.

Al-Kindi was an unusual Muslim philosopher, because his faith in religious dogma was sustained and even strengthened through the philosophical insights gleaned from Greek thought. His successors, including those from his own school, soon succumbed to religious scepticism. It seems that the power of rationalist thought and abstract speculation, chiefly prevalent among Mu'tazilite sympathisers, led to religious doubts, particularly about post-biblical prophecy, doubts shared by Karaites and the arch rationalist Gaon, Shmuel ben Hofni.

Al-Razi (864–925/32)

Al-Razi was interested in every aspect of knowledge, including philosophy, but challenged some basic Muslim beliefs and was regarded as an iconoclast. He was also no respecter of persons,[8] a trait he shared with ibn Ezra. Al-Razi was essentially a Platonist, whose goal was that the soul should divest itself of its material body:

> God created man and imparted Reason to him from the "essence of His divinity", so that Reason might eventually rouse the Soul from its earthly slumber in man's body and remind it of its genuine destiny as a citizen of the higher (intelligible) world and of its duty to seek that world through the study of philosophy.[9]

Ibn Ezra advocates a similar practice, but encourages the observance of the mitzvot, as well as the honing of the intellect. He therefore succeeds in keeping intact the volitional side of humanity, as delineated by traditional religion.[10]

Al-Farabi (ca. 870–950)

Two features of al-Farabi's theories are relevant to ibn Ezra, namely his neoplatonic, emanationary system and his theory of language. According to Fakhry, the whole of Muslim neoplatonism is contained in the *Enneads* and *Liber de Causis*, which discuss:

> the utter transcendence of the First Principle or God; the procession or emanation of things from Him; the role of Reason as the instrument of God in His creation and the locus of the forms of things as well as the source of the illumination of the human mind; the position of the Soul at the periphery of the intelligible world and the link or "horizon" between the intelligible and the sensible worlds; and finally the contempt in which matter was held, as the basest creation or emanation from the One and the lowest rung in the cosmic scale.[11]

Although ibn Ezra is greatly influenced by such views, he finds it difficult to reconcile the idea of emanation with the traditional view of creation *ex nihilo*. He appears to take an intermediate position in this respect between al-Kindi and the neoplatonists, suggesting that creation took place out of primordial matter. However, his attitude to matter itself is ambivalent. He definitely encourages the view that the soul should free herself from the body. However, when attacking philosophical and religious systems which he regards as overly other-worldly, and whose adherents misunderstand the typical *pshat* straightforward textual interpretations, he praises the body at the expense of the spiritual. It would appear, then, that his stance is dictated as much by political as linguistic or philosophical concerns.[12]

Al-Farabi played a seminal part in the popularisation of Greek philosophy in the Muslim world. His account of Aristotle's *Physics*, in which he discussed the dualism of matter and form, efficient and final causes of motion and the non-physical first principle of motion (the Prime Mover), is especially relevant to an understanding of ibn Ezra. Al-Farabi's cosmology was based on a combination of Aristotle and Ptolemy. The intelligence of the last sphere, the moon, is known as the 'active intellect', which presides over the sublunar world. This active intellect 'conveys forms to the world, thus constituting the rational structure of the universe. It also actualizes the potential intellect of the individual.'[13]

Al-Kindi's original ideas were thus developed by al-Farabi. A person who attained the 'acquired intellect' approached the level of the active intellect, where the intelligiser, intelligised and intellect would combine, becoming free from matter. This state could be viewed as approaching the divine, and such a person was considered a philosopher or sage. If he also possessed a perfect imagination, he could be considered a prophet. The Aristotelian agent, or active, intellect was known in the neoplatonic tradition as intellect or mind. Ibn Ezra combines both forms of terminology because of his desire to defend Jewish tradition from pure emanationary theories.[14] Even a person who does not reach the ultimate goal of acquired intellect is assured of an insight into the rational processes of the mind and the structure of the world.

Ibn Ezra describes the instigating role of both the heavens and the active intellect; al-Farabi describes the importance of insight, which is derived from active intellect, but is not identical with it. This divine faculty relates to the objects of imagination in similar fashion as senses to objects. The celestial principles are present in us as objects of imagination. Unlike the intellect, therefore, imagination is connected with sense impressions. Imagination is responsible for both dreams and prophecy. For al-Farabi, therefore, the philosopher is superior to the prophet, being further removed from reliance on the senses. However:

> the effect of prophecy on the philosopher is to transform his imagination in such a way that he acquires the skill of using persuasive expressions and stories to those less perfect than him in the intellectual truths, and possibly in the practical aspects of life too.[15]

This is how ibn Ezra justifies the *drash* methods of the early rabbis: as language deliberately chosen to educate a mass audience, but which cannot be taken as the literal truth.

Al-Farabi's theory of language resembles ibn Ezra's approach in some, but not all respects. Al-Farabi follows Plato's *Cratylus*:

> which he describes as an investigation of the power of language to inform and a critique of the notion that the

meaning of words is a sufficient source of knowledge as to the nature of things.[16]

This can be contrasted with Loewe's analysis of ibn Gabirol's approach to language, which was emulated by ibn Ezra. Here:

> speech is something more than a convenience of human communication; the corollary of which must be a respect for the integrity of the Hebrew language, as constituting the raw material of both Jewish aesthetic self-expression and Jewish creative response to spiritual vocation.[17]

Loewe suggests that, although ibn Ezra anticipates Rambam in believing that 'the highest vocation of man is a spiritually dedicated intellectualism', the latter would not have appreciated ibn Ezra's attitude to language. Rambam was highly influenced by al-Farabi, whose view was that:

> in Arabic, philosophers speak of the essence of a thing as its thatness. Al-Farabi's easy assertion that this notion (of factuality) is found in all languages provides fascinating evidence against the vulgar misuse of Whorfian ideas in the popular thesis that language sets the bounds of thought.

For al-Farabi:

> logic ... deals not with pure concepts but with concepts as they are signified by words.... Language does not impose but does reveal the underlying structure of reality.[18]

In his polemic against the midrashic approach, ibn Ezra goes some way to agreeing with al-Farabi's view of language. Nevertheless, he certainly esteems the 'playful' quality of Hebrew. He regards it as superior to all other languages, not simply as the medium of divine speech, but as the matrix of continuous creative re-interpretation. Goodman claims that al-Farabi's analysis forms the:

> roots of al-Ghazali's profound, ultimately Aristotelian idea that this world is a symbol system, whose unriddling leads us to the supernal world of the divine, the heavenly kingdom, Malakut, which the Ikhwan al-Safa [Brothers of Purity] identified with the realm of Platonic ideas as elucidated by al-Farabi.[19]

In contrast to both al-Farabi and ibn Sina, ibn Ezra agrees with al-Ghazali that religious tradition is superior to philosophy. Nevertheless, he would also concur with al-Farabi's view that true understanding ultimately transcends the sensible, by internalising knowledge. For al-Farabi, as for ibn Ezra, grammar is the key to such thinking, because it 'recognises the same formal relations in all.'[20] Al-Farabi interprets Aristotle as believing that:

> words indicate ... *impressions* in the soul rather than concepts because he wants to include all that arises in the soul when the sensory objects are no longer present to perception.

For al-Farabi:

> [l]anguage develops, in the first instance, as a representation of the notions in our soul; and they, in turn, represent what is external to it. For abstract notions do not occur outside the soul.[21]

Concerning the respective roles of mind and language, ibn Ezra strikes a balance between al-Farabi and the midrashists. Where the two thinkers differ, however, is in the relative importance they place on philosophy and religion. We shall see that ibn Ezra attacks the Ge'onim, maybe unfairly, for holding that religion is merely the handmaid of philosophy. On the other hand, he attacks the midrashic approach, preferred by the religious majority, just as al-Farabi attacks *kalam* for using persuasion rather than rational proofs. For al-Farabi, linguistic usage depends on:

> convention and agreement.... Once words are established as signs of ideas and so ordered that they are capable of signifying the actual nature of things, indirection ... and figurative usage come into play... Thus arise figurative and metaphoric usage.... Metaphor... is not a main source but a derivative of the primary, referential use of language.... Poetry... is not the mother but the daughter of plain prosaic speech. And so it must be if our reference to things is to be by way of concepts that refer to their real natures. For unlike images, words have no resemblances to their referents; and the images words may stand for have real reference only through the concepts whose outlines they suggest to the emerging intelligence.[22]

In contrast to this view of language as 'referential', ibn Ezra regards Hebrew as the very structure by which supernal knowledge can be attained. He does not allegorise away, but regards an intimate knowledge of Hebrew as both the means and the end to this knowledge.

In discussing poetry, al-Farabi uses the term 'usages' to describe how a group agrees on interpretation:

> Any divergence from its usages is barbarous in his ears. One who circulates among such people can preserve in memory the linguistic achievements of the poets and orators of the past – along with the traditions and customs they contain.[23]

Ibn Ezra uses similar language when describing Karaite ignorance of Hebrew usages (*totza'ot*), despite their obvious knowledge of the language. For ibn Ezra, true understanding of language includes shared cultural, religious and contextual, as well as linguistic, criteria. In this emphasis he is amazingly modern. The Karaites, however expert they might be in grammar, do not accept Oral Torah, related to the collective memory of the Jewish people, and thereby betray Judaism.

Al-Farabi maintained that writing appears when oral tradition becomes too cumbersome for memory. His overview of this development, in which scholars begin to collect, compare notes, classify and formulate rules, can be compared to the formalisation of the Talmudic hermeneutic rules, discussed above. Farabi's conclusion that language is a 'tool', rather than a 'cage', and that philosophers of all nations speak to each other via logic and reason, preferring Greek to Arabic,[24] is in complete contrast to ibn Ezra's views on Hebrew. Ibn Ezra is totally opposed to the idea that language can be sacrificed to meaning, although he does aim to achieve intellectual insight, rather than 'multiple meanings' for their own sake. Goodman even suggests that al-Farabi formulated a type of universal grammar, based on logic, and bequeathed it to the Brothers of Purity. Ibn Ezra's concept of grammar, by contrast, is grounded entirely in the structure of the Hebrew language.

Al-Farabi's arguments in favour of the right balance between religion and philosophy are relevant to ibn Ezra:

> If the philosophy grounding the adopted religion is sound but expressed solely or largely in the language of parables,

leaving tacit its apodeictic basis, the religious symbols will likely be mistaken for truth itself.[25]

Moreover, al-Farabi's suggested outcome of such an erroneous approach actually happened to the Jewish midrashic traditions: eventually philosophers attacked religion, being unaware that religious texts could be considered as comprising 'parables of philosophic matter'.

Awareness of arguments similar to those of al-Farabi may be one of the reasons for ibn Ezra's attack on contemporary midrashic anthologies. In his view, their compilers lack the sophistication of the originators of midrash, who knew when it was appropriate to interpret literally or symbolically. Al-Farabi emphasised the importance of correct religious behaviour. For ibn Ezra, correct theoretical understanding leads to correct practice, which in turn results in correct theoretical understanding. In ibn Ezra's opinion, this 'truth' has been internalised by the upholders of Oral Torah.

Thus, ibn Ezra attempts to harmonise two completely different concepts. He introduces Judaism to philosophical ideas regarding the fusion of the acquired and active intellects. To this he adds his own notions concerning the divinity of Jewish spiritual leadership, particularly with respect to interpretation of sacred texts.

The debate between Matta and al-Sirafi (932)

This debate concerned the relationship between language and meaning and the impact of the Greek philosophical tradition on Islam. The participants in the debate were the Nestorian Christian translator and logician, Matta, and the Muslim grammarian, jurist and theologian, Said al-Sirafi. Christian thinkers had already used language and ideas which appealed to pagans, in order to convert them, whilst rejecting certain aspects of Platonism which they found idolatrous. Nevertheless, it appears that many Muslim philosophers accepted the Greek view that souls emanate from God, despite their belief in God the Creator.

As in the case of Judaism and Christianity, there were internal as well as external reasons for the appearance of philosophical arguments in Islam. The concepts of *ta'wil* (figurative) and *zahir* (obvious) interpretations first appeared as legal devices with philosophical relevance. We have seen how Faur equates *ta'wil* with rabbinic *drash*. There were also Muslim arguments from analogy, which appear to resemble some of the Talmudic *middot*.

Aristotelian logic helped clarify concepts in Islamic law which were already utilising a form of internal reasoning. Philosophers used logical demonstration, whereas theologians generally used accepted dialectic. *Kalam* had arisen to safeguard Islamic theology, encouraging the question and answer approach. Just as the Jewish traditionalists (Rabbanites) living in Muslim countries had to fight their external and internal rivals with the tools of grammar, so too did the early *mutakallimun*. The *kalam* was therefore considered as a defensive method:

> a science which involves arguing with logical proofs in defence of the articles of faith and refuting innovators who deviate in their dogmas from the early Muslims and Muslim orthodoxy.

Al-Ghazali, a staunch defender of 'religion' against neoplatonism, was highly critical of the followers of *kalam*, because:

> they relied on premises which they took over from their adversaries, being compelled to admit them either by uncritical acceptance, or because of the community's consensus, or by simple acceptance deriving from the Qu'ran and the Traditions. Most of their polemic was devoted to bringing out the inconsistencies of their adversaries and criticising them for the logically absurd consequences of what they conceded. This, however, is of little use in the case of one who admits nothing at all except the primary and self-evident truths.[26]

This rebuke is similar to ibn Ezra's attacks on the Ge'onim and midrashists. For instance, although Sa'adiah Gaon attacked the Karaites in order to preserve Oral Torah, he used Karaite premises and methods, based on *kalam*, in the course of his attack. On the other hand, the midrashists rely on irrational premises which, when taken literally, are open to ridicule and do not further the cause of truth or Oral Torah.

During the debate in question, Matta, whose native language was Syriac, was chided by al-Sirafi for espousing Greek logic, whilst being totally ignorant of the Greek language, and only slightly conversant with Arabic. Matta's view was that logic is concerned with concepts and is therefore unaffected by translation, serving merely as a tool for distinguishing correct from incorrect usage. Al-Sirafi refuted this claim, stating that logicians need to use the Greek language in order to master logic. Matta advocated reliance on translations, which faithfully reproduce the basic semantic values of Greek into Arabic. For him, the linguistic nuances lost in translation are not essential to the overall meaning. Al-Sirafi disagreed. He suggested that Matta should make a detailed study of Arabic rather than concentrate on Greek concepts. For al-Sirafi, logic is not a way of reasoning, but of speaking properly. Language, as the science of grammar, can be transformed into philosophy. Knowing a particular language thoroughly is thus the root to all knowledge. Matta uses 'balance' imagery to describe logic as the:

> "instrument" of "speech" by which correct "speech" (*kalam*) is known from incorrect and unsound meaning from sound. It is like a balance, for by it I know overweight from underweight and what rises from what sinks.[27]

Ibn Ezra's view is that logic has its place, but that, ultimately, the grammar of a particular language, Hebrew, is the best means of attaining 'philosophical grammar'.[28] Moreover, the upholders of the Oral Torah knew this, so that even when they appeared to interpret illogically, or against grammatical convention, in reality they really understood the text better than we do.

It is this belief in the importance of the Hebrew language that impels ibn Ezra to characterise the Karaites as totally ignorant of 'the deeper senses [*totza'ot*: usages] of the Holy Tongue'. This is why they 'consequently get lost in grammatical mazes'. Like Matta, the Karaites were usually more interested in the quality of the translations, because they wrote in Arabic script. For ibn Ezra, as for al-Sirafi, unless one goes through the physical step of mastering a particular language, 'basic semantic values' will remain elusive. In complete contrast to Matta, ibn Ezra is interested especially in the nuances of language, those aspects that cannot usually be translated adequately.

Faur has shown how Arabic-speaking Jews transformed semiotic and semantic levels of language. He quotes the authoritative massorete, Aaron ben Moses, who was contemporaneous to this debate, as stating that 'lexical meaning is comprised in the [semantic] sense, and the sense is in the synthesis of the mind'. Faur differentiates the Greek metaphysical view of the world, in which 'the mind is eternal ... it can only be', from the rabbinic 'semiotic' view, where everything is 'decoded as speech and writing.'[29] In following this same rabbinic view, ibn Ezra goes further even than al-Sirafi. He maintains that Hebrew script and terminology are essential to providing a true reading of the sacred text.

It is therefore unlikely that ibn Ezra would have agreed with al-Sirafi's concept of logic as a way of speaking properly. For Muslims, the Qur'an was God's speech. To some Mu'tazilites it was the 'direct creation of God and at the same time multiple and temporal . . . created on the lips of him who recites it.' However, the canonisation of Hebrew scripture rendered the '"written" character' of the latter 'too essential to permit them [the Jews] to adopt this kind of explanation.'[30] For Jews, interpretation replaced speech as the key to the tradition. Even Jewish Mu'tazilites, including the Ge'onim mentioned by ibn Ezra, attempted to harmonise all extraneous influences within the Jewish tradition.

In the Middle Ages Judaism was not a powerful political entity, and Hebrew never rivalled Arabic as a dominant world language. Thus, Hebrew did not originally possess its own science of language. It eventually acquired such a science from the Muslims. The Ge'onim, followed by ibn Ezra, used this research to counter Karaite linguistic expertise, questioning previous traditional interpretations as they did so. The dispute between religion and philosophy was to continue in Muslim and Jewish circles and was still current in ibn Ezra's time. Admittedly, the problems raised by these two approaches were not entirely the same for Judaism as for Islam. Jewish tradition is unthinkable without Hebrew at its core. Ibn Ezra was understandably concerned at the role of Arabic in the formulation of Jewish tradition, as demonstrated in both Karaite and Rabbanite writings. On the other hand, Arab traditions, Muslim and non-Muslim, incorporated both Arabic and non-Arabic speakers. Al-Sirafi had to cater for the latter as well. In keeping with Jewish tradition, ibn Ezra emphasised interpretation, not speech. These differences reflect the contrasting views of the two traditions towards their holy books, and thus towards their self-image, in the mediaeval period.

The Ash'arites

The Ash'arites were a group who broke away from the Mu'tazilites, determined to champion tradition at the expense of philosophy. There was a gradual cleavage between the systematic neoplatonic philosophy initiated by al-Farabi, and that espoused by followers of al-Kindi, who sought to build their system on the foundation of dogma. In 912, a more traditional interpretation of Islam was initiated by al-Ash'ari, who had himself studied Mu'tazilite philosophy. The Ash'arites emphasised the importance of tradition as well as reason. We are reminded of ibn Ezra's stress on traditional authority, at least in theory, in contrast to Karaite and Ge'onic emphasis on reason.

In fact, the Mu'tazilites were not closer to philosophy than the Ash'arites, but were rather theologians who used philosophical arguments. The Asharite rejection of philosophy did not entail a similar rejection of reason, as the rational faculty is endorsed by the Qur'an itself. This rational approach also appealed to the Karaites. They rejected Oral Torah and, it must be said, often 'secular' philosophy too, but generally encouraged the use of reason as dictated by the scriptural text. One of the difficulties faced by ibn Ezra was that the 'enemies' of the Karaites, the Ge'onim, the authorised interpreters of rabbinic law, were also attracted by Mu'tazilite doctrine, with its emphasis on philosophy.

Leaman argues that by abolishing prophecy, Muhammad increased the significance of reason, aided by written and oral Muslim Law. Ibn Ezra, however attributes prophetic skills not only to God's chosen Jewish prophet, Moses, but also, through the chain of tradition, to the spiritual descendants of Moses, the early rabbis. Moreover, reason is incapable of explaining those Jewish religious laws which appear to be irrational. Traditionalists held these to be as important as the rational laws.

For the same reason, philosophy had its detractors even within the Muslim intelligentsia. In both religions many philosophical conclusions contradicted the sacred text and tradition, and were thus regarded as an 'alien' way of thinking. Al-Farabi had therefore tried to argue that Greek philosophy at the very least had Arabic, if not Muslim roots. Similarly, ibn Ezra maintained that the early rabbis were well versed in Greek philosophical concepts.

In order to be acceptable to Islam, any new belief or practice had to show compatibility with the Qur'an. Traditional Judaism avoided this difficulty in relation to the biblical text, by revering the interpreters, and their innovations, perhaps even more than the sacred text itself. The normative Muslim approach, therefore, to have had more in common with the Karaites, whose tradition remained oral rather than written.

One of the main differences between the Mu'tazilites and Ash'arites concerned the question of free will. According to the

Ash'arites, it was blasphemy to believe that anyone other than God was responsible for human actions at all times. They disapproved of the use of reason to explain phenomena pertaining to revelation or faith. They maintained that neither God, nor good and evil, could be known independently of revelation. To safeguard the idea of God as creator, they defined the world as being composed of atoms and accidents, respectively enduring and being created continually by Him.

The atomist theory supported an idea of God much more suited to the theological idea of divine free will than the mechanical Aristotelian causal view. The 'atomist' theory remained unpopular in Rabbanite and most Karaite circles, probably because it undermined the idea that science exists, or that there are such things as natural processes. It also failed to account for the phenomenon of motion. Nevertheless, the Ash'arites became the accepted school in Muslim circles.

The Ash'arites assumed a central position on the question of Qur'anic anthropomorphisms, neither completely accepting nor denying the literal meaning of the text. In *Second Path Four* ibn Ezra's own ambiguity towards anthropomorphisms is evident. He does not accept interpretations which refer to God in literal fashion, but he chides Sa'adiah for figurative interpretations of miracles.

The Ash'arites, therefore, re-emphasised the authority of religious tradition at the expense of reason. A parallel is to be found in ibn Ezra's attack on the Ge'onim in *Path One*, and on the Karaites in *Path Two*. However, the Ash'arites did not reject reason completely, stating that its use was encouraged in the Qur'an. Nevertheless, they were fully aware that many religious laws are incapable of being explained by reason alone. In line with Jewish tradition, ibn Ezra regards the upholders of authorised tradition as experts in these matters, whereas the Ash'arites referred the practitioner back to the sacred text, thereby demonstrating their similarity to the Karaites rather than the Rabbanites.

Ibn Sina (980–1037)

Unlike the previous philosophers, ibn Sina's influence on ibn Ezra was direct.[31] Ibn Sina's views on the internal senses enable us to understand ibn Ezra's own ideas on the subject. Especially useful is ibn Sina's contention that there is a philosophical chain linking memory and oral wisdom. It is ibn Ezra's unique achievement to have equated this philosophical chain with the Jewish interpretative chain which links the idea of Torah from Sinai with rabbinic tradition.

Ibn Sina popularised al-Farabi's work. He was the prime target of al-Ghazali's attack on Muslim neoplatonism. Ibn Sina was interested in the usual Greek–Muslim culture described above, but was also influenced by the Isma'ilis and the Brothers of Purity. He believed that contemporary Aristotelianism was good for the general populace, but that 'the true science' was to be divulged only to those who fully understood the truth. As well as developing al-Farabi's theory of cosmology, ibn Sina expressed views on demonstrative argument, which:

> depends on ... certain indemonstrable principles which are directly apprehended, such as the objects of sense, empirical maxims, beliefs accepted on authority, possible or probable opinions universally believed, and finally those primary principles of knowledge on which all proof rests and which are intuitively certain.[32]

Ibn Sina's theory of physics and motion was similar to that of his predecessors. He described original motion as creative, generated by an infinite and incorporeal power which acts through:

> a corporeal power or Soul naturally disposed to receive the incorporeal action.... [A]nimal and human life arise by virtue of the action of these heavenly bodies. But the Soul, as the principle of life, is an emanation from the lowest of the "separate intelligences" or active intellect, the true agent of generation and corruption in the sublunary world and "giver of forms" ... in it.

According to ibn Sina, the soul is unified, but possesses a series of faculties at each of its three levels, ranging from the vegetative, through the sensuous and the imaginative–retentive to the rational. Ibn Sina refines Aristotle when he speaks of:

> the close correlation between the *sensus communis* and the imaginative faculty ... and the introduction of a separate inner faculty, which he calls the estimative ... whereby the animal discriminates instinctively between what is desirable and what is repugnant. Such perceptions are stored in the

retentive faculty, analogous in this respect to the imaginative, in which the ordinary sensible perceptions are stored away.[33]

These ideas significantly increase our understanding of ibn Ezra. Wolfson gives a detailed definition of the 'internal senses' in various mediaeval thinkers. 'External senses' are the five senses: sight, hearing, taste, smell and touch, whose importance ibn Ezra underlines in *Path Three*. The internal senses are those which 'reside *within* the *brain* and operate *without bodily* organs.'[34] Originally, the internal senses were synonymous with Aristotle's 'common sense.'[35] However, there arose two main groups of classification of the internal senses in Muslim and Hebrew literature. Ibn Ezra belongs to the group which includes ibn Gabirol and Rambam.

In ibn Gabirol the three internal senses are *hargashah* (inherent creativity), *makhashvah* (thought) and *binah* (understanding). For these, ibn Ezra substitutes the terms *da'at* (knowledge), *tevunah* (understanding) and *hokhmah* (wisdom), thus retaining a link with the biblical text. *Exodus* 31:3 refers to Bezalel, God's chosen architect of the holy Tabernacle, precursor of the Temple. This Bezalel is '*filled ... with the spirit of God, with wisdom, understanding and knowledge*, as well as all manner of workmanship.' We shall have occasion to return to the Tabernacle later on in this section. For the moment let us pursue the interesting link between wisdom and memory in ibn Ezra's scheme. According to earlier philosophers:

> there are two kinds of memory, one belonging to sense-perception or imagination and the other belonging to thought.... Furthermore, recollection, as distinguished from memory, is according to Aristotle a sort of investigation ... and syllogistic reasoning ... and is therefore only found in man, who has the power of deliberation....[36]

Thus the third internal sense, memory, can refer to either memory of intellectual conceptions, or to 'recollection', which is how ibn Gabirol interpreted 'understanding'. For ibn Ezra, however, memory is linked with 'wisdom', rather than understanding:

> to the intellectual conceptions themselves which form the contents of intellectual memory, or to the intellectual process involved in recollection, for ... he says: "And 'wisdom' refers to the forms [=intellectual forms] which are stored up in the

posterior [ventricle] of the brain in the cranium". In another passage Ibn Ezra speaks definitely of recollection and says: "Know that in the posterior [ventricle] of the brain is recollection, and that place is the storehouse of the forms, so that recollection includes memory."[37]

Ibn Gabirol and Rambam link the first internal sense, imagination, with inherent creativity, whereas ibn Ezra links it with knowledge. Ibn Gabirol and Rambam link the second internal sense with thought, whilst ibn Ezra links it with understanding. To demarcate the exact role of this faculty as a mediator between imagination and memory/wisdom, ibn Ezra uses phrases such as 'weighed in the scale of the balance of the mind'. Ibn Ezra describes the faculty of understanding, and our ability to recognise it, as having being implanted in us by God's wisdom. By asserting that this cognitive balancing act is the foundation to all greater knowledge, even mystical experience, ibn Ezra reminds allegorists that it is related to the external senses, which their allegorising proclivities tend to ignore. Therefore, if a scriptural passage does not contradict the bounds of reason it should be interpreted 'according to its plain meaning (*pshat*) and the normal function [of the wording] (*mishpat*). These two terms are related in Hebrew.[38]

Ibn Ezra concludes that a balanced approach to the text is the true meaning of the mystery of the Tree of Knowledge. He sums up the conjoined physicality and spirituality of this mystery in one phrase: '*ke-milat-basar*'. This phrase can be interpreted in two ways, which represent for him the essence of Judaism (circumcision) and Christianity (the word [made] flesh) respectively. The Jewish interpretation of this Hebrew phrase is 'like the circumcision of flesh'. Circumcision, so repugnant to St. Paul and his followers, represents the covenant between God and the Jewish people. On the other hand, the 'word [made] flesh' is an allusion to Christ who, for Christians, transcends the 'word'. This idea is alien to mainstream Jewish thought, which regards the written word as divine, and exegesis as the most holy of pursuits.[39] This small phrase is typical of ibn Ezra's ability to defend Judaism theologically and linguistically, whilst simultaneously attacking her perceived foes. For him, nature in all its plurality need not be the enemy, but can actually serve as a guide to the whole of life, including the spiritual.

In *Second Path Two* ibn Ezra appears to suggest that the relationship between the Written and Oral Torah parallels that between the external and internal senses. On the other hand, he considers that contemporary advocates of midrash have unfortunately lost the knack of cognitive balancing in their interpretations.[40]

In *Second Path Four*, ibn Ezra defines the three methods of approaching both Written and Oral Torah. Ibn Ezra suggests that if these methods prove fruitless, we must either resort to figurative language, or admit our intellectual inferiority to the earlier sages. The methods are *shakhul ha-da'at ha-yesharah* (weighing of direct knowledge), *derekh sabara* (using our common sense) and *ha-kabbalah ha-nigmara* (relying on the complete tradition). It is possible that these three methods reflect the second, first and third internal senses respectively: balanced reason, the senses and tradition/wisdom, the last including collective memory.

However, there is one passage in the *Introductions* which most clearly depicts ibn Ezra's genius in utilising his multi-levelled approach. This passage occurs at the end of *Second Path Five*, the culmination of his *Second Introduction to the Torah*. Here he states that contemporary sages are no longer skilled in grammar, and therefore need some assistance from him. Alluding to the holy Tabernacle, ibn Ezra sets out his approach to teaching grammar, but uses vocabulary which could just as well refer to the construction of an edifice. He talks about 'foundations, conjugations, usages and details'. It is evident from the context that ibn Ezra is drawing an incisive parallel between the structure of grammar and the structure of God's dwelling-place, thus re-emphasising the link between hermeneutics and divinity in Jewish tradition. Moreover, *binah*, understanding, the second, and balancing, internal sense, is linked in Hebrew to the word *tavnit* (the prototype of the Tabernacle which God showed to Moses on Mount Sinai),[41] as well as to *binyan*, conjugation/construction in grammar.

Ibn Ezra demonstrates that he is not merely using language here in order to pun or poke fun, like some mediaeval Oscar Wilde. In ibn Ezra's hands language opens up all kinds of marvellous possibilities, like a kaleidoscope, forever changing shape and colour, pointing us in directions we would not have believed possible had we stuck to our normal one-dimensional approach.

To emphasis this point, let us investigate the passage on grammar further. *Mossad* is a basic vowel, but also the foundation of knowledge. *Binyan* is not simply a construct, physical or mental, but also a breakthrough. *Totza'ah* is the origin of pronunciation, correct usage, effect and consequence. Lastly, *inyan* signifies a particle (the little thing that adds flavour), matter, thing, context, detail and real meaning. The genius of Hebrew lies in its tiny vocabulary: the same word can signify a minute physical particle and the most sublime metaphysical concept. They are equal. For ibn Ezra the allegorical approach is mistaken when it discards the shell for the kernel. Through his multi-levelled interpretation, ibn Ezra alludes to his four-fold hermeneutic structure, which starts at the foundation, builds up, branches out and eventually acquires meaning. The *Second Introduction* concludes decisively with the phrase, 'afterwards they will stand at its/grasp its feet', referring to the gaining of true understanding at the four corners of the Ark of the Tabernacle.[42]

We can thus see that ibn Ezra was particularly indebted to ibn Sina for his ideas on the internal senses, which influenced his views on the link between memory and Oral Torah. However, these ideas merely served as a basis on which ibn Ezra constructed his own, unique hermeneutic, based in Hebrew grammar, but culminating in knowledge of God.

The Brothers of Purity (Ikwan al-Safa)

The philosophical ideas of this group influenced many Jewish neoplatonic thinkers, such as ibn Zaddik, ibn Gabirol and Moses ibn Ezra, all of whom had an impact on ibn Ezra. In addition, the Brothers' theme that man is a 'microcosm', the epitome of the universe, also influenced Sa'adiah Gaon, Israeli, ibn Pakuda, Halevi and ibn Ezra. Some of the Brothers' language theories also influenced ibn Ezra.

The Brothers' work, known as the *Epistles*, was imported into Spain in the eleventh century and was compared by them to 'a garden of untold splendour', containing 'a hidden ... wisdom that should be disclosed ... only in part'[43] to the chosen few. There were a number of subjects on which the Brothers held views similar to those of ibn Ezra: number, astrology, self-knowledge and the compatibility of prophecy with science and philosophy.[44]

The Brothers compared 'form' in the Universal Soul to 'a craftsman's plan'. This description is reminiscent of the midrashic view of the Torah as the prototype of God's creation. The Brothers wrote that:

> Knowledge, or science, is the form of the object known in the soul of the knower, and art is the expression of that form by its imposition on matter. Education is bringing out ... of

intellectual potential, making the mind actually intelligent, developing the inner likeness of man to the divine and leading us to the supernal realm and immortality.[45]

Ibn Ezra sympathises with this view to the extent that it allows for a certain activity of the will, avoiding the necessary emanation which was advocated by neoplatonic purists. He also agrees with the Brothers that 'words without meanings are like spiritless bodies, and thoughts without any word to express them are like bodiless spirits'. The brothers followed Plato 'in locating a referent for all significant expressions.'[46] Similarly, ibn Ezra demonstrates that *pshat* is of paramount importance, embracing within itself all possible meanings.

The Brothers regarded the differences between religion and philosophy as merely methodological. The more developed the person, the more he could 'rise above the literal or 'overt' meaning of Scripture.'[47] Unlike the neoplatonists, the Brothers questioned if celestial providence and the stars were totally responsible for all terrestrial events. They were very keen to remove all barriers between religion and philosophy, 'and to bring metaphysics and science from the inaccessible heights of pure speculation down to the market place of active, practical concern.' Although they divided believers into three classes, they suggested that it is preferable that beliefs should be understood by as many people as possible, using reason and the sacred text.[48] Ibn Ezra holds similar views.

Like al-Farabi, the Brothers regarded language as conventional.[49] There are some who have the same view of ibn Ezra:

Words are only labels for concepts, like bodies covering souls. Different words may label the same concept.... [T]he presence or absence of the word *and* is insignificant. This strikes a heavy blow to typical midrashic interpretation, where an entire law could be derived from the presence or absence of so small a word as *and*.[50]

Muslim criticism of midrashic anthropomorphisms, together with their preference for philosophical and grammatical analysis, encouraged the negative Ge'onic reaction to midrash, resulting in a reappraisal of *pshat* and *drash*. In this respect ibn Ezra is a true successor of the Ge'onim. However, he also regards words as possessing their own intrinsic mystery and worth, a point he claims was understood by the early sages, if not by his own contemporaries. However, the redefined Ge'onic *pshat* approach:

> required historical perspective, rationalism and linguistic and literary sophistication. By dint of its fairly secular orientation, this method allowed Jewish interpreters to argue the meaning of Scripture on common ground with partisans of other faiths. [This approach] emerged in the Orient and spread to Spain, where grammarians, such as Ibn Janah, and synthetic commentators like Ibn Ezra, defined its decisive application to biblical studies.[51]

Ibn Ezra's positive attitude to the 'body' is articulated in *Path Four*. Here he disparages midrashic explanations 'as mere clothes to the pure naked truth'. The 'clothes' of midrash are impediments to the 'naked truth' of *pshat*, where *pshat* is etymologically related to *pshut* ('naked'). Just as the *guf* ('body') of the beloved is an invitation to hidden pleasures, so the naked truth of a text can elicit a myriad of meanings. The creative exegete is nothing less than the lover of the Hebrew God, revealed as textual interpretation. The more adventurous the lover, the greater the pleasure. The more creative the exegete, the more meaningful the text. This is a far cry from Greenstein's one-sided picture of ibn Ezra as depicted above.

To the Brothers, language was the most spiritual of all the arts, although it 'is not the source but the expression of ... our intellectual susceptibility to divine commands, that renders the soul immortal':

> Indirection too ... is a source of linguistic power. That helps to explain why ambiguity is not an embarrassment but a blessing: it is a guarantor of privacy but also an evidence of the larger, mental reality than underlies our use of language.

The Brothers regarded linguistic logic as the 'branch', and philosophy as the 'root' of their system, leading them to regard words as 'only the conventional signs of ideas'. Rhetoric is one of the lower forms of discourse:

> In higher as in worldly persuasion testimony and reasoning are relied upon; logic is the standard of sound argument, as calibrated weights and measures are the standard of sound value in the marketplace.[52]

These arguments resemble ibn Ezra's description of cognitive balance. He differentiates between linguistic and philosophical logic only when it is necessary to 'emend' (*taken*) grammatical structure in order to reconcile text and traditional interpretation in legal passages.[53] The purely philosophical concept from which the Brothers wished to create a syncretic religion thus becomes the lynchpin of ibn Ezra's scheme for preserving Jewish particularism.

For the Brothers, philosophical logic is impossible without an understanding of linguistic logic. Ibn Ezra equates philosophical logic with Oral Torah. It thus becomes easier to understand his rejection of the Karaites. Despite their linguistic ability, 'they are completely devoid of the deeper senses (*totza'ot*) of the Holy Tongue.' Just as ibn Sina's ideas on the internal senses may have influenced ibn Ezra to equate memory with wisdom, and specifically Oral Torah, we may speculate that the Brothers' view of two different types of logic had some bearing, even if indirectly, on ibn Ezra's equation of Oral Torah with philosophic logic.

Another way in which the Brothers may have influenced ibn Ezra is in their concepts of 'straight' and 'circular'. These terms derived from the Muslim definition of Muhammad's ladder of ascension, at his death, from the mosque at Mecca (changed at a later date to Jerusalem) to the 'further mosque' of Allah in heaven. The Brothers developed the 'ladder' image to depict the 'neoplatonic upward way or "the straight path" ... which the Qur'an commends in numerous passages.'[54] This path is contrasted with the downward, 'ill-directed', or 'crooked' path. The idea was further elaborated by an older Spanish Muslim contemporary of ibn Ezra, ibn al-Sid al-Batalyawsi (1057–1127), in his *Book of the Circles*. According to this book, the Universal Soul:

> encompasses the globe of the spheres. It has ... two circles ... and a straight line ... and the first circle is contiguous with the [all-] encompassing sphere, the latter being its [viz. The Universal Soul's] supernal limit. The second circle is the lowest limit, and its place is the centre of the earth ... between its supernal limit and its lowest limit there is a line ... which connects [the two circles], which they call "the ladder of the ascensions". It causes [Divine] inspiration to reach the pure individual souls, and on it descend [the angels] and ascend the purified spirits to the supernal world. ... In the "straight line" ... connecting the uppermost and the lowest circle we recognise the Qur'anic term "The straight

path" ... which the Ikhwan apply to the upward way.... The ladder or "straight line" ... becomes a symbol of the souls' return to their home.[55]

This book became popular in mediaeval Jewish circles, where the phrase, 'straight line', was translated as *kav yashar*. Many Jewish thinkers used the concept of the 'ladder of ascension' in order to interpret the motif of Jacob's ladder. It is thus highly likely that in his *Introduction* ibn Ezra uses similar images when depicting God as the centre of a circle, to be reached by as straight a path, or grammatical an approach, as possible.

It is feasible, therefore, to conclude that there are several areas in which the Brothers may have influenced ibn Ezra. They gave a philosophical emphasis to their hermeneutic approach. They included the idea of the 'will' in their system, thus countering the emanationary theories threatening monotheistic religion. They viewed man as microcosm. They depicted various paths to God as circular or straight. However, their view of language as a mere pointer to the truth is only partially shared by ibn Ezra, who occasionally accentuates the opposite view: language contains within itself the seeds of its own interpretation. However, the Brothers' differentiation between linguistic and philosophical logic is useful in appreciating ibn Ezra's desire to uphold grammatical accuracy only when Oral Torah is not threatened. Perhaps their greatest influence on ibn Ezra was, however, in their syncretic approach, their belief that abstract truths should be reflected in correct behaviour, and last but not least, in their emphasis on community.

Al-Ghazali (1058–1111)

Al-Ghazali was an important influence on Judah Halevi, ibn Ezra's older contemporary and closest friend. He epitomised that conflict between philosophy, religion and mysticism in Muslim thought which was also present in several Jewish thinkers, including ibn Ezra. Well versed in Ash'arite theology and Sufi mysticism, al-Ghazali's goal was to find the ultimate truth that could not be deceived by sense perception or reason.[56]

Like Halevi and, later, ibn Ezra, al-Ghazali tested the views of a number of groups to discover if they really possessed the truth. His most vehement attack was aimed at the philosophers, represented by ibn Sina. Al-Ghazali believed, nevertheless, that:

"only one who has mastered the science [of philosophy] to such a degree that he can vie with the most proficient in that science" and even excel them would be qualified to show the incoherence of their doctrine.[57]

Here, al-Ghazali resembles Halevi far more than ibn Ezra, whose criticisms are sarcastic and generalised, rather than sober and particularistic. Al-Ghazali's main aim was to attack those who repudiated Muslim beliefs and neglected ritual worship because of their adherence to Greek philosophy. He felt, more than ibn Ezra, that the study of physics and metaphysics could lead to heresy.

Al-Ghazali attacked three neoplatonic propositions: the eternity of the world; God's ignorance of particulars; and the denial of bodily resurrection. The first two are of relevance to ibn Ezra's *Introductions*. Al-Ghazali was one of the first systematic Muslim expositors and refuters of the theory of the eternity of the world. He attacked three aspects of this theory: creation, time and potentiality.

Regarding creation, he first tackled the question of matter and form. Unlike ibn Ezra, he believed in pure creation *ex nihilo* and attacked the neoplatonic view of emanation.[58] Like ibn Ezra, al-Ghazali was careful to attack his opponents on their own ground, but went even further, suggesting counter-arguments to his own. Belief in creation *ex nihilo* assumed that God pre-dated the world and therefore time, despite the apparent absurdity of such a view. Al-Ghazali countered the theory of potentiality with the assertion that something comes from nothing when God decides, thereby stressing the importance of God's will and questioning the existence of causality. He espoused the Ash'arite view which opposed the idea that secondary causes were responsible for efficacy in the natural order. Instead, he stated that there was nothing *'necessary* in the relation between cause and effect',[59] for God's will acted as mediator. Ibn Ezra *does* espouse the theory of secondary causes, in which angels and planets act as God's 'agents', but he dismisses the idea of necessary effects, if this is one of the correct translations of *totza'ot*. Ibn Ezra believed that people should constantly strive to use their own free will to make conscious decisions at every moment, in imitation of God's workings on nature.

Al-Ghazali denied that the order of nature was a matter of chance, asserting that a 'hidden syllogistic power' is embedded in the world, which somehow enables it to continue regularly. Like ibn Ezra in *Path Three*, he compared the structure of the natural world to the logical reasoning process. He accepted ibn Sina's structure of causal connection, but not its impersonal and non-divine nature. He therefore permitted the study of the rules of natural science only if God was recognised as being responsible for 'natural connection'.[60] On this subject, ibn Ezra takes a middle position between ibn Sina and al-Ghazali.

Al-Ghazali's attack on the study of physics would have drawn only a guarded sympathy from ibn Ezra, as al-Ghazali's real quarrel was with those who denied the divine origin of the laws of causality. However, ibn Ezra shared many of al-Ghazali's concerns, especially regarding the study of metaphysics *per se*. Judging by *Path One*, ibn Ezra appears to take a compromise position between al-Ghazali and the neoplatonists, who were the prime object of al-Ghazali's attack.

In conclusion, al-Ghazali tackled many philosophical views which appeared to contradict traditional beliefs and traditions. Like Halevi and, to a lesser extent, ibn Ezra, he was extremely well-versed in the philosophies he criticised. His mystical leanings may also have influenced ibn Ezra's stance, as we shall see below. Like ibn Ezra, he defined his system by outlining the views of four groups. Unlike ibn Ezra, he did not need to advance a separate path, since he embraced the views of one of the groups, the Sufis.

Sufism

The rise of Sufism is relevant to ibn Ezra because of his unusual role in the history of Jewish thought, certain commentators believing him to have been a precursor of Jewish mysticism.[61] Altmann links the idea of 'the true love of God'[62] in Islam and Judaism to the quest for self-knowledge, relating both to the idea of man as microcosm. In his emphasis on adherence to the mitzvot, ibn Ezra may also have been influenced by the Sufi teaching of correct practice.

It will be recalled that four groups were investigated by al-Ghazali, the last one of which were the Sufis, amongst whom he found 'the answer to his own intellectual and spiritual quest'. He was far more learned than any of his Sufi masters. He 'pledged his full support to orthodoxy and bent his efforts to bringing everything he cherished into harmony with it'.[63] To this end he utilised:

> the koranic concept of a Supreme Being, wholly other than the world, which He created by an unconditioned act of free will [al-amr] ... the Neo-Platonic hierarchy of being, in

which Reason serves as the link between God and His Creation; and ... the Hallajian concept of God dwelling in the Soul and using it as an instrument... .[64]

Al-Ghazali therefore united concepts from sources as disparate as the Qur'an, philosophy and ecstatic mysticism, to formulate 'a mystical creed essentially compatible with orthodoxy', even though, in his non-mystical works, he wholeheartedly criticised philosophy. Al-Ghazali used light imagery, based on a Qur'anic verse, in order to demonstrate that reason 'has a greater analogy to God, who created Adam, the prototype of rational nature, in His own likeness' than does sight.[65] Ibn Ezra also uses a variety of sources to delineate his *pshat* approach and shares al-Ghazali's view of Adam.

Al-Ghazali equated the Qur'an and other revealed scriptures with the spiritual and luminous world, of which our world is a mere shadow. Mystics had 'attained the pinnacle of reality and risen above the "plane of metaphor"', realising that the true reality is 'God's face'.[66] Al-Ghazali and ibn Ezra held similar views on the senses, reason, prophecy and religious practice. Prophecy can be described only in figurative terms. Experience is of the highest importance. Al-Ghazali did not, however, advocate total identity with God. His mysticism is:

> an attempt to give the monotheistic ideal of Islam a greater degree of metaphysical cogency.... The doctrine of Ghazali is Semitic monotheism seen through the prism of Neo-Platonism.[67]

We can thus see that there are many areas of similarity between al-Ghazali and ibn Ezra. Firstly, they are well versed in the philosophies which they criticise. Secondly, they use these philosophies to support religious tradition. Thirdly, they emphasise experience of God through practice. In addition, they justify themselves by quoting scripture and their respective religious tradition. On the spectrum between philosophy and mysticism, they are mystics grounded in the philosophic tradition.

Ibn Bajjah (Avempace: died 1138/9)

From the eighth century Spain became one of the most brilliant political and cultural centres in the history of Islam, as well as 'the bridge across which Greco–Arab learning passed to Western Europe in the twelfth century.'[68] Despite the rivalry between Babylon (Iraq) and Spain, cultural relations and ideas were exchanged and, from the ninth century, scholars travelled from one domain to another. After an anti-philosophical interlude, the study of philosophy and science was revived by the middle of the eleventh century, with a tendency towards syncretism.

Ibn Bajjah continued the tradition of al-Farabi and influenced Jewish thought through the work of ibn Rushd and Rambam. He advocated a solitary life, leading to the immortality of the intellect through philosophic study rather than mystical practice. Following al-Farabi and ibn Sina, ibn Bajjah's aim was:

> "contact" or "conjunction" (*ittisal*) with the active intellect, i.e., the attainment of a spiritual or intellectual condition in which the mind is united with this supermundane agency and thereby becomes a part of the intelligible world.

In contrast to theologians and jurists, philosophers and Sufis had considered the theoretical and practical sides of philosophy to be complementary, leading to the soul's happiness in this life through the acquisition of knowledge. The Sufis had emphasised the practical and personal side of this quest, and aimed for 'union', whereas the philosophers, led by ibn Sina, emphasised the theoretical side, their goal being 'contact' or 'conjunction'.[69] Ibn Ezra explicitly posits intellectual contact with God, whilst implicitly sympathising with the Sufi experiential position.

Ibn Bajjah described man as 'one of the intellectual or "spiritual forms"'. At this stage 'the "solitary" is able to rise to that condition of permanence or immateriality which is the characteristic of all spiritual forms.' Then 'he becomes truly divine and joins the ranks of the intelligible substances.' All the Muslim neoplatonists had this aim, which was later developed in Aristotelian fashion by ibn Rushd. Like al-Ghazali, ibn Bajjah described the last stage of the journey in philosophical terms, as being 'brought about by an infusion of a light', which al-Ghazali had called the '"key to all forms of knowledge"'.[70]

Ibn Bajjah's philosophy, regarding 'contact' between the 'acquired' and 'active intellects', has been identified by Sirat as the object of Halevi's erudite criticism in his *Kuzari*, a Jewish apologia, which paralleled the work of al-Ghazali. Halevi disliked this type of philosophy because it did not discriminate between religions. It posited only a socio–legal system: 'the perfect man, the philosopher, may live in it and attain his ultimate objective: conjunction with the Active Intellect'.[71]

Pines has, nevertheless, identified ibn Bajjah's influence on that section of the *Kuzari* pertaining to the 'divine spark' or '*amr ilahi*', which distinguishes the Jewish people from all others. We have seen above how, in al-Ghazali's Sufism, *amr* represented the 'free will' by which God created the world. To philosophers, the term meant a supernatural way of living. To Shi'ite circles, it embodied the divine spark, transmitted by heredity. To Isma'ilis, it symbolised the divine word, action or will.[72] It is therefore irrefutable that ibn Bajjah was widely read in those Spanish Jewish circles of which ibn Ezra was a member. Ibn Ezra shared with Halevi the desire to retain the individuality of the Jewish tradition. Nevertheless, it is true that when Goodman says of ibn Bajjah:

> he sees in the mystic quest no rival to the sciences but their culmination and fruition. Scientific knowledge is constitutive of the comprehensive inflow of the forms that is the true goal of the adept. Further, science ... is not the value-free or value-neutral enterprise we may associate with the term.... Comprehensive knowledge ... does not exclude moral and spiritual truths. They are, in fact, explications of our own nature and role,[73]

he could be echoing ibn Ezra's own *Path Three*.

Ibn Tufayl (1100–85/6)

Ibn Tufayl's only philosophical work to survive is *Hayy ibn Yaqzan*, 'an allegorical novel in which he develops the esoteric themes of the solitary which Ibn Bajjah had placed at the center of his ethical and metaphysical system.'[74] According to Fakhry, 'once the solitary has apprehended truth through unaided reason, he is able to verify ... the harmony of philosophy and dogma, of reason and revelation'.

Ibn Tufayl aimed to venture even further than ibn Bajjah, and expound the 'illuminative wisdom'[75] of ibn Sina as a mystical experience, rather than as merely the result of pure speculation. This was also the aim of al-Ghazali and many of the Muslim neoplatonists. Ironically, it was also one of the aims of the Almohad rulers, who invaded Spain in the 1140s, causing many non-Muslims to flee, as we saw in Chapter One. Ibn Ezra wrote a very similar allegorical work to *Hayy*, which is discussed in detail by Greive. In ibn Tufayl's work, as in ibn Ezra's, knowledge of the Supreme Being is gained not through bodily means, but through the soul, which is akin to the necessary being, the object of knowledge. For ibn Tufayl, however, as for the Sufis, the ultimate goal is 'annihilation of the self or its absorption in God'.[76]

To attain this goal, one has to dwell on both the positive and negative aspects of God's nature. The positive aspects involve knowledge of His absolute unity. The negative aspects go beyond our consciousness, leading to a type of intoxication, possibly culminating in union with God. Here ibn Tufayl amalgamates neoplatonic and Sufi doctrines in a similar manner to al-Ghazali. *Hayy* develops the theme of harmony between reason and revelation, and between philosophy and religion. Scripture is correct in using anthropomorphisms, since most people can only understand 'similes and sensible representation'. This is exactly ibn Ezra's argument in *Path Four* against the literal understanding of midrash.

Fakhry reproaches ibn Tufayl and ibn Bajjah for endorsing a system in which philosophical truth attained through experience or reflection is vouchsafed the privileged few, whereas the masses understand only religious truth. Ibn Rushd and Rambam developed this bifurcation, whereas Halevi and ibn Ezra regarded it as a danger to Oral Torah and, therefore, Jewish tradition. Whilst themselves utilising philosophical arguments, they attempted to safeguard both tradition and the community from the inroads of philosophy. Ibn Tufayl found that 'language, culture, religion and tradition are not necessary for the development of a perfect mind but may well impede its progress'.[77] Halevi and ibn Ezra completely disagree.

It is not surprising that their low opinion of the masses led ibn Bajjah and ibn Tufayl to support the idea that language could be transcended. Ibn Tufayl thought that 'the biases of language could be overcome by reason', not because of the relativity of human thought, an idea he gleaned from al-Ghazali, but because of 'the traditional dichotomy between thought and language' discussed by the Brothers of Purity.

In ibn Tufayl's view, language is biased towards the sensory world, whereas thought depends neither on language nor on imagination. He favoured the use of rhetoric to 'free language' and to act as:

aids to ordinary men, suggesting higher ideas by way of symbols, practical and poetic.... Symbols become an obstacle only when they lose transparency and are taken for the truth itself.

Once again, in *Path Four*, ibn Ezra can be seen to draw the same conclusions as ibn Tufayl, if not for the same reasons. For ibn Tufayl also felt that words are aids to thought, as laws are aids to real virtue. Both are a means to an end. 'Language is a passive tool in all this, not neutral, but not fatal either. Wisdom fulfils itself by cutting clear of it.'[78] We saw in the last chapter how Christian tradition expressed a similar view of language and rhetoric.

Ibn Ezra's attitude to language, and particularly Hebrew, prevented him from embracing this view. When ibn Ezra compared meanings positively to words, it was in the context of a community which took all the nuances of Hebrew and tradition for granted. Ibn Ezra was aware of contemporary Muslim trends towards unity of disciplines, which had been evolving into a two-tiered belief system. He did not endorse this method himself. In *Path One* he even criticises the revered Babylonian Ge'onim, 'great sages ... in Muslim realms', for espousing ideas which were 'far above the contemporary mind', and thus liable to aid divisions. However, he had nothing against using the arguments of these elitists, in order to counter the alleged enemies of traditional Jewish teaching.

Ibn Rushd (Averroes: 1126–98)

Although it was practically impossible that ibn Ezra could have read ibn Rushd's work, he might well have picked up the general ambience in which they were written. Ibn Rushd is particularly well known for his attack on al-Ghazali's anti-Aristotelianism, which itself was a critique of ibn Sina's interpretation of Aristotle. Ibn Rushd's main teachers were ibn Bajjah and ibn Tufayl. He shared their view that religious laws were mere pointers to philosophical truths, which only philosophers were capable of understanding. They held that the truth must be hidden from the general public and revealed only to the chosen view. However, ibn Rushd was far more meticulous in dissecting Aristotle's text and grappling with the relationship between philosophy and dogma than either al-Farabi or ibn Sina had been, and is thus critical of most previous Muslim philosophy.

His solution to the relationship between philosophy and scripture, especially with regard to unacceptable anthropomorphisms and the absence of an authorised teaching authority, was to resort to *ta'wil*, or figurative explanations. He thus recognised philosophy and scripture as equal sources of truth. He therefore resembled the earlier al-Kindi rather than ibn Sina, who sacrificed scripture to philosophy. As was stated above, within the rabbinic tradition the existence of authorised interpreters somewhat eased the problem of authority in interpretation, although the problem was very real in the Karaite community, as ibn Ezra illustrates in *Path Two*.

Ibn Rushd tried to solve the problem of the absence of authorised interpretation by suggesting that only God and philosophers are able to interpret Qur'anic ambiguities correctly, through *ta'wil*. It could be argued, therefore, that the relationship between 'the philosophers' and ibn Rushd is similar to that between the *Bet Din* and ibn Ezra. The '*Bet Din*' acts as a sort of supra-authority with regard to scriptural interpretation.

Following Aristotle, ibn Rushd named three types of argument: demonstrative, dialectical and rhetorical. These are used by philosophers, theologians and the masses respectively. He added that the theologians 'have unlawfully divulged the secrets of interpretation', causing heresy in Islam.[79] Although ibn Ezra attacks various types of interpretations and modes of knowledge, he does not classify their adherents in the same way as ibn Rushd. Instead, he hopes that everyone following the rabbinic tradition, whether scholar or otherwise, can be led to the correct observance of religion through perfect understanding, which he aims to teach them through his *Introductions*. It is the very fact that the Ge'onim appear content to remain sole experts in *ta'wil*, without attempting to educate the masses, that leads to ibn Ezra's critique of their approach. Those later Ge'onim who put the needs of the community first are exempt from this criticism, as we shall see.

According to ibn Ezra, therefore, the rational faculty alone does not lead to God. The Jewish masses of Christian Europe who 'chase' after the rhetoric of midrash, are deemed closer to God than the learned Ge'onim. The reason for ibn Ezra's somewhat surprising show of support for these rhetoricians may be the reverence they display towards Jewish tradition and the *Bet Din*. However, ibn Ezra does resemble ibn Rushd in believing that the earliest writers of midrash knew the 'real' meaning of ambiguous verses better than present-day exponents of the methodology.

Ibn Rushd referred to contemporary exponents of the Qur'anic text as 'theologians' who:

> misunderstanding the nature or purpose of this language, have extended to it the process of interpretation and thereby confused the masses and repudiated the divine wisdom underlying its use.[80]

Ibn Rushd complained that none of the theologians, literalists, or esotericists were capable of true interpretation, mainly because 'their arguments or interpretations are "innovations" which have no basis in tradition'. Moreover, scripture itself contains all three types of proof. Here ibn Rushd uses an argument similar to that of ibn Tufayl, his mentor, namely that the Qur'an addresses each person according to their understanding. Ibn Rushd defines *ta'wil* as:

> the act of extending the connotation of the term from the real to the figurative meaning, *without violating the linguistic usage of the Arabs*, which allows for giving a thing the name proper to its equal, its cause, its accident, or its concomitant.[81]

Ibn Rushd was particularly annoyed with al-Ghazali for divulging the secrets of *ta'wil*. Traditionally, the occasions when *ta'wil* should be used are when no 'consensus' is possible, where scriptural passages contradict each other and when philosophy or natural reason are in conflict with the text. This definition follows closely that of Sa'adiah Gaon, whose language ibn Ezra echoes in *Second Path Four*.

Ibn Rushd was concerned to accommodate philosophy and scripture, suggesting that, when properly understood, they are always in harmony with each other. In addition, the philosopher must subscribe to Qur'anic beliefs. The first belief, according to ibn Rushd, is that God is Creator and providential ruler of the world, but not in the different ways argued by Aristotle, ibn Sina and the Ash'arites. Rather, one should use the Qur'anic arguments 'from invention (or creation) and . . . from providence or design.'[82] Most of the other core beliefs are also found in the Qur'an, and some are endorsed by nature (as suggested by ibn Ezra with respect to Jewish tradition). One example given by ibn Rushd is especially relevant to ibn Ezra. There is nothing in the Qur'an which states that '"God existed together with non-Being" and subsequently the world came into being after it was not'. The Qur'an actually suggested to ibn Rushd that:

The "form" of the world is created in time, whereas both its duration and matter are uncreated. Thus the verse (Koran II, 6) "He who created the heavens and the earth in six days, while His throne rested on water" implies the eternity of water, the throne, and time, which measures their duration. Similarly, the verse (Koran 41, 10) "Then He arose toward heaven, which consisted of smoke" implies that the heaven was created out of preexisting matter, smoke.[83]

In *Second Path Four* there is an almost identical description, based on midrash, of the coexistence of God, the Torah and the Throne of Glory, before the creation of the world.

Ibn Rushd admitted that there were places where reason was unable to provide an explanation of the text. Here, it was necessary, as al-Ghazali had said, to rely on scripture. In similar cases, ibn Ezra resorts either to grammatical structure, or, in legal cases, to Oral Torah, but never to the text *per se*. Ibn Rushd was practising eisegesis, not exegesis, implying that only a philosopher was capable of choosing correctly from one of three possible types of interpretation.

I mentioned above that, in order to rehabilitate Aristotle, ibn Rushd attacked both ibn Sina and al-Ghazali. One of the methods he used was to introduce the idea, later taken up by Rambam, that one cannot use the same language of God as of creation, but that all the attributes applied to God are nevertheless valid. Ibn Rushd also criticised as verbal sophistry the Ash'arite view that there is no causal nexus, only 'efficient causation'. He argued that without a causal nexus there would be no action and that therefore God's role, as posited by al-Ghazali, would be void. Moreover, real knowledge involved 'eliciting the causes underlying a given process'.[84] To deny causality is to deny reason, order in creation, and a wise Creator. To do this not only contradicts philosophy, but also the Qur'an, 'which describes the world as the perfect workmanship of God.'[85]

On a different tack, ibn Rushd attacked al-Farabi and ibn Sina for confusing Aristotle with Plato. He declared their emanationist doctrine to be non-Aristotelian and illogical, as it limited the scope of God's power 'to a single mode of production.'[86] To prove his theory, he discussed three theories of the origin of the world: creation *ex nihilo*; its opposite, latency; and Aristotle's theory, as mediated by Alexander of Aphrodisias. The theory of latency most resembles ibn Ezra's views. Here the agent 'brings form and matter together' and 'reduces what is potential in the patient into actuality'. To say that God 'creates' or 'makes' the world is simply an analogy.[87] Ibn Rushd also reproached ibn Sina for suggesting that essence precedes existence and is capable of being defined independently of the existence of its object.

Despite these attacks, with many of which ibn Ezra would have sympathised, ibn Rushd approved of ibn Sina's theory, taken up by ibn Bajjah and ibn Tufayl, that the material intellect conjoins with the active intellect.[88] He also agreed with them that this goal is possible only for the select few, most people being capable only of moral excellence. For ibn Ezra, moral excellence, exemplified by keeping the mitzvot, is equal in importance to intellectual excellence. In fact they have a reciprocal relationship.

Ironically, ibn Rushd had far greater influence on Jewish philosophy than on his co-religionists. Through Jewish translations he eventually entered the stream of consciousness of the Latin west, where he was known as Averroes. In some ways he was the arch synthesiser; in others the pure Aristotelian, who wished to strip away neoplatonism. He is the last Muslim philosopher whose ideas may have filtered through to ibn Ezra.

In this chapter I have shown how Muslim hermeneutics and philosophy were utilised by ibn Ezra to define his own system. Muslim philosophers attempted to integrate Greek philosophy within their religious tradition, emphasising rationalism. This development affected the definition of *pshat* among Jewish scholars residing within the Muslim world. *Pshat* gradually came to mean the 'plain' meaning of the text. The concept of *ta'wil* was also explored further, and led to a more philosophical approach to allegory. Metaphorical statements could either be reduced to idiomatic expressions, or subsumed under allegory. *Drash* was thus increasingly dismissed as rhetoric by Jewish scholars, or elevated as a figurative device. Mystical trends also influenced the Jewish milieu, and practical teachings on this subject can be compared with some of ibn Ezra's descriptions. The ultimate impossibility of unifying all possible interpretations of a text led, in some quarters, to a double faith theory, positing a two-tiered system of interpretation. Ibn Ezra attempted to counter this trend, as he was afraid it would lead to a break-up of the Jewish community.

There is no proof that most of these philosophers influenced ibn Ezra directly, but he was aware of contemporary currents and philosophical developments. His approach was eclectic. He chose only those aspects which supported his own system and buttressed his definition of Jewish tradition. However, some Muslim thinkers directly influenced the Karaites and the Ge'onim, who are specifically discussed by ibn Ezra in his *Introductions*. These groups are the subject of the following two chapters.

6

THE KARAITES

... watch
The Master work, and catch
Hints of the proper craft, tricks of the tool's true play.
(Robert Browning, 'Rabbi Ben Ezra': XVIII)

The Karaites play an important role in a study of ibn Ezra's *Introductions*, because they raise the very issue which concerns him most: the status of commentary in the Jewish tradition and the relative importance of Oral and Written Torah. Through his sometimes viciously sarcastic comments on the Karaites, it becomes evident that ibn Ezra actually wishes to define himself by their approach. He often criticises in them tendencies which one suspects he recognises in himself, but which he endeavours to curb, in order to safeguard rabbinic tradition and the continuity of the Jewish community, as he sees it. It is noteworthy that elsewhere in his Torah commentaries, ibn Ezra adopts a far more respectful approach to individual Karaite exegetes. This is all the more surprising, since ibn Ezra is generally regarded, together with Sa'adiah Gaon, as the most virulent critic of the Karaite stance. In his *Introductions*, however, he maintains that he will be 'no respecter of persons'[1] in exegetical matters, and he certainly keeps to this assertion.

In order to understand how Karaism arose, it is helpful to examine the political and social factors current in Babylon from the time of Muslim rule. Before the rise of the Ge'onim, the two major rabbinic academies of Sura and Pumbedita had been simple scholastic institutions, which developed Oral Torah. Under Muslim rule the prestige of the Jewish lay leader, the exilarch, declined, whilst the influence of the two academies increased. Their presidents now assumed the title of Gaon, 'eminence'. Additional legislative powers entailed a greater bureaucracy than had been the case under the exilarch, increasing the financial burden upon the Jewish community. In Talmudic times the heads of the academies had been chosen by their colleagues. Now they were chosen by the exilarch, with the result that often the community was represented by men of questionable learning and spiritual development.

A legacy of the Muslim conquest was the access of new territories to which there was mass emigration from the newly-named Iraq:

> The remoteness of these frontier settlements from the metropolitan center of Iraq made them practically independent, in both religious and secular matters, from exilarchic and Geonic authority.[2]

Many of these Jewish emigrants were greatly influenced by their Persian Shi'ite neighbours and questioned the legitimacy of the Jewish leadership, which had, in any case, become open to corruption. This was the origin of the movement which later became known as 'Karaism'.

The name 'Karaite' is usually interpreted as referring to those Jews who adhered solely to scripture rather than Oral Torah.[3] The origins of the 'scripturalist' approach to the text have been discussed above in Chapter Three. The alleged Karaite link with the Sadducees of Second Temple times was very real to ibn Ezra, who saw the rabbinic tradition as following the radical and innovative interpretative tradition of the Pharisees. However, it is incorrect to assume that the Karaites were purely scripturalists, for the very important reason that it is difficult to totally reject tradition in interpretation. Rather, the Karaites were against the notion of a compulsory, divine *rabbinic* tradition. Instead, they developed one of their own, known as *sevel ha-yerushah* ('yoke of inheritance'), based on non-biblical customs accepted by the Jewish community.

It is not only their attack on the rabbinic tradition, but also their proposal of an alternative tradition, which incites ibn Ezra against them in *Path Two*. It is possible that he himself had first-hand experience of the Karaite tradition and 'usages' in Spain. There was a short-lived Karaite centre there at the end of the eleventh century. It was eventually banned by the Castilian government at the request of the traditionalists, mainly because of its missionary activity among the Jewish population. This may be one of the reasons why ibn Ezra alleges Karaite ignorance of Hebrew and grammatical 'usages' (*totza'ot*). He stresses their use of Arabic instead of Hebrew in biblical exegesis, but does not acknowledge that they have their own tradition, despite, or even because of, their expertise in Hebrew and rabbinic traditions. Ibn Ezra believes that if the Karaite 'tradition' takes over, the Jewish community will be led into grievous sin.

The first Karaite capable of writing systematically about his theology was Anan ben David. He established the principle: 'Search thoroughly in the Torah and do not rely on my opinion.'[4] Rather than bolstering the Hebrew Bible as sole source of law, which was his avowed aim, Anan's dictum led to the disintegration of the new movement after his death. According to the early tenth-century Karaite, al-Kirkisani, no two Karaites ever agreed on religious matters. In addition, Anan took several doctrines from extra-Talmudic and Muslim sources, increasing the severity of religious practice.

In order to refute Sa'adiah's sophisticated arguments against them in kind, the Karaites produced scholars every bit as learned and philologically adept as their traditionalist counterparts. Their 'Golden Age', lasting for three centuries until 1200, parallels that of the Jews of Spain. However:

> in a series of polemical tracts Sa'adiah proceeded to attack and refute the doctrine and practice of Karaism, and to demonstrate to his own satisfaction that the Karaites were not just harmless deviators to be mildly chided for their error but complete apostates who should be ostracized from the community of Israel. Sa'adiah's leadership showed that Rabbanism had the seed of reform within itself, and the exclusion of the Karaites from the Jewish community made it impossible for them to participate in this reform, and at the same time, cut them off from the main stream of Jewish thought and social progress.[5]

Karaite interpretations were based very much on the type of *pshat* approach in which context and customary usage are paramount. Traditional rabbinic ideas are accepted only as a support or to clarify ambiguities, and not as a source of divine inspiration. If conscience dictated, it was perfectly in order to change former opinions. As we have seen, ibn Ezra's own approach to 'tradition' is not as unambiguous as he sometimes implies. This can be demonstrated by comparing the *First* and *Second Introductions*. In *First Path Five* he repudiates the Karaites for suggesting that traditionalists contradict 'the written biblical text and grammatical rules.' However, he himself advocates independence in interpreting non-legal passages and, in *Second Path Five*, he even offers to teach the religious authorities the rudiments of grammar and philology. Moreover, in *Second Path Four* he sees tradition as only one of three categories necessary for correct exegesis, the other two being common sense and reason.

The contradictory stance taken by ibn Ezra appears to be symptomatic of his real fears of Karaite encroachment on traditional rabbinic terrain. No doubt, this was a major reason for his desire to leave Spain and ensure, by his teaching efforts, that traditionalists in non-Sephardi lands became aware of the 'correct' grammatical approach to exegesis. Only thus, in his view, would Jewish tradition remain safe from the two-pronged attack of foreign conquerors and internal 'heretics'.

An analysis of the major Karaite thinkers

In this section I review the work of ten Karaite thinkers, chronologically: Anan ben David, Benjamin Nahawandi, Daniel al-Kumisi, Jacob al-Kirkisani, Salmon ben Jeroham, Jafet ben Ali, Hasan ben Mashiach, ben Zuta, Joseph the Blind and Jeshua ben Judah. Anan, Benjamin, ben Mashiach and Jeshua are heavily criticised by name in *Path Two*. Only the first two, Anan and Benjamin, are ridiculed in *Second Path Two*. In the Torah commentaries themselves, chiefly those on *Genesis* and *Exodus*, Jafet, ben Zuta and Jeshua are discussed on an equal footing with the Gaon, Sa'adiah. Jafet and Jeshua are treated particularly respectfully. Al-Kirkisani and Joseph are not mentioned at all by ibn Ezra, but both are important philosophers who admired Sa'adiah. It is highly likely that ibn Ezra knew their work, and they are therefore included in the following analysis.

Anan ben David (eighth century)

It appears that ibn Ezra placed far more importance on Anan's contribution to Karaism than did subsequent Karaite thinkers. His name is immortalised by ibn Ezra in the wonderfully sarcastic pun on his name in *Path Two*: 'And if a dark cloud [*anan*] should dwell on earth'. In *Second Path Two*, ibn Ezra ridicules Anan's attitude to sexual intercourse!

Benjamin al-Nahawandi (830–60)

Benjamin was regarded by later Karaites as second only to Anan in importance:

> ... while Anan freely used Rabbanite exegetical and juridical methods, he came to entirely divergent conclusions, in direct contrast to Benjamin al-Nahawandi, who employed distinctly Karaite methods of legal exegesis, but came to many conclusions identical with or closely parallel to Rabbanite legal norms.[6]

According to al-Kirkisani, Benjamin was extremely knowledgable in both rabbinic and scriptural teaching. He disagreed with much of Anan's teachings, and later Karaites did not accept all his views. It is possible that he influenced Sa'adiah's concept of an intermediary between God and creation, known as *kavod*, or 'glory', which is based on the *kalamic* view of the 'creative word'.

In *Path Two* ibn Ezra refers to the scholastic anarchy initiated by the divergences between Anan and Benjamin. He puns on the name 'Benjamin', 'son of the right hand', and also on its last three letters, *min*, connoting 'heretic':

> This is the way of Sadducees, such as ... Benjamin ... as well as every other [type of] heretic who does not believe in the words of the authorised keepers of the religious tradition. Deviating left or right, each of them interprets the verses as he wishes, even when they concern commandments and statutes.... For how can one rely on their opinion regarding the commandments, if they meander from one side to another every moment, according to their [contextually constrained] thought?

However, despite ibn Ezra's contention that the Karaites 'are completely devoid of the deeper senses [*totza'ot*: usages] of the Holy Tongue', it appears that Benjamin actually wrote 'all his works in fluent and idiomatic Hebrew'.[7] Furthermore, Benjamin acknowledged that pure scripturalism could be impractical, because of changing conditions. In actual fact, ibn Ezra greatly admired Benjamin's exegesis. However, he also lampoons Benjamin mercilessly in *Second Path Two*. Benjamin is typecast as an example of those who:

deny the words of the copyists who were all *zaddikim* [spiritually elevated]; sometimes they [the Karaites] are within the point [i.e., reach the truth] and sometimes surround it. Sometimes they are outside its circumference, like Benjamin, who was both 'left' and 'right' [*yamin*]. For, like every heretic [*min*], he refused to believe the words of our esteemed forefathers.

Here the Karaites are described as occasionally straying completely outside the circle of truth, just like the 'allegorical' Christians of *Path Three*. The pun on *yamin* is extended to include the concept of *min*, a term often used to describe the Christians. It also happens to be the Hebrew term for 'gender', extended to include 'sex'. Elsewhere ibn Ezra compares Benjamin to the serpent in the Garden of Eden. It is therefore not impossible that here, as in *Path Three*, ibn Ezra intends to ridicule the sexual prowess of the unfortunately misguided exegete. As well as being prevented from penetrating the centre of the circle through the correct attitude to exegesis, a person who vacillates on the subject of communal allegiance is also liable to come unstuck in his manhood. Be that as it may, it is clear that Benjamin was an interesting and innovative Karaite, to whom ibn Ezra related in a most contradictory manner![8]

Daniel al-Kumisi (ninth–tenth centuries)

Al-Kumisi, the first eminent Karaite to settle in Jerusalem, differed greatly from both Anan and Benjamin, regarding Anan as a 'champion fool'.[9] According to al-Kirkisani, al-Kumisi was devoted to pure reason beyond all else. His overwhelming intellectual honesty led him to inform followers whenever he reformulated previous ideas, so that they could correct copies of his work. He had an excellent knowledge of the scriptural text and the Hebrew language. His most complete extant work is a commentary on the *Minor Prophets*. In it he bitterly criticised the corruption of the rabbinate and the degeneration of the Jewish people through worldly occupations and pleasures. He blamed the rabbis for the exile of the Jews. He was hostile towards both secular studies and rabbinic tradition. The:

> struggle for the fundamental exclusiveness of the biblical canon incorporates an absolute rejection of "a commandment of men learned by rote" (i.e., the Oral Law) side by side

with the vigorous rejection of "alien wisdom." Thus ... he describes the sins of "the exiles": "They did not return to God to learn from the Law of Moses, but wandered among the nations and [followed] their customs and learned their writings, which are vain writings, alien wisdom, an abomination to God. They did not realize that it was not proper for them to rely on those who smite them, that they would never find any remedy from them...."[10]

This negative reference to 'alien wisdom' can be compared to ibn Ezra's criticism of the Ge'onim in *Path One*. Ibn Ezra is, however, primarily interested in motivation. Secular science is useful when it supports tradition: not in its own right. It must be said, however, that ibn Ezra's commentaries and the *Introductions* are themselves full of lengthy digressions, which show off his own scientific expertise to perfection! Al-Kumisi's negative attitude to Oral Torah and science did not prevent him from encouraging rigorous and rational analysis of the biblical text.

Jacob al-Kirkisani (early tenth century)

Al-Kirkisani was very knowledgeable in all areas of Muslim, Christian and traditional Jewish learning. Although he could be harsh towards the rabbis, he is never as abusive as other Karaite polemicists, 'and toward Sa'adiah Gaon, the bête noire of all tenth century Karaite writers, he preserved throughout a tone of respectful and calm disagreement',[11] making extensive use of the latter's interpretations. Like Sa'adiah and ibn Ezra, al-Kirkisani had a positive attitude to textual commentary, science and reason, using figurative interpretations only sparingly. However, unlike some of the Karaites, he wrote only in Arabic, and was probably never translated into Hebrew. Even Arabic-speaking Karaites were indifferent to him, possibly because he was 'scathing' about Karaite sectarians, including Anan.[12]

In outlining his principles of biblical exegesis, al-Kirkisani promises to explain every detail, especially ambiguities and contradictions 'pointed out by dissenters and deviators.' Here he resembles ibn Ezra who, in *Path Two*, describes the Karaites as 'meanderers ... deviating....' In *Path Five*, ibn Ezra adds:

I shall ... thoroughly, and to the best of my ability, seek the grammatical [form] of every word. Then I shall do my utmost

to explain it.... Heaven forbid that we should get mixed up
with the Sadducees [Karaites].

Whether criticising Karaites or Ge'onim, al-Kirkisani generally
anticipates ibn Ezra's style. Possibly bearing in mind al-Kumisi,
al-Kirkisani further asserts that there is nothing to fear from
philosophy, because it is the key factor in the understanding of text
and religion alike. Ibn Ezra differs from him in believing that reason
plays an important, although not totally exclusive, part in exegetical
comprehension. This does not prevent ibn Ezra from exaggerating
or undermining the role of reason in his system when he feels it
necessary. However, when al-Kirkisani suggests that to deny reason
is akin to denying sense perception, he finds an echo first in
Sa'adiah, his great mentor, and then in ibn Ezra. In *Second Path
One*, ibn Ezra states: 'A person who denies knowledge [reason]
should be compared to someone who denies their own senses.'

For al-Kirkisani there are four sources of knowledge, the first
three being sense perception; things evident in themselves, such as
the fact that lying is bad and blameworthy; and demonstrative
knowledge. The fourth, traditionally transmitted knowledge,
depends on the first three.[13] In theory, if not in practice, these
four sources seem almost identical to ibn Ezra's sources, and
certainly to Sa'adiah's.

Al-Kirkisani used scriptural texts to validate reason, concluding
that 'these are the rational proofs built upon the knowledge based
on sense perception'. However, ibn Ezra acknowledges that text,
senses, reason and tradition are all separate entities, and that,
occasionally, the last three cannot be employed in understanding the
first. In this case, he suggests, one has to employ *pshat* in a certain
'grammatical' way, where apparent anomalies are explained as
'secrets', which 'only the wise will understand.'[14] Using *Psalms* 19:8
as a prooftext, al-Kirkisani suggests that the heart is satisfied
'because of the truth of the premises and conclusions contained in
the commandments.' In mediaeval times the heart was regarded as
synonymous with the mind. Ibn Ezra depicts it as the actual
repository of wisdom, corresponding to the second internal sense,
as we saw in the discussion on ibn Sina in the previous chapter.

Another passage of al-Kirkisani's, which may have influenced
ibn Ezra, states that:

Scripture as a whole is to be interpreted literally, except where
the literal interpretation may involve something objectionable

or imply a contradiction. Only in the latter case, or in similar cases which demand that a passage be taken out of its plain meaning – e.g., where a preceding or a following passage requires it in order to avoid a contradiciton – does it become necessary to take the text out of the literal sense.

An example of ibn Ezra's views on biblical statements which describe 'seeing' God, has been given in the section on al-Kindi in the previous chapter. Commenting on the very same verse, *Exodus* 24:10, al-Kirkisani anticipates ibn Ezra by stating that it 'must not be taken literally and does not signify seeing with one's eye, since it is contrary to reason to assume that the Creator may be perceived with man's senses'.

Another instance of similarity between the two exegetes emerges from al-Kirkisani's maxim that '[t]he Hebrew language is the primordial tongue in which God addressed Adam and the prophets.'[15] This is a remarkable statement for someone who wrote only in Arabic. Moreover, it casts doubt on ibn Ezra's motivation in accusing the Karaites of not knowing Hebrew and thence being incapable of interpreting the scriptural text. However, Sirat emphasises that al-Kirkisani, like most of his fellow Karaites:

> tended to use Arabic characters even for the Pentateuch and books of prayers translated in Judeo–Arabic, and this is an unique phenomenon. On this subject Kirkisani expresses a surprisingly modern opinion: the content of the words is important and not their language or their script. This idea is opposed to the Jewish consensus, which considers the Hebrew language and the Hebrew alphabet as the sacred language of humanity.[16]

Al-Kirkisani's view of language may be 'modern', but many would now have more sympathy with the 'Jewish consensus' described by Sirat. Moreover, she concedes that this same 'Jewish' attitude is expressed by al-Kirkisani 'in another place'. In *Alternative Path Three*, ibn Ezra imitates al-Kirkisani by comparing the structure of Hebrew to the structure of language itself:

> If we find in the Torah [something] unacceptable to reason, we should add or emend [the text] to the best of to our ability, following the structure of language which primordial Adam carved out/decreed'.

The big difference is that ibn Ezra replaces God by Adam. It is Adam who 'carves out' language. This change is probably due to the fact that ibn Ezra's practical approach could not allow him to regard individual languages, even Hebrew, the holy tongue, as other than conventional, i.e., produced by human beings. What is innate, in his view, is the structure of language in general, together with the knowledge of how to interpret it, which has been 'implanted' in humanity by God.

Following on from his 'conventional' view of language, another of al-Kirkisani's principles was that 'Scripture addresses mankind in a manner accessible to their understanding and about matters familiar to them from their own experience.'[17] Ibn Ezra criticises the midrashic approach for ignoring this view of language. Both exegetes use this principle to explain biblical anthropomorphisms, such as 'seeing' God.

The Muslim philosopher, al-Kindi, influenced al-Kirkisani's ideas on physics and cosmology. The Mu'tazilites influenced his ideas on atomism. The greatest influence of all, however, was Sa'adiah. Al-Kirkisani, in turn, influenced many Ge'onim, including the arch-rationalist, Shmuel ben Hofni, who is mentioned by ibn Ezra in *Path One*. It is ironic that al-Kirkisani's positive attitude to science as a tool for understanding scripture had greater influence on ibn Ezra than on fellow Karaites.[18]

Salmon ben Jeroham (tenth century)

According to Karaite tradition, Salmon had been Sa'adiah's teacher, but in fact, Salmon outlived Sa'adiah by a number of years. Moreover:

> Salmon's principal work is his polemical epistle against Rabbanism in general and Sa'adiah in particular, written while the latter was still living.... .[19]

Only the Hebrew version of this epistle has survived and is written in rhymed quatrains. Many of Salmon's arguments, but not the poetic style or aggressive manner, were borrowed from al-Kirkisani. Although Sa'adiah and ibn Ezra both ignored Salmon as unimportant, he is relevant to ibn Ezra's *Introductions*, because of the similarities of style and polemic.

In his rhymed polemic against Sa'adiah, *Book of the Wars of the Lord*, Salmon denies that the Oral Torah was given at Sinai, since it was later written down, not by Moses, but by those who 'altered God's alleged words'. In his view this constituted a great offence. Moreover, the Mishnah was written in contemporary language, without those signs or miracles which accompanied the giving of the Written Torah. In addition, it contradicts itself, allowing two points of view on one issue, and containing 'no law of logic', or reason. Salmon would rather have 'weighed the word of the Lord' than listen to arguments between two human scholars. He asserts that everyone should be entitled to their own opinion in interpreting Written Torah, and therefore can dispense with Oral Torah. For Salmon, interpretation, the raison d'être of rabbinic tradition, belies divinity.[20]

Salmon's polemical poem is similar to ibn Ezra's *Introductions* not only in subject matter and style, but also in vocabulary. 'Paths' denote life-styles. Knowledge is 'weighed' or 'balanced' by reason. Even the word 'testimony', used sarcastically by ibn Ezra in *Path Two*, in order to promote the superiority of Oral Law to Karaite conventions, is used first by Salmon in contemptuous dismissal of Oral Law:

> Now if Israel and Judah are all united concerning the validity of the oral Law which is, as they say, perfect, let them offer their testimony, and let their voice be heard.

Salmon also anticipates ibn Ezra in the following statement: 'I have seen an end to every human purpose, but there is no end to the speaking about the majesty of His ordinance and utterance'. This sentiment is actually based on *Ecclesiastes* XII: 12–13: '*of making many books [there is] no end ... let us hear the end of the matter*'. Ibn Ezra finishes *Path Four* by imitating both *Ecclesiastes* and Salmon: 'and the end of the matter is that to *drash* there is no end'.

The most striking similarity, however, comes towards the end of Salmon's poem, where he states that all the difficult questions:

> in the songs of the Prophets and other seers, All these things are already mentioned and are contained therein; They are bound and fastened therein as firmly as with ropes, And they do not follow from thy words and thy worthless traditions.

Salmon asserts that the Bible is self-explanatory and does not need Oral Torah or rabbinic tradition to explain it. In his *Introductory Prayer*, ibn Ezra sets down his own textual approach:

This is the Book of the straight path by the poet, Abraham.
Bound by cords of true grammar. To be deemed fit by the eyes
of knowing judgment. And make happy all those who uphold
it.[21]

Ibn Ezra's apparently bold preliminary declaration may, in fact, be
regarded as a defensive parry in the opening bout between himself
and would-be detractors of tradition and Oral Law. For Karaites
such as Salmon, truth was 'bound up' in the scriptural text,
whereas for ibn Ezra it was 'bound up' in interpretation, through a
marriage of philology and tradition. Salmon's polemic criticises all
knowledge not obtainable from the text itself, including science and
rabbinic tradition.[22] The polemic demonstrates the classic argument
between Karaite adherence to Written Torah and traditional
rabbinic adherence to Oral Torah. Salmon is a 'peshatist' in
Rawidowicz' narrow sense of the term, described in Chapter Three.
Ibn Ezra was actually the very opposite:

> ... vis-à-vis the Karaite belief that all who add to Scripture
> lose even their basis in Scripture, ibn Ezra holds the opposite
> view, namely, that one who goes no farther than Scripture
> loses even Scripture itself.[23]

Jafet ben Ali (late tenth century)

Jafet is of immense importance for an understanding of ibn Ezra.
Although he is mentioned more than any other Karaite exegete in
ibn Ezra's Torah Commentary, he does not feature in either of the
far more polemical *Introductions*. This omission is possibly due to
the fact that Jafet was a sober commentator, who avoided most of
the excesses of Karaite exaggeration, despite being virulently
critical of Sa'adiah. Like al-Kirkisani he was a great Bible
commentator, who wrote only in Arabic. His commentaries have
led to comparisons with Sa'adiah and even Rashi. Like Sa'adiah, he
translated the Hebrew Bible into Arabic. Jafet's exegesis was
extremely literal, often breaking the rules of Arabic grammar. His
commentaries included theological discussions and polemics
against Christianity and Islam, which would have attracted ibn
Ezra. He also wrote on law, Hebrew grammar and history. His
exegesis was not original and he admits that he relied on his
predecessors:

... and occasionally borrows from Rabbanite sources, the Targumim ... the Talmud, and the works of the Karaites' archenemy, the Gaon Sa'adiah. Nevertheless his commentaries enjoyed great favor and exerted a powerful influence upon later Karaite exegetes and also upon the Rabbanites, including among the latter no less an authority than Abraham ibn Ezra.[24]

Sirat compares Jafet to al-Kirkisani and distinguishes him from Salmon. However, Salmon and Jafet both followed al-Kumisi, rather than al-Kirkisani, in their negative attitude to science. Unlike al-Kirkisani, Jafet posited three, not four, sources of knowledge: rational knowledge (including sense perception), revelation and true tradition. He also emphasised the limitations of human knowledge. By contrast, al-Kirkisani actually found 'evidence' within the biblical verses themselves in support of secular study.

Jafet's views on textual exegesis are similar to, but not identical with, those of ibn Ezra. Only when 'contradicted by *reason* or by a *clear text*' should one refrain from interpreting literally, because the words must have 'been used in some metaphorical or improper sense', especially in cases of anthropomorphisms.[25] Jafet also anticipated ibn Ezra's non-traditional view, expressed in *Path Four*, that humanity is not the goal of creation.

According to Sirat, Jafet's work epitomises the three most important Karaite ideas of this era: the quest for rational knowledge; the certainty that this knowledge is given by God through the Scriptures and not through Oral Torah; and the feeling that only the Karaites possess the key to truth, 'which is expressed in vigorous polemics'. One of the polemics included the attack on Sa'adiah and his school, mentioned above. Jafet described:

> ... the vanity of the *traditionalists* like *El-Fayyumi* [Saadiah], who have destroyed Israel by their writings; who maintain that the Commandments of God cannot be known by study, because it leads to contradictions; so that we must follow the tradition of the successors of the prophets, viz. the authors of the Mishnah and the Talmud, all of whose sayings are from God. So he has led men astray by his lying books; and vouches for the veracity of anyone who lies against God.[26]

As we shall see in the following chapter, Sa'adiah had nothing against Bible study, as long as tradition could play a part in elucidating its awkward passages. As ibn Ezra says in *Path Two*:

> We ... do not learn from the Torah what is entailed in 'witnessing' the month.... It is not clearly explained in the Torah of Moses how to ascertain the number of months in the year.... This is the reason why all these commandments need the received Oral Tradition.... For [in reality] there is no difference between the two Torot, as both are handed down to us by our ancestors.

Here ibn Ezra demonstrates, by various specific examples, the inability of Written Torah alone to explain certain crucial legal questions. He ends by linking the two Torot as of equal importance in the chain of tradition, thus answering criticisms made by Karaites such as Jafet.

When analysing Jafet's exegesis in his *Commentary* on *Exodus*, ibn Ezra occasionally agrees with him, comparing him favourably with other Karaites, especially ben Zuta and Jeshua ben Judah. Sometimes he gives an alternative interpretation, without criticising Jafet. Sometimes he agrees with Jafet's conclusions, but not with his arguments. At other times he criticises him for using non-contextual or midrashic argument. Occasionally, he criticises Jafet's knowledge of Hebrew grammar; inaccurate citations from traditional sources; and ignorance of scriptural 'short cuts'. It is noteworthy that ibn Ezra is never rude about Jafet, but uses his approach to demonstrate the lack of Karaite uniformity in exegesis.

Whereas Sirat has described the similarities between al-Kirkisani and Jafet in their attitude to science, Simon has emphasised the differences. Whilst al-Kirkisani was in favour of secular studies, Jafet condoned only those scientific explanations which could be supported in the scriptural text. He quotes scripture to demonstrate how:

> anyone who adds (that is, who makes assertions that cannot be proven from Scripture) is detracting from the truth of God's word, and merits punishment as one who errs and leads others astray.[27]

In *Second Path Two*, ibn Ezra uses the same terminology to defend both the early rabbis and oral tradition from Karaite attacks:

> We have received the Written Torah from the hand of our fathers, and likewise heard the Oral Torah from their mouths. Heaven forbid that they should add to or subtract from what

we have received and heard. If there is no truth in Oral Torah, then there is also no cure in the Written Torah, for in Holy Scripture there is not one commandment satisfactorily explained.

Hasan ben Mashiach (tenth century)

Ben Mashiach is described by the fifteenth-century Karaite chronicler, ibn al-'Hiti, as having lived in Baghdad, where he held religious disputations with a Christian scholar. Ben Zuta states that he also held religious disputations with Sa'adiah, but this is chronologically unlikely, although he did write a polemical treatise against him.[28] Ben Mashiach is mentioned in *Path Two* as one of four Karaite 'heretics' who disbelieve Oral Torah. Otherwise, he does not appear in ibn Ezra's work.

Ben Zuta (tenth–eleventh centuries)

Otherwise known as Sahl ben Masliah and Abu al Surri Sahl, ben Zuta was a younger contemporary of Jafet. He had a conflict in Cairo with Jacob ben Samuel, an important and zealous follower of Sa'adiah. Jacob wrote a sharp letter to ben Zuta, attacking Karaism in general, and himself in particular, for having come to stir up trouble among traditionalists with his missionary activity. Ben Zuta's answer was given in the form of a long epistle, written in Hebrew, which included the words: 'I shall perhaps make a translation of this work into Arabic, so that it might be read by those who do not know Hebrew.' He thus contradicts ibn Ezra's subsequent depiction of him in *Second Path Two* as the prototype of Karaite ignorance of Hebrew:

> For they do not understand philological structure, nor have they heard it in their land, like [for example] ben Zuta, who sinned in all his interpretations.

Ben Zuta's rejoinder to Jacob ben Samuel has been described as:

> ... of outstanding importance. It represents the earliest complete example, so far discovered, of practical Karaite propaganda, couched in simple terms and addressed not to the learned and privileged classes of Rabbanite Jewry but to the man in the street.

As stated at the beginning of the chapter, Karaite missionaries were inspired by their radical contemporaries within Islam. Unlike them, Karaites were unlikely to be executed, but might be expelled from the area, as happened in ibn Ezra's childhood.

Ben Zuta was extremely prolific. His works included a refutation of Sa'adiah's critique of Karaism, and a pointed attack on rabbinic hypocrisy. He asserted that Karaism considers each individual to be responsible for their own soul. He used scripture in order to demonstrate that three factors: the text, 'analogy' (an hermeneutic method inspired by Islam) and 'testimony' are all needed in order to verify the truth of Oral Torah:

> There is no duty resting upon us to follow our fathers unconditionally; rather it is our obligation to scrutinize their ways and to set up their deeds and judgments over against the words of the Law. If we find them identical, without deviation, we must accept and obey them without change and follow them. But if their words contradict the Law, we must reject them and ourselves search and investigate, using the method of analogy, because the precepts and other things written in the Law of Moses are in no need of any sign or witness to testify whether they are true or not, whereas the words of the fathers require a sign and a trustworthy witness, that you may know whether or not they are true.'[29]

At the very end of his *Introduction*, ibn Ezra uses similar terminology to make the opposite point, that scripture, especially the legal part, is dependent on traditional rabbinic teaching:

> However, concerning [verses dealing with] laws, statutes and regulations, if we find two [possible] meanings to a verse, one of which follows the exegesis of the official interpreters [of Oral Torah], *zaddikim*, every one of them, we must, without a doubt, lean with all our might on their true [interpretation]. Heaven forbid that we should get mixed up with the Sadducees [Karaites], who say that their tradition[al interpretation] contradicts the written biblical text and grammatical rules. In fact, our esteemed forefathers were true, all their words are true. . . .

According to ibn Ezra, the upholders of tradition know from the context which criteria to use in making an exegetical decision. By occasionally accepting a textual explanation based on extra-scriptural arguments, the Karaites are behaving inconsistently. Ben Zuta admits that occasionally Karaites use rabbinic or rational arguments in exegesis, but for him intellectual freedom is the key factor.

I shall now consider ibn Ezra's views on ben Zuta, as expressed in his commentaries on *Exodus*. In *Exodus* 20:22, ibn Ezra berates him for making a point without bringing scriptural analogies which could contradict it. He describes him as 'dazzled with blindness'. In verse 23, ibn Ezra ridicules ben Zuta's ignorance of contextual criteria and everyday speech. The prooftext reads '*Nor shall you climb up by steps [be-ma'alot] unto My altar, so that your nakedness is not uncovered upon it*'. In the *Second Commentary* ibn Ezra cites proofs both from other verses and from idiomatic speech to demonstrate that the phrase '*be-ma'alot*' means '*by steps*' and not '*by sacrifices*'.[30] In order to drive his point home and ridicule ben Zuta, ibn Ezra uses the very words from the biblical text:

> ... but Ben Zuta thought to go up the ladder of wisdom in his vanities, but his nakedness was uncovered upon it. This is how we shall describe every heretic who does not believe in the words of our esteemed forefathers.

In the earlier *First Commentary*, ibn Ezra refers to ben Zuta as 'one of the Sadducees' who by this error:

> ... really did 'sin' against the Lord, by interpreting the commandments according to his own opinion, and also because he has no knowledge of philological structure.... His sin uncovered his nakedness, for the words actually mean 'by steps'.

Ibn Ezra adds that the meaning of the ambiguous phrase is well-known from Mishnaic and Talmudic sources. He thereby implies that if ben Zuta had adhered to tradition, the correct grammatical form of the verb would have been known to him. It is this link between traditional interpretation and grammatical accuracy which makes ibn Ezra unique among exegetes.

In his commentary on *Exodus* 21:24, ibn Ezra criticises ben Zuta for his literal interpretation of the law of talion ('*an eye for an eye ...*'). Ibn Ezra explains that Sa'adiah utilises the traditional rabbinic argument based on reason or common sense, which demands monetary compensation, rather than retaliation, for an injured eye. The victim's actual loss can never be assessed completely accurately. In his retort ben Zuta uses another scriptural prooftext, but fails to counter Sa'adiah's argument that a preposition (here *tahat*) can have more than one meaning. In context, the correct interpretation is 'to fine', rather than 'to inflict physical damage'.

Ben Zuta then brings a proof from a non-Pentateuchal verse, but Sa'adiah's view is that this verse refers to an equivalent, but not identical, punishment, and is therefore invalid. Sa'adiah thus demonstrates the indispensability of Oral Torah in deciphering the meaning of Written Torah, using a technical argument to conclude that there is no difference between the two in practice.

In both commentaries on *Exodus* 21:35 ibn Ezra criticises ben Zuta for making a stupid statement based on a grammatical error which could have been avoided had he been aware of traditional interpretations. The prooftext reads:

> And if a man's ox hurts his neighbour's [*rey'ehu*] ox so that it dies, then they will sell the living ox and divide up its financial worth, and they shall also divide up the dead [ox].

Once again, ibn Ezra cannot resist exploiting the prooftext in order to ridicule his opponent: 'and the ox has no fellow [*rey'a*] except for Ben Zuta.'[31]

In his commentary on *Exodus* 22:28, ibn Ezra compares the views of Sa'adiah, Ben Zuta and Jafet. The verse reads literally: '*Your fullness [mele'atkha] and your trickling [dim'akha] you shall not delay. The first-born of your sons you shall give to Me.*' Ibn Ezra agrees with Sa'adiah that '*fullness*' and '*trickling*' refer to 'new wine' and 'pure oil' respectively, and that both allude to Torah scholars. His allegorical interpretation follows the context, in which the first-born son is also offered to God. However, ben Zuta interprets the two words as signifying 'pregnancy' and 'semen' respectively. He regards the verse as an example of the scriptural command to '*be fruitful and multiply*' (*Genesis* 1:28). However, as ibn Ezra points out, if this were the case, the word order should have been reversed to *finish* with pregnancy!

In conclusion, in both the *Introductions* and the Torah commentaries, ibn Ezra is far more critical of ben Zuta than of any other Karaite commentator. This is possibly because ben Zuta's exegeses occasionally led to absurdities, as we have just seen. In addition, he strayed outside the sphere of exegetical polemics, in order to attack social mores by appealing to the masses over the heads of the rabbis. Finally, he claimed to find scriptural proof for the indispensability of Muslim hermeneutics in substantiating Oral Torah. From ibn Ezra's point of view, therefore, he was a very dangerous opponent of traditionalism and thus unworthy of any respect.

Joseph the Blind (Joseph ha-Ro'eh al Basir: early eleventh century)

I have not been able to find an instance of ibn Ezra's mentioning Joseph.[32] He was one of the most important Karaite authorities, a philosopher who studied the Talmud and other rabbinic literature, as well as Mu'tazilite doctrine. He gave priority to reason over revelation as the fourth source of truth. He supported the atomist theory and attempted to reconcile the Muslim *kalam* with Karaite dogmas. Like many Karaites, he criticised the *Shi'ur Qoma*, an early anthropomorphic rabbinic work written in Palestine. However, he also criticised Sa'adiah's philosophical work, *Emunot ve-Deot*. Nevertheless, his own work is similar to Sa'adiah's.[33]

Jeshua ben Judah (Abu al-Farag Furkan ibn 'Asad: late eleventh century)

Jeshua was one of the foremost Karaite figures of the eleventh century, and the last Karaite scholar to live in Palestine. He was an expert both in Arabic philology and Jewish law. He wrote a legal treatise entitled, like ibn Ezra's Torah commentary, *Sefer ha-Yashar*. He translated the Torah into Arabic, providing two philosophical commentaries. He also composed a homiletic commentary specifically on *Genesis*. Jeshua is mentioned derogatorily in *Path Two*, but with great respect in the *Commentary on Exodus*. His biblical exegesis was actually greatly admired by ibn Ezra. Jeshua occasionally produced polemics against the traditionalists in general and Sa'adiah in particular. However, his arguments were of such power and insight, and his tone so calm and moderate, 'with an undercurrent of respect for Sa'adiah's learning and sincerity',[34] that he was bound to be taken seriously, even by non-Karaites. His role was enhanced by translations into Hebrew by Byzantine and Spanish Karaites, thereby reaching the wider, non-Arabic speaking Jewish world.

Like Joseph, Jeshua adopted the atomic theory, but opposed the view that God creates atoms from moment to moment, and that there are therefore no natural and necessary sequences in the world.[35] Rather, he considered the world to be created by an agent. The *kalam* maintained its supremacy among Karaites until the end of the Middle Ages: 'Karaite thinkers resisted the trend toward Neoplatonism and Aristotelianism which characterized Islamic and rabbinic philosophy.'[36]

Weiser mentions nineteen occasions where Jeshua appears by name in ibn Ezra's commentaries, mainly in *Exodus*. Here he is treated with respect and his views are occasionally endorsed.[37] When ibn Ezra does disagree with him, the reasons are based on context, philology, common-sense, knowledge of geography, Jewish tradition, psychology, biblical proof-texts and semantics. Ibn Ezra appears to agree with him on three occasions. On the first occasion, ibn Ezra follows Jeshua's allegorical interpretation rather than Jafet's common-sense argument. On the second occasion, ibn Ezra uses Jeshua's argument to amplify his own views. On the third occasion, he agrees with Jeshua on a semantic interpretation, disagreeing with the traditional view based on the Mekhilta and Rashi. Sometimes ibn Ezra states Jeshua's views without comment.

There are two examples in the commentaries which are relevant to the *Introductions*. In his commentary on *Exodus* 35:5 ibn Ezra uses everyday speech to decide whether the letter *vav* is superfluous or meaningful in context.[38] In his commentary on *Leviticus* 23:11 ('*and he shall wave the sheaf before the Lord ... on the day after Shabbat ...*') ibn Ezra discusses the correct time for waving the *Omer*. This is the barley offering, which marks the beginning of the seven-week period between the festivals of Pesach and Shavuot. The 'time' of the waving is not defined precisely in the Bible.

According to ibn Ezra the biblical term *Shabbat* can refer to a festival occasion, as well as the weekly rest day. He dismisses Sa'adiah's interpretation, preferring Jeshua's argument that Scripture mentions several possible interpretations of *Shabbat*. However, and this is the nub of ibn Ezra's general anti-Karaite critique, Jeshua makes 'mistakes' in his analysis by following Written Torah alone, filling in the 'gaps' in the text by his own reasoning. Ibn Ezra, however, uses Oral Torah to come up with the 'correct' interpretation that no precise date is given for Shavuot, because of the traditional onus on each individual to count the *Omer* himself.[39] It is thus essential to ibn Ezra that the means, as well as the ends, of interpretation be seen to be 'kosher'.

The above notwithstanding, it can be seen that in his Torah commentaries ibn Ezra treats Jeshua as a fellow exegete, worthy of serious scrutiny. In his polemical *Introduction*, however, he attacks him – and other Karaites – for failing to acknowledge the superiority of rabbinic tradition over philosophical and linguistic expertise.

This chapter has demonstrated that ibn Ezra's view of the Karaites was ambivalent. He admired, and even emulated, much of their exegetical work, but denigrated their rejection of Oral Torah and Jewish tradition. As their greatest tool was their exegetical skill, ibn Ezra attacks them with these same weapons in his polemical *Introductions*, whilst conceding their ability in the body of his commentaries. Their great linguistic skill, combined with their rejection of rabbinic tradition, made the Karaites a fearsome foe in ibn Ezra's eyes.

The individualistic approach of the Karaites promoted anarchy. They also posed a threat by using rational and common-sense arguments to demonstrate apparent absurdities in Oral Torah and the stupidity of those who upheld it. In his *Introductions*, therefore, ibn Ezra feels obliged to emphasise the perfect knowledge and religious behaviour of the rabbinic authorities, which enables them to lead the Jewish masses to the 'truth'. By adopting this defensive attitude, ibn Ezra defines his own approach whilst, at the same time, attempting to convince himself of the validity of his anti-Karaite stance.

7

THE GE'ONIM

'Let me discern, compare ...'
(Robert Browning, 'Rabbi Ben Ezra': XVII)

I now turn to the Babylonian Ge'onim, in whose hands the Talmud became the key to continuity of the Jewish people. These were the forerunners who, more than any other group, influenced ibn Ezra in his negative attitude to the Karaites and alerted him to the necessity of trying to effect a union between law (Talmud) and exegesis (Bible).

The Talmud has already been discussed in Chapter Three. It was not itself a code of law, but it 'became the basis and the final court of appeal for all the later Codes.'[1]

> In earlier generations, when the oral law adhered closely to the written law, the latter served, *inter alia*, as an instrument for reminding the student of the *halakhah* derived from each verse. This use of the biblical text not only as the legal and logical basis for oral law but also as a mnemonic aid was carried over to the talmudic literature and Jewish literature in general. It created the concept of *asmakhta* (support), that is citing a biblical text that is not the direct source of the *halakhah* but that is combined, by some exegetic method, with a known *halakhah* to serve as a mnemonic aid. Use of this method was so widespread that sometimes it was almost impossible to distinguish between the authentic commentary and that which serves merely as an *asmakhta*.[2]

Ibn Ezra describes *asmakhta* as a 'mere support' when he refers to those parts of the tradition which contradict the scriptural text. He states that this use of *drash* as 'a reminder and a mere support' implies a full rabbinic endorsement of *pshat* interpretations. However, sometimes the ordinary reader needs 'a reminder and a sign', in order to understand the text at his own level. Moreover, even according to *pshat*, it can occasionally prove difficult to understand biblical statements. Ibn Ezra's solution in these cases is to appeal to popular, non-literal conceptions.

According to Steinsaltz, the earlier rabbis were totally uninterested in philosophy and had an empirical, non-theoretical approach to the text. Most importantly, they did not take their own midrashim literally. Whether Steinsaltz is totally correct in his assessment of the interests of the Amoraim, it is true that philosophical and scientific disciplines were never regarded by them as other than tools. Ibn Ezra's fear of forays into 'gentile wisdoms' therefore leads him to attack the Ge'onim, just as he had attacked the Karaites for over-emphasising the scriptural text.

From the end of the sixth to the eleventh centuries the Ge'onim were recognised as the highest authority of instruction by the majority of Jewish communities. In *Path One* ibn Ezra calls them 'the great sages who were yeshivah scholars in Muslim realms', i.e., Babylon–Iraq and its sphere of influence. By interpreting the Talmud,[3] the Ge'onim aimed to make it the accepted arbiter in all social and religious matters. Their academies were simultaneously supreme law courts and educational institutions. The Ge'onim issued new regulations, or *takkanot*, based on the Talmud, with reference to contemporary needs. These *takkanot* had legal validity because the Ge'onim regarded themselves as the Sanhedrin of their day and as spiritual descendants of the original prophets in Israel. More importantly, they were regarded with the highest respect by the mass of the Jewish people.[4]

> The logic employed by the Talmud is often expressed in a few bare words and is therefore dependent upon a transmitted interpretation. The technical expressions used in the Talmud also require the guidance of a student well versed in that dialect.[5]

The Ge'onim were thus regarded as 'retaining the key to the fuller and competent understanding of the talmudic text' and the Babylonian Talmud became the exclusive object of study.

In addition, the Ge'onim introduced responsa, codes and glossaries, thereby initiating new areas of halakhic study. It was probably the responsa system, whereby the Ge'onim would answer questions requiring 'authoritative decisions on points of day-to-day Jewish law', which was the main reason for the supremacy of the Babylonian Talmud. A responsum differed from academic discourses, or legal codes, by dealing with one question at a time, as quickly and as concisely as possible.

> The solution must be practical and in keeping with the mainstream of legal thought, custom and practice. As the basis of his decision the respondent may use intuition, literary sources, prevalent custom, tradition, precedent, analogies, or any other resource guided by his own legal philosophy and methodology.[6]

It was this literary activity of the Gaon, rather than any priestly or legal status, 'which determined that future development of Jewish law and practice should derive principally from that same Babylonian Talmud.' The relationship between the Ge'onim and the Talmud constituted a 'unique interaction of forces' and 'a mutual, self-renewing conferment of status'.[7]

As early as the eighth century, however, Ge'onic writings differentiated between aggadic and legal statements. There were both internal and external reasons for this. The desire to codify and make practical decisions rendered hyperbole and other forms of figurative language irrelevant.[8] By the tenth century, if not earlier, aggadah was becoming an embarrassment in rabbinic circles.[9] As we have seen, attacks on aggadah, and especially on anthropomorphisms in the Talmud, as well as the Bible, increased from within Judaism, as well as from outside sources. The Muslims attacked aggadic methodology by using logic, a practice soon found necessary by the Ge'onim themselves, although it was already present in Talmudic reasoning. Christian attacks on aggadah generally occurred later, spurred on by Jewish converts to Christianity. Very often these attacks were aimed, none too politely, at the authority of the sages themselves.[10]

However positively the writers of the Talmud regarded their own midrashic and aggadic interpretations, by Ge'onic times the aggadah 'appears as a potential source of trouble that must be neutralised.'[11] One method was to stress the *pshat* method of interpretation, which was increasingly being redefined as the 'plain', or 'simple' rather than the 'authoritative' or 'contextual' meaning. However, this new definition itself involved a change in attitudes to *pshat*, which extended to the scriptural text, and sometimes led to a denial of the authority of anthropomorphic statements in works such as the *Shi'ur Qoma*. Whereas Sa'adiah and Shmuel ben Hofni questioned the authority of this work, the

Ge'onim, Sherira and Hai, as well as ibn Ezra, 'sought to defend its authenticity.'[12] Some Ge'onim respected aggadot which appeared in the Talmud more than those found elsewhere, but were not averse to disagreeing with certain aspects even of these.[13]

As *drash* waned in importance, *pshat* definitions were extended to include metaphor.[14] Greenstein describes the change of attitude to *drash* as a recognition:

> ... that multiplicity in the Bible's significance not only inheres in the nature of the text, but also results from divergent methods or dimensions of reading it.[15]

The onus is thus now put on the reader as well as on the text. Ibn Ezra is aware of both these approaches. In *Path Four* he reminds the exponents of midrash that: 'no text can be deprived of its *pshat*'. In *Path Five*, however, he states that 'the path of *pshat* does not deviate on account of *drash*, since "there are seventy faces to Torah."'[16]

We now find ourselves in the interesting position of seeing *pshat* replace *drash* as the most potent rabbinic interpretative weapon in the war against internal and external opponents alike. The rise of *pshat* was inevitable. Whereas the sacred canon could elicit multiple meanings, its authorised interpretations could not be allowed this luxury. By the time of ibn Ezra, however, the authorised interpretations had themselves become 'canonised' in certain circles. They elicited the same methods of investigation as the original sacred text.

'The great sages ... Yeshivah scholars in Muslim realms'

According to ibn Ezra, the hermeneutic approach of the Ge'onim is too difficult for the average person. It lies 'far above the contemporary mind'. We shall see however, that ibn Ezra disingenuously uses the Ge'onim to define his own approach, and often criticises them for traits present in his own exegesis. Ibn Ezra names three scholars who 'have trodden' this path: Rav Isaac, Sa'adiah Gaon and Shmuel ben Hofni. Rav Isaac is difficult to identify. Weiss Halivni identifies the author of the *Yitzhaki*, a book others associate with 'Rav Isaac', as the philosopher, Isaac Israeli. Simon makes a convincing case for its being the Spanish grammarian, ibn Janah. Others favour another Spanish grammarian, ibn Yashush.[17] In my view, the most likely 'Rav Isaac' to be associated by ibn Ezra with the Ge'onic approach, whether or not he is also the author of the *Yitzhaki*, is Isaac Israeli, who corresponded with Sa'adiah.

Isaac Israeli (855–955)

Israeli was mentioned in Chapter Five, because he was influenced by the Muslim philosopher, al-Kindi and through his own role in the development of the theory of the internal senses. Israeli's theory of creation influenced the great Spanish Jewish poet and philosopher, ibn Gabirol, and thence ibn Ezra. Israeli was the first Jewish philosopher to unite neoplatonism and traditional Jewish thought, by linking Proclus' theory of 'union', known in Hebrew as *devekut*, with the 'bliss' of paradise. To know oneself is to know the 'all'. Israeli may also have influenced ibn Ezra through his disciple, Dunash ibn Tamim, who wrote a commentary on the mystical *Sefer Yetzirah*. This work certainly influenced Sa'adiah's theory of the 'created glory'.[18]

In *Path One* ibn Ezra offers four separate criticisms of Rav Isaac's *Commentary on Genesis*. He is long-winded. He discusses 'the belief in the powers of light and dark'. He speaks at length on diet. Finally, he introduces irrelevant secular sciences into biblical exegesis. All these descriptions fit Israeli's commentary.

Firstly, no less a person than Rambam attests to Israeli's 'windy imaginings and empty talk.'[19] Secondly, in his *Book of Elements*, Israeli discusses the respective roles of light and dark in the creation of the world, and his disciple, Dunash ibn Tamim, cites similar Manichean teachings.[20] Thirdly, in the *Second Introduction*, ibn Ezra accuses the Ge'onim of digressing on *Genesis* 1:12 by discussing the medical efficacy of fruit and herbs. Ibn Ezra refers to a work which he calls *The Medical Book*. Israeli wrote a book entitled *Medical Ethics*, a 'half-medical and half-philosophical treatise, probably part of a commentary on Genesis.' This may refer to one of the two commentaries on *Genesis* 1, mentioned at the outset by ibn Ezra.[21] Lastly, Israeli was incapable of adhering to any subject, without producing evidence from irrelevant sources.[22]

In the light of the above evidence, together with the fact that 'Rav Isaac' probably refers to someone living outside Spain at the same time, or slightly before, Sa'adiah, Isaac Israeli is a more likely contender for ibn Ezra's faint praise than ibn Janah or ibn Yashush, who were grammarians living in Spain well after Sa'adiah's time.

Sa'adiah Gaon (892–942)

Sa'adiah is of immense importance for an understanding of ibn Ezra, who held him in great respect, despite criticising him in his *Introduction*:

> ... in presenting Saadiah ben Joseph, generally called Saadiah Gaon, it is usual to quote Abraham ibn Ezra: "Saadiah Gaon was the chief spokesman in all matters of learning", meaning that Saadiah first introduced the cultivation of all branches of Jewish knowledge, and this statement is so true that one cannot avoid citing it.[23]

Like ibn Ezra later, Sa'adiah was fearless in both exegesis and personal morality, secure in the knowledge of his great learning and spirituality. Sa'adiah's contributions to halakhah, exegesis and philosophy are all relevant to the development of the Ge'onic tradition. His halakhic work is also interesting for its hermeneutic approach. Sa'adiah's exegetical and philosophical work overlap, as they are both based on his philological–hermeneutic approach.

Sa'adiah's books of halakhic decisions differ considerably from those of his predecessors. He was the first to write halakhic works in Arabic, thus setting a trend for his successors. He would first give clear definitions before citing examples, as ibn Ezra set out to do in his Torah commentaries. Sa'adiah was also the first to introduce biblical quotations into Talmudic rulings, in order to add a moral and ethical dimension to halakhic questions.[24] In this respect Sa'adiah was a role model for ibn Ezra, who does not differentiate between Written and Oral Torah and strongly berates those who do, such as the French exegete, Rashbam.

Sa'adiah's philological activity was influenced by the growing Muslim interest in the structure of Arabic, and lay the groundwork for the scientific study of the Hebrew language. This approach was continued by his disciples and culminated in the Spanish school of philology, whose last exponent was ibn Ezra.

Sa'adiah also introduced new ideas to the writing of poetry. He broke the dominance of the flowery school of the *piyyutim*, liturgical poets from Palestine, whose style was increasingly ill-suited to the abstemious intellectual rigour of those Jews living under Islam. Whereas ibn Ezra describes the language of Kallir, the greatest *paytan*, as a 'breached city with no walls', he absolves Sa'adiah, alone of the *payyetanim*, of the same 'four blunders'. Sa'adiah's prayers are written in biblical style, pay attention to grammar, omit figurative allusions and avoid midrash.[25] Ibn Ezra's sombre attitude to poetry was in evidence in Chapter Six, when his *Introductory Prayer* was compared to the style of the Karaite, Salmon ben Jeroham.

Sa'adiah thus relied on both Jewish and Muslim traditions to develop the Hebrew style in religious and secular poetry from which the Spanish School would benefit. However, prose writers had no stylistic role model in Hebrew. They could therefore choose either Hebrew or Arabic as the language through which they expressed themselves, without having to pay attention to the rules of 'purity'.[26] These 'rules of purity' are of course discussed by ibn Ezra in his greatest work on grammar, *Sefer Zahot*, written shortly after he completed his *Commentary on the Torah*. Unlike so many Jewish writers of his background, including Sa'adiah, ibn Ezra chose to write his prose works in Hebrew too, thus demonstrating his originality and desire to reach the mass of the Jewish people. It is this resistance to compromise that ibn Ezra holds against the Ge'onim, including Sa'adiah.

Sa'adiah's philological approach was greatly influenced by the grammatical tradition exemplified by his Muslim contemporary, al-Farabi. This tradition was important to Sa'adiah for:

> ... anchoring Biblical exegesis on sound philosophic footings
> ... his regular practice is to resolve metaphors and other figures to their referential senses.

This is not 'passive reading', but 'articulates an awareness of the structure and logic of imagery.' As I have already noted, Sa'adiah was 'impatient of aggadic embroideries' and even devised rules for the figurative evaluation of the biblical narrative.[27] As part of the tendency to downplay *drash* and elevate *pshat*, Sa'adiah attempted to demonstrate the indespensability of the recently recognised massoretic text. Ibn Ezra, by contrast, chooses to attack massoretic writers for one aspect of their work, use of midrash.

Sa'adiah's two translations and commentaries on the Bible are relevant to the above overview of his philological approach, as well as to ibn Ezra's strictures. One translation is 'fairly literal; the other is rather a kind of paraphrase and commentary intended for cultivated readers.'[28] These commentaries, often highly anti-Karaite in flavour, influenced ibn Ezra's own polemics against the Karaites, as well as his linguistic and philosophic research.

In *Path One*, however, ibn Ezra criticises Sa'adiah for digressing, and in his commentary on *Genesis* 2:11, he criticises him for interpreting without the support of tradition. It is possible, however, that ibn Ezra's real disagreement with the Ge'onim concerned their use of Arabic in biblical exegesis, which he conflates with their culling of views emanating from Muslim intellectual centres. We may therefore conjecture that he does not object to 'foreign opinions' *per se*, as much as the use of a foreign tongue in which to introduce them into a commentary on *Genesis*. The miracle of creation should be accompanied by the use of the Holy Tongue.[29] This may provide yet another reason for ibn Ezra's self-imposed 'exile' to lands under Christian rule, which did not read Arabic, in order to compose his own commentaries. It is possible that biblical commentaries written in Hebrew may not have been taken so seriously in Spain, where, following Ge'onic precedent, most prose writings were in Arabic. One could argue that, in leaving Spain, he was safeguarding, as well as disseminating, the choicest fruits of Muslim scholarship for posterity, and thus preserving Jewish tradition.

Ibn Ezra was an advocate of the many-sided and imaginative approach to hermeneutics initiated by Sa'adiah, as stated above. For the Spanish scholars who followed Sa'adiah:

> ... philology and theology are interrelated disciplines, each protecting the other: philology worthy of the name protects against errors of doctrine, while pure belief shields against philological errors. Hebrew linguistics and Scriptural exegesis are both holy labors, because the scientific endeavour has far-reaching results in the realm of doctrine – just as it can illuminate the texts it can also befog them.[30]

This 'pure belief' is not limited to the Bible, but also extends to Jewish tradition. 'Scientific endeavour' can 'befog' the text when introduced for its own sake (as in the case of the Karaite 'dark cloud'), rather than for the sake of tradition. In his savage polemics against the Karaites, which were described at length in the previous chapter, ibn Ezra is merely following in Sa'adiah's footsteps.

Let us now turn to Sa'adiah's theory of knowledge, in which he was greatly influenced by Israeli. Sa'adiah recognises three universal sources of knowledge: sense perception, certain judgment and logical inference. In addition, the Jews possess a fourth source, known as 'authentic tradition'. Influenced by the double faith theory then current in the Muslim world, Sa'adiah posits two types of religious understanding. The intellectual elite is capable of understanding religious truths primarily through their rational faculty, whereas the intellectually inferior experience revelation through the senses. Sa'adiah resorts to figurative interpretations when faced with scriptural verses which contradict reason. For him, reason precedes 'tradition'.[31]

The second source of knowledge, which is translated by ibn Ezra as 'knowledge of reason', is known in Hebrew as *med'a ha-sekhel*, the self-evident truths, or Aristotle's first principles. Ibn Ezra came to this interpretation through Bahya ibn Pakuda, a Spanish thinker who lived in the second half of the eleventh century. Bahya defines this second source of knowledge as 'that which grasps the intelligible things by itself [*be-atzmo*]'. This type of knowledge includes secular studies, as well as value judgments.[32]

The importance of Bahya's paraphrase is that it links directly to ibn Ezra's use of the term *etzem* in his *Introduction*. He specifically states in *Path Two* that the Karaites 'thought that they were standing at the very point itself'. It is now possible to view ibn Ezra's comment as more than a vague rhetorical attack on Karaite ignorance of God. Ibn Ezra's precise language demonstrates that it is part of Jewish tradition (that tradition initiated by Sa'adiah, influenced by Muslim models) to understand the meaning of self-evident truths. This cannot be achieved without first relying on sense perception, the primary source of knowledge. By rejecting tradition, the Karaites are not only rejecting Oral Torah, as they think, but also reason, grounded in sensory perception, which is the sole means whereby they can eventually reach the centre of the circle and gain true understanding. In ibn Ezra's system, *etzem* comes to mean divinity itself, as was discussed in Chapter Three.

I have already commented on ibn Ezra's role as the first Jewish thinker to posit the Aristotelian union of thinker, thinking and thought. This is the nearest that Jewish philosophy ever comes to suggesting union with the divine. It is ibn Ezra's genius to have combined the idea of such an intellectual union, based on a paraphrase of Sa'adiah by Bahya, with the concept of a personal journey, which every genuine seeker after God must make, to the centre of the circle of Jewish tradition, to that 'still small point' where He can be found. Ibn Ezra thus finds the solution to his quest to unite knowledge and tradition. Through correct exegesis the two unite, quite literally, in God, the point itself. Moreover, knowledge without tradition, and tradition without knowledge, imbalances the perfect 'weighing' mechanism of the rational faculty.

The Spanish school, which followed the Ge'onim, reduced the three sources of knowledge to two, sense perception and reason. In *Second Path Four* ibn Ezra uses the phrase 'direct balance of knowledge' (*shakul ha-da'at ha-yesharah*), to convey the idea of intuitive or necessitated knowledge, a combination of the original second and third sources, certain judgment and logical inference. The sources of knowledge correspond to ibn Ezra's interpretation of the internal senses, which were discussed in Chapter Five with reference to ibn Sina. Wisdom, the third internal sense, linked to memory, can now be seen to represent Jewish tradition, which was originally the fourth source of knowledge.

Memory can be both active and passive, as exemplified by the two different versions of the Ten Commandments (in Hebrew *dibbur*: word) issued by Moses at different junctures during the exodus of the children of Israel from Egypt to the promised land. The first time Moses issues these words, which are something completely new in the experience of the children of Israel, he descends from Mount Sinai and tells them to '*Remember the Sabbath day . . .*' (*Exodus* 20:8), using the verb *zakhar*, which depicts masculinity and drive. At this juncture, he is thus encouraging a very active and vigilant form of memory. However, at the end of his leadership, when the children of Israel are about to cross over into the promised land with a new leader, Moses says '*Preserve the Sabbath day*' (*Deuteronomy* 5:12), using the verb *shamar*. Here he suggests a less obviously active approach. Now memory should be nurtured.

However, equally important as a prelude to these later words is Moses' reminder to the assembled people that '*The Lord did not make this covenant with our fathers, but with us personally, all those of us who are alive today*' (*Deuteronomy* 5:3). In other words, scripture itself tells us that memory is never completely passive. Even collective memory, that most Jewish of traditions, should be regularly honed, re-thought and re-articulated in the light of the present context. By equating wisdom with memory and tradition, ibn Ezra thus posits a creative approach to the exegetical endeavour. It is this creativity, not merely habit, which will ultimately 'preserve' the Jewish people. 'Keeping' and re-membering' are not the same thing.

Sirat echoes this view when conveying Sa'adiah's explanations in a way compatible with normative Jewish tradition: 'True tradition' is:

... founded on the historical experience of the Jewish people and ... none of the other religions cast any doubt on the historical reality of the Exodus and the Jews' sojourn in the desert.

The link between tradition and intellect should be forged as follows:

... first, that traditionally transmitted knowledge should become firmly anchored in the intellect; secondly that we may answer detractors of the Law.... All the various kinds of knowledge that scientific effort may uncover are in conformity with the true tradition. Saadiah was convinced that *Torah* and science spring from the same branch; they cannot contradict each other in any way, and, if there is an apparent contradiction, this is due to our faulty reasoning or to our failure to interpret the revealed text correctly.[33]

Ibn Ezra does not quite say this.[34] In *Path Five* he merely states that if there are two possible meanings to a legal verse we must follow the official interpreters, otherwise we will be playing into the hands of the Karaites, who maintain that traditional interpretations contradict both the written text and grammatical rules. Ibn Ezra's argument here is not very convincing. In *Second Path Five*, he emphasises that he will rely on traditional interpretations only in legal matters. However, he ends by saying that he hopes to teach contemporary sages the rules of grammar. Then, after all, grammar and tradition will remain compatible as they were in days of yore!

Weiss Halivni asserts that Sa'adiah was the first rabbi 'to ascertain the superiority of peshat over derash', based on his delineation of the three modes of knowledge. However, he 'has not yet connected the inviolability of peshat ... with the dictum of the Talmud (profusely quoted later on) "No text can be deprived of its peshat."' Although Sa'adiah was more lenient than some of his Ge'onic successors in defining and applying *pshat*, he nevertheless limited the occasions when non-*pshat* interpretations could be made, usually when the text was in conflict with experience or reason. In these cases, the passage should be interpreted figuratively.[35] However:

in order to prevent metaphorization of the commandments ... he attempted to establish clear and objective guidelines for determining when non-literal interpretation (*ta'wil*) is required. This view of metaphorization has two facets: just as it is forbidden to resort to metaphor whenever it is not absolutely necessary, so it is forbidden to refrain from it when it is clear that the verse cannot be understood literally.[36]

In *Path Three* we see evidence of Sa'adiah's influence on ibn Ezra with respect to legitimate and illegitimate allegorisations. *Path Two* echoes:

> ... the belief in the binding authority of talmudic tradition, whose status as Oral Law was equivalent to that of the Written Law. This belief in the truth of talmudic tradition – which was principally halakhic and only secondarily historical or exegetical – and in its harmony with the philological–contextual meaning of the Torah, was deemed utterly logical: the striking absence of complete and comprehensive information on most of the precepts and the lack of proportion between what was written and what was only alluded to, attest to the fact that from the first, the Torah was not intended to stand on its own.

Simon rightly call this attitude '[a]nother limit to exegetical freedom which was intended to serve as a bulwark against the danger of Karaitic anarchism.'

Despite the legacy that Sa'adiah bestowed on ibn Ezra, Simon offers perhaps the best explanation of ibn Ezra's ambivalence towards him:

> Just as talmudic tradition clarifies and complements the Torah but does not flow from it, so should the Bible be explained in the light of philosophy and the sciences, but it is neither necessary nor obligatory to base these areas of knowledge on the scriptures.... Recognition of the independence of talmudic tradition on the one hand and scientific knowledge on the other is to be found already in the work of Saadiah Gaon, and Abraham ibn Ezra drew from it a weighty conclusion concerning the commentator's duty: he must minimize as far as possible the imposition of both halakhah and science on the Bible (a procedure characteristic of the Geonim). The Torah was given to all the children of Israel, "the educated and the uneducated" (Long Commentary on Exodus XX:1), hence it contains only a very few allusions to

philosophy and the sciences which require lengthy study. As the commentary must, in his view, suit the character and objective of the Bible itself, it should include only those scientific introductions that were essential for an understanding of the text, and those allusions meant solely for the educated.[37]

For Malter, however, Sa'adiah's importance lies in his desire to prove:

the superiority of Judaism as compared not only with other religious systems, but also with the various doctrines of the philosophers, and of the compatibility of Jewish tenets with reason. Saadiah was ... the first Jewish philosopher fully conscious of the basic difference between the Jewish and the philosophic conceptions of truth, and he gave especial emphasis to the fact that Judaism is primarily and essentially a religion based on historical experience; philosophic reflection being required only for the purpose of furnishing secondary evidence of the genuineness and worth of its manifold teachings.[38]

Ibn Ezra would not have agreed with Malter's assessment of the secondary role of philosophy in Sa'adiah oeuvre. By ibn Ezra's time however, dialogues, both internal and external, had altered. For ibn Ezra in the twelfth century, the role of philosophy was proving more of a hindrance than an aid in the preservation and development of the Jewish tradition. The double faith theory engendered by philosophy was gradually causing a dangerous split in the spirit of *klal Israel* (the collectivity of the Jewish people). It challenged the very genius of the Pharisees, who had decided before the destruction of the Second Temple in 70 CE that Jewish interpretation was now to be available to all Jews, on an equal footing. It was this intellectual and psychological rift that ibn Ezra wished to repair.

Shmuel ben Hofni (died 1013)

Immediately after criticising aspects of Sa'adiah's exegetical approach, ibn Ezra turns to the Gaon, Shmuel ben Hofni. He accuses him of being digressive, verbose, non-specific and overly rationalistic. The last tendency can be linked to Shmuel's approach to Talmud, an area in which he excelled. Although Shmuel exceeded Sa'adiah's rational approach to both Bible and Talmud, ibn Ezra links the two Ge'onim, seemingly aware that Shmuel's commentary on the Torah was a direct continuation of Sa'adiah's. However, in his own commentary, ibn Ezra takes Shmuel's exegesis seriously, just as he had done with the Karaites and Sa'adiah.

In line with his rational approach, Shmuel extended the meaning of the term *pshat*, to the detriment of *drash*. He:

> was the first one, according to the extant literature, to interpret the word peshuto in the celebrated dictum to mean simple or plain meaning and to make the dictum imply the invincibility of peshat. R. Shmuel's interpretation spread rapidly throughout the Jewish world.

The 'celebrated dictum' refers, of course, to the Talmudic statement regarding the status of *pshat*: 'no text can be deprived of its *pshat*'.

> There is ... an interesting difference between R. Shmuel ben Chofni and the others with regard to the full significance of the dictum ... which R. Shemuel connected with plain meaning. *R. Shemuel*, who took the idea of the invincibility of peshat from R. Saadya and who in turn most likely took it from the Arabs, both sources of which give, if not an overwhelming endorsement of peshat (with exceptions), at least a very strong preference for peshat over derash, understood the dictum ... to mean that *no text can be deprived of being interpreted exclusively according to peshat.* The derash has to be rejected. In contrast, R. J. ibn Ganach, Rashi, ibn Ezra, and others understood the talmudic statement to mean that peshat and derash co-exist. The derash is not to be rejected.... Such was R. Shemuel's reliance on Arabic sources ... that he refracted the dictum in the Talmud in such a way that would make it comply with what he derived from these sources. The claim was made there that in general peshat ought to be the exclusive meaning of a text, and the dictum in the Talmud was made to fit that claim. Ibn Ganach and the others had no such reliance and, guided by the words of the dictum, understood them to mean that a bona fide derash has a legitimate claim, so that while a text can never be deprived of its peshat, neither can the peshat deprive the text of its legitimate derash.[39]

So far did Shmuel go in his sole adherence to reason that he is quoted as saying that '. . . if the words of the sages contradict reason, we are not obligated to accept them.'[40] Ibn Ezra is more ambivalent in his adherence to reason and *pshat*, because he also wishes to preserve the role of traditional interpretations and interpreters.

Apart from criticising Shmuel for relying excessively on reason and science, ibn Ezra also accuses him of unnecessary digressions. This tendency might have been due to Shmuel's excessively orderly and analytical approach, in which he was even 'somewhat more systematic than Saadya',[41] and prone to explain points in great detail. In contrast, ibn Ezra does not criticise Shmuel's legal writings, which he regarded as part of the chain of tradition which preserved and interpreted Jewish law and practice. This tradition was continued by the Spaniard, Shmuel ha-Nagid, who forged a link between the Ge'onim and the Spanish intellectual school.

Ibn Ezra mentions Shmuel in six places in his own commentary.[42] Here his treatment of Shmuel is similar to that employed with the Karaites. His method is to compare the view of various predecessors, including Shmuel, before occasionally giving his own view. For instance, commenting on the serpent's speech in *Genesis* 3:1, ibn Ezra considers how the serpent actually spoke. He condemns those who identify the serpent with Satan, as he regards this midrashic interpretation as non-contextual. He then cites Sa'adiah's view that an angel interceded and spoke on behalf of the serpent, because no animal is naturally endowed with speech and intellect. Shmuel disagrees with Sa'adiah's view. Ibn Ezra then presents ibn Gabirol's refutation of Shmuel. Ibn Ezra concludes that the words should be interpreted at face value. His reason, taken, ironically, from midrash,[43] is that originally the serpent could speak and stand upright, like a man. He disagrees with Sa'adiah that an angel could speak for the serpent, because of his own elevated view of angels as obedient emissaries of God. This is an instance where ibn Ezra disagrees with all predecessors and actually uses midrash when it appears to make as much sense as any other interpretation, and has the added bonus of safeguarding tradition.

Ibn Ezra continues by discounting any resemblance between the two appearances of the word *arum* in the text, even though they appear in adjacent verses, and could therefore be judged contextually significant. In this case, he wishes to safeguard the 'purity of language' In *Genesis* 2:25, *arum* is translated as 'naked', reflecting the state of Adam and Eve before they sinned. In *Genesis*

3:1, *arum* refers to the serpent, and is translated as 'cunning'. In this case ibn Ezra avoids the popular midrashic explanation in which the juxtaposition is regarded as highly significant.

Genesis 28:10–11 introduces Jacob's dream of a ladder reaching up to heaven, with angels moving up and down it. Here, Shmuel takes over Sa'adiah's commentary. Ibn Ezra expresses astonishment at Shmuel for confusing ordinary dreams with Jacob's prophetic dream. This is no doubt why, in *Path One*, he criticises Shmuel for dream interpretation. Ibn Ezra suggests that only experts can interpret dreams accurately and that Shmuel is therefore digressing.

Exodus 4:24–5 relates how Moses' son is circumcised by his wife rather than by Moses himself. Moses has omitted this important task, because of his self-doubts as leader of his people. The verse: '*And it came to pass, on the way at the lodging place, that the Lord met him and sought to kill <u>him</u>*' is normally interpreted as a euphemism for Moses' sudden illness, brought on as a punishment for vacillating. Thus, Zipporah '*cut off the foreskin of her son and cast it at <u>his</u> feet*', connecting Moses with her action. Shmuel questions the usual interpretation of the words '*him*' and '*his*'. He thinks they refer to the son, Eliezer, rather than to Moses. However, ibn Ezra counters Shmuel, using common-sense arguments.

In *Exodus* 8:6 Pharaoh agrees to free the children of Israel, as long as the plague of frogs is removed from his land. Shmuel argues from custom, but ibn Ezra goes strictly by the text and finds a plausible explanation for Pharaoh's a-typical behaviour. However, with respect to *Exodus* 19:13, ibn Ezra agrees with Shmuel, as against Sa'adiah, that the phrase '*and they shall ascend the mountain*' does not refer to Israel collectively, but specifically to its leaders, Aaron, Nadab, Abihu and the seventy elders. Shmuel uses the proof-text *Exodus* 24:1, which appears later in the narrative, but *Exodus* 19:12 already strictly prohibits '*the people*' from ascending the mountain.

Commenting on *Leviticus* 16:8–9:

And Aaron shall cast lots upon the two goats; one lot for the Lord, and the other lot for the scapegoat. And Aaron shall bring the goat upon which the Lord's lot fell, and offer it as a sin offering,

ibn Ezra discusses the disagreement in interpretation between Shmuel and Sa'adiah, without giving his own view. Sa'adiah does not interpret the word *az'azel* as 'scapegoat', but as 'mighty mountain'. Shmuel disagrees, basing his argument on the exact order of the letters in the name. In his opinion, both goats are marked *'for the Lord'*. Ibn Ezra counters that 'scripture does not require his explanation ... because the scapegoat is not a sacrifice, since it is not slaughtered.' Shmuel's view is therefore controversial and lacks scriptural backing.

From the above examples it can be seen that in the commentaries on the Torah, as opposed to the *Introductions*, ibn Ezra takes Shmuel's views very seriously. He even occasionally supports him against Sa'adiah and ibn Gabirol, acknowledging his adherence to the text and context. Even when he disagrees with his exegesis, he often acknowledges that Shmuel's reasoning is relevant. His only outright criticism is of Shmuel's confusion over different types of dream.

We can therefore conclude that despite his admiration for both Sa'adiah and Shmuel, ibn Ezra had doubts about certain aspects of their approach. In the *Introductions* he practically links them together as one entity. In the *Commentaries*, by contrast, their separate views are highlighted and often opposed, in order for ibn Ezra to appear to be taking a compromise position. Two further Ge'onim, Sherira, and his son, Hai, are important for our purposes. Their textual approach is influenced by that of Sa'adiah and Shmuel. They, in turn, influenced the Spanish school. Most importantly, they are not mentioned by name in the *Introductions*.

Sherira Gaon (ca. 906–1006)

Sherira was one of the most active responsa authors of Babylonian times. He also researched the authorship of the Talmud, including the part played in its redaction by the Ge'onim themselves. Both Sherira and his son, Hai, acknowledged the supreme authority of the Babylonian over the Jerusalem Talmud. Although Sherira was less interested in Arabic literature than Hai, he nevertheless wrote some responsa in Arabic.

Sherira regarded Sa'adiah with great respect, disagreeing with him only reluctantly on points of law. Sherira also rekindled an interest in mysticism, which had been encouraged by Sa'adiah, but rejected by Shmuel. Sherira's approach had certain similarities with that of ibn Ezra, who normally explained anthropomorphisms philosophically, but occasionally, like Sherira, regarded them as inexplicable deep mysteries. On the other hand, Sherira tended to approach aggadic material rationally: '... we do not rely on aggadic utterances; that portion of their words which is confirmed by reason and the Biblical text is correct.' Sherira's adage that 'there is no end or limit to the aggadot' is imitated by ibn Ezra at the end of *Path Four*, 'and the end of the matter is that to drash there is no end'.

Hai Gaon (939–1038)

Hai went even further than his father in rejecting non-rational interpretations:

[A]ggadic sayings are not like authentic tradition. Rather, each sage expounded as it occurred to him, as if to say, 'Perhaps,' or 'One might say,' and not as something definite. Therefore we do not rely on them.

As Goldin says:

By now *ein somekhin al aggadah* [we do not rely on aggadah] is itself become a fixation, a kind of immovable tenet of about one third of the classic Oral Law curriculum.[44]

The Spanish school, starting with Shmuel ha-Nagid, a correspondent of Hai, developed this line of thought, which culminated in the ideas of ibn Ezra. Ibn Ezra occasionally followed Hai in explaining anthropomorphisms as examples of the phrase, 'the Torah spoke in the language of men'. Such statements were to be considered 'not in accordance with their apparent meaning, but as analogies and comparisons with things known to us by the senses'.

A theological axiom has become the standard against which the aggadah is measured; those statements that do not conform to the standard are not totally dismissed but are interpreted. According to this approach, neither prophets nor sages intended their assertions about God to be understood literally, they used graphic language because this is the only way the average human being can understand the abstract notion being expressed. This use of the phrase "The Torah spoke in the language of men" to emphasize the need for metaphoric interpretation of statements about God became a cornerstone of Spanish philosophical exegesis.[45]

Hai is especially important for the links he forged between the schools of Babylon and Spain. In his opinion, only traditionalist Jews are authorised to use *ta'wil* interpretations. This view helps us understand ibn Ezra's criticism of the Karaites and Christians for attempting to divorce exegesis from rabbinic tradition. Despite being an expert in Arabic himself, Hai was concerned about Muslim influences on the Jewish community, especially in the realm of philosophy. He was critical of his father-in-law, Shmuel, among others, for reading non-Jewish works. He also dismissed as alien to Judaism Shmuel's view that miracles could be performed only by biblical prophets. Hai encouraged ideas which he held to be more compatible with Jewish tradition, for example that angels were created by God as a medium of communication between the divine and the human. Whereas Shmuel had stressed Sa'adiah's rational tendencies, Hai emphasised his mystical approach.

As well as forging a link with the newer Jewish centre in Spain, Hai was also largely responsible for forging a link backwards with the Talmudic sages of the past. He was able to do this because of the reciprocal relationship between the Jewish communities and the Babylonian Academies. Hai recognised that 'the tradition of that community' was 'ultimately authoritative in matters of religious practice.'[46] The Ge'onic legacy was regarded as having 'been deposited, transmitted, and received in tradition from father to sons ... from the days of the prophets unto the present time.'[47] Veracity of practice was authenticated by the behaviour of the traditionalist community, which was regarded as being of even greater importance than study of Oral Torah.[48] The community were the sole interpreters of *ta'wil* because they were 'the authorities of its language, the transmitters of its text, and the proclaimers of its veracity'. They had 'received it from the Prophets verbally [i.e., directly], as well as its meaning and *ta'wil*.'

For instance, Hai used to discuss scripture in a friendly manner with the head of the Syrian Church, but only at the plain, or *sharah* level. It was felt that figurative interpretations depended on a deep understanding of the Hebrew language and Jewish tradition. In contrast, surface-level knowledge could be gleaned through translations or rudimentary Hebrew. This attitude helps us understand ibn Ezra's attitude to allegorists outside Jewish tradition: their interpretations are simply not valid, because they are not descended from those who received all possible interpretations from the earliest Jewish sages.[49]

Sherira and Hai represent a tendency in Ge'onic thought which endeavoured to attenuate the rigid rationalism of Shmuel ben Hofni. Whilst recognising that aspects of Muslim and Greek thought could be beneficial tools in the elucidation of law and Scripture, these two Ge'onim knew that mystical and popular folk elements also contributed to the tradition. By stressing the importance of the community of believers and practitioners, they succeeded in making the religion more accessible, as well as ascribing sole interpretative authority to their own followers. It may be for these reasons that they are not singled out for criticism by ibn Ezra, whose prime aim was to safeguard the community.

The rise of the Ge'onim, despite all their individual differences, contributed considerably to the cultural milieu inherited by ibn Ezra. They encouraged those aspects of Muslim hermeneutics and philosophy which they judged to be compatible with Jewish self-understanding. In addition, they redefined and thus upheld the importance of Oral Torah, laying the foundation for the Spanish school, which further developed the study of philology.

Ibn Ezra's criticisms of non-traditionalist groups were anticipated by the Ge'onic definition of figurative interpretation as lying solely within the orb of the believing community. Ibn Ezra depicts this idea quite literally in his *Introduction*, through his circle imagery. Moreover, ibn Ezra's ambiguity towards midrash, outlined in *Path Four*, is a development of the Ge'onic emphasis on both the rhetorical and philosophical possibilities inherent in this genre.

The Ge'onim had an all-embracing attitude to knowledge emulated by ibn Ezra himself, and which he subsumed under his term 'grammar'. If he criticised the Ge'onim for being overly rationalistic, it was largely because this tendency was present in himself.[50] Ibn Ezra realised that in order to persuade a contemporary Ashkenazi readership of the superiority of his 'grammatical' path, emphases other than the purely rationalistic and linguistic were to be required. With this decision, ibn Ezra transcended his heritage, and made a novel contribution to Jewish intellectual history.

8

INTRODUCTION TO THE TORAH: TRANSLATION AND COMMENTARY

Thence shall I pass, approved
A man, for aye removed
From the developed brute; a god though in the germ
(Robert Browning, 'Rabbi Ben Ezra': XIII)

The text

The edition of ibn Ezra's *Introduction* and *Commentary* used in this book is Weiser (1977), which also includes the *Second Introduction* and *Commentary*. The Menorah (1988) annotated English translation of the *Introduction* is based on the version in the standard *Mikra'ot Gedolot*, but the majority of its comments rely on Weiser.[1]

The present translation and commentary

Quite apart from his esoteric allusions intended only for the 'wise', ibn Ezra's writings in general are far from clear. Commentators who wish to act as a bridge between text and reader should be gifted in two ways. They must understand the text on which they are commenting, but must also be able to communicate that understanding to their readers. To some, ibn Ezra has only the first gift. He is too concise and at times incomprehensible, omitting necessary supplements and clarifications.[2] In my translation I have attempted to overcome this difficulty by adding in square brackets material which I have judged to have been part of ibn Ezra's thought process. It is hoped that important ideas not addressed in the previous chapters are satisfactorily explained or cross-referenced in the commentary accompanying the translation.[3]

TRANSLATION

Introductory prayer

In the name of the Great and Awesome God
I shall begin expounding the meaning of the Torah.[1]
I beseech Thee, Oh God of my father, Abraham,
Deal mercifully with Thy servant, Abraham.[2]
And let it come to pass[3] that the opening of Thy words[4] enlighten
Thy servant, son of Thy servant, Meir.[5]
And from the salvation of Thy countenance[6] let sustenance come
To the son of Thy hand-maiden, he who is named ben Ezra.[7]
This is the Book of the straight path[8]4 by the poet,[9] Abraham.
Bound by cords of true grammar.[10]
To be deemed fit[11]5 by the eyes of knowing judgment.[12]6
And make happy all those who uphold it.[13]
Thus saith Abraham the Spaniard,[14]
Who is mindful of the five paths taken by the Torah commentators.[15]

Commentary on Introductory Prayer

[1] This description of the deity is taken from one of the most important parts of the daily synagogue service, the *Amidah*. It directly follows the linking of God with the three Hebrew patriarchs, Abraham, Isaac and Jacob. Here the expression sets the grave and serious tone intended by bn Ezra.

[2] The first 'Abraham' refers to the biblical patriarch, the second to ibn Ezra himself. The biblical Abraham was the first monotheist, symbolised in Jewish tradition by the attribute of *hesed*, mercy or kindness. In the biblical narrative, Abraham is called by God to leave his country, Ur of the Chaldees, and father a great nation in Canaan, later the Land of Israel. Abraham gains many converts for the new religion of monotheism. Similarly, ibn Ezra leaves Spain and travels to

---

Numbers in square brackets relate to the Commentary. Remaining numbers relate to endnotes

unknown territory. Here he hopes that God will treat him with *hesed*, enabling him to win adherents to the grammatical method of exegesis. In this way he will father a great grammatical movement which will preserve Jewish tradition for posterity. It must be remembered that ibn Ezra outlived all but one son, ironically named Isaac, just like the son of the patriarch, Abraham. Ibn Ezra's son, Isaac, converted to Islam. It is possible that these circumstances influenced ibn Ezra's desire to father spiritual children who would continue his exegetical approach in virgin territory. Ibn Ezra must also have been aware of the burden of being the first great Spanish biblical exegete, setting out to introduce a completely new methodology on new and hostile terrain. Like his namesake, he regarded this new terrain as the future safeguard for the Jewish people.

[3]   Note the biblical style.

[4]   Compare with the very first words of the *Amidah*, 'Oh Lord, open my lips and my mouth shall declare Thy praise.'

[5]   Ibn Ezra's father's name, Meir, means 'enlightener'. Ibn Ezra hopes to fulfil the potential inherent in his father's name.

[6]   See *Psalms* 80:4, 8, in which a link is made between God's countenance and human enlightenment. Also see *Psalms* 118:19–22, part of the festival *Hallel* prayers.

[7]   A pun on the name 'Ezra', signifying 'help', both material and spiritual. For possible biblical connection, see *Psalms* 121:1–2. By describing himself as God's 'hand-maiden', ibn Ezra acknowledges his passive role in relation to God. The phrase can also be translated 'son of Thy truth', implying 'bearer of God's truth'. Ibn Ezra may also be thinking of Eve's role as 'helpmeet' to Adam, a phrase indicating a far more active role than the translation conveys. Ibn Ezra sees himself as God's interpreter to the Jews of Lucca, who do not know the rules and secrets of Spanish exegesis. Having described himself and his role, ibn Ezra now broaches the nature of the *Commentary* itself.

[8]   The term *yashar* denotes frank, undeviating, moral integrity.

[9]   Ibn Ezra's views on poetry as a discipline have been discussed above.

[10] In Chapter Six I suggested a link between this phrase and the style of the Karaite, Salmon ben Jeroham. Ibn Ezra offers his poetic *Introduction* as a restrained and disciplined festal offering. For the link between God's enlightenment of

humanity and the binding of the festival cords in sacrifice, see the *Hallel Psalm*, 118:27. For a possible link with Abraham's preparations to sacrifice his son, Isaac, known as the *Akeda*, or binding, see *Genesis* 22:9.

[11] Literally 'kosher'. Ibn Ezra continues the metaphor of the animal prepared for ritual slaughter. He hopes that his readers will prepare themselves for study and thus also 'digest' his poetic offering in the correct or fitting manner. A biblical precedent for 'ingesting' words of truth appears in *Ezekiel* 3:1–3.

[12] This phrase combines the ideas of enlightenment and wisdom.

[13] See *Proverbs* 3:18. Having already compared his *Commentary* to a festival offering, ibn Ezra now compares it to the Tree of Life. His use of biblical metaphors emphasises ibn Ezra's divinely-inspired role.

[14] Ibn Ezra reintroduces himself as a quasi-prophet, simultaneously drawing attention to his Spanish origins and their superior cultural overtones.

[15] Ibn Ezra will now elucidate five methods of exegesis. Throughout, he emphasises development through motion, rather than intellectual study, which can lead to stasis. He continues to use the verb *halakh* and the noun *derekh* when he describes the paths as methods of reaching the centre of a circle. '*Halakh*' gives rise to *halakhah*, the traditional Jewish method of carrying out God's will according to Jewish Law. I have already discussed the tension experienced by ibn Ezra in his desire to mediate between correct exegesis and *halakhah*. Ibn Ezra's restless life of continual travel northwards was not only the result of his wish to educate the Jews of Christian lands, but also a personal expression of his aim to find the right path to God.

Path One

Path One is long and wide, far above the contemporary mind. If truth be compared to the central point of a circle, then this path must be like the circumference, or like a thread surrounding it from the start.[1]7, 8 Within it have trodden the great sages who were yeshivah scholars in Muslim realms.[2] An example is Rav Isaac, who compiled two [whole] books on the text '*In the beginning*' [*Genesis* 1:1] up to '*and were completed*' [*Genesis* 2:1], yet he himself did not complete [them], on account of the number of issues [discussed in them].[3] [In his commentary] on the verse, '*let there be light'* [*Genesis* 1:3], he mentioned the belief in the powers of light and dark, yet he himself was walking in the dark without knowing it.[4]9 In his comments on [the verse] *'and the earth brought forth'* [*Genesis* 1:12], he himself brought forth words from his own mind, speaking of trees and vegetation, small and large. Moreover, in his comments on [the phrase] *'living souls'* [actually singular: *Genesis*.1:20, 21, 24 and 30], he [even] cited gentile wisdoms.[5]10

Even Rav Sa'adiah, the Gaon of the Diaspora, pursued the very same route.[6] He introduced non-Jewish ideas into his comments on *'let there be luminaries'* [*Genesis* 1:14], in order to inform us about the measurements discussed by astronomers.[7]11 Similarly, Rav Shmuel ben Hofni had [only] *'gathered wind in his fists'*[8] in commenting on [the phrase] *'and Jacob went out'* [*Genesis* 28:10], due to his plethora of details. He mentioned every [biblical] prophet by name, how many times he was exiled from his place,[9] and the benefits of travelling on the path.[10] Yet this commentary [itself] has no benefit and its only merit is its length.[11] His [comments on the phrase] *'and he dreamed'* [*Genesis* 28:12] aspire to be [nothing less than] a [full] interpretation of dreams, and [an exploration of] why people see [things] whilst slumbering.[12] However, anyone who wishes to acquire insight into the secular sciences is better advised to study them from books by experts in the subject. Only then will they be able to weigh up their evidence and arguments,[13] as to their validity. The Ge'onim, however, cited such opinions in their books without evidence. Some of them were even ignorant of the methods of the ancient [non-Jewish] sages, as well as of the sources whence they derived their knowledge.

Commentary on Path One

[1]   In this first path, ibn Ezra likens God to the truth which is at the centre of the circle. However, the Paris manuscript replaces 'truth' by 'men of truth'. All five paths are depicted in terms of comparative proximity to this centre. In this first path, the Ge'onim, or Babylonian sages, are described as attaining only the outer edge of knowledge, depicted as the circumference of the circle. True knowledge lies within this circumference. The Karaites of the second path are depicted as 'meanderers', 'deviating' from the right path. The Christian allegorists of the third path are situated outside

the circumference, as they are ignorant of its centre. The followers of the fourth path, midrash, however, are very close to the centre, lacking only the mental discipline to actually grasp it. In the *Second Introduction*, written in France, ibn Ezra changes his descriptions. He is more positive about the Ge'onim, admitting that they occasionally reach the centre. The Karaites are described as erratic: sometimes they reach the centre, presumably when their exegesis agrees with ibn Ezra's; sometimes they remain on the circumference; and sometimes they are completely outside it. The Christian allegorists remain beyond the circumference, because their *exegesis* negates Jewish tradition, whereas Karaite *exegesis* does not necessarily do so. Midrashic writers alternate between the centre and the circumference.

[2]   The Ge'onim, mainly from Babylon. Ibn Ezra's respect for Muslim culture was enormous. However, he was also concerned that the scientific and philosophical approach which had aided Jewish culture under Islam might eventually undermine Jewish tradition, by encouraging contempt for the early authors of the Talmud, whose successors now lived largely in lands ruled by Christians.

[3]   A pun on *kalah*, signifying 'completion'. Ibn Ezra imitates the biblical phrase as a form of mockery of Rav Isaac for his longwinded commentaries on it!

[4]   A pun on 'dark' and 'ignorance'. It is generally thought that ibn Ezra refers here to the Zoroastrian religion which predominated in Babylon before the onset of Islam.

[5]   Literally 'alien wisdoms', probably denoting secular sciences. Karaite use of this phrase against the Ge'onim was discussed above in Chapter Six. Ibn Ezra reproaches the Ge'onim for citing their sources out of context and without evidence.

[6]   Literally 'climbed the same track'. Not only does this phrase continue the metaphor of movement, but also emphasises the arduous nature of the Ge'onic scientific quest for God.

[7]   The most straightforward translation of *middot* in context is 'measurements' or 'ratios'. However, given ibn Ezra's penchant for double entendre, the term may also refer to the *norms* of interpretation, as well as *levels* of spiritual development, since he regarded the planets, like the angels, as emissaries of God. Here ibn Ezra criticises the Ge'onic emphasis on love of scientific learning for its own sake, although he himself espouses similar tendencies!

[8]   Here ibn Ezra puns on Shmuel's name, which can be
      translated as 'fist'. See *Proverbs* 30:4. According to him,
      Shmuel's interpretation can be compared to 'thin air'.
[9]   Or, 'Shmuel frequently goes off the point'. The term *maqom*
      can mean place of abode, or more figuratively, subject-matter.
      In addition, it is a common euphemism for God Himself. In
      this short phrase ibn Ezra suggests that, because Shmuel tends
      to digress, he is in danger of forgetting the divine goal of his
      exegetical task. In his standard commentary on the *Minor
      Prophets*, written later in France, ibn Ezra himself gives
      details of each prophet. In this context he obviously deems
      such details relevant!
[10] Once more, ibn Ezra's sub-text includes the religious duty of
      disciplined interpretation, attained by following the right
      'path'. He is not simply discussing the value of travel for its
      own sake, as in Shmuel's case.
[11] A sarcastic put-down. Ibn Ezra will argue that his own path is
      short and direct.
[12] This refers to Jacob's famous 'ladder' dream at Bethel. See
      Genesis 28: 10–19
[13] *Az yitbonen berey'utam* can also be translated as 'contem-
      plate their creation'. This may be an allusion to midrashic
      interpretation of *Proverbs* 8:22, in which God is described as
      consulting with the Torah (personified as wisdom), before
      creating the world.

Path Two

Path Two was chosen by meanderers,[1]12 whether they were
Israelites[2] who thought that they were standing at the very point
itself,[3] or others who did not even know its place.[4] This is the
way of Sadducees, such as Anan, Benjamin, ben Mashiach and
Jeshua[5] [the Karaites] as well as every other [type of] heretic[6]
who does not believe in the words of the authorised keepers of the
religious tradition.[7]13 Deviating left or right,[8] each of them
interprets the verses as he wishes, even when they concern
commandments and statutes.[9] Actually, however, they are
completely devoid of the deeper senses[10] of the Holy Tongue
and consequently get lost in grammatical mazes.[11] For how can
one rely on[12] their opinion regarding the commandments when
they meander[13]14 from one side to another every moment,
according to their [contextually constrained] thought, given that

it is impossible to find in the text of the Written Torah a single commandment that is so sufficiently explicated as to cover every case of its application?[14]

I will [merely] mention here one which is of great significance to those who acknowledge it. For its sub-cases all include [the punishment of] being cut off from the community of believers.[15] [This punishment would be meted out] for eating on Yom Kippur; [for consuming] hametz on Pesach [and the original paschal sacrifice], incorrectly performed by people who were inappropriately purified; for [not] desisting from work on the seven [festival] rest-days; [for not observing correctly the commandments of] festival sacrifices, building a succah and blowing the shofar. For the [rules governing the periodical] yearly laws and statutes are not spelled out in the Torah in exact detail, nor how we should reckon the months [and dates therein].

'*And those who are desolately poor*' in knowledge '*are cast down*'.[16] They have made their mark based on the verse '*for signs*[17] *and for appointed seasons*' [*Genesis* 1:14]. However, they did not realise that [the phrase] '*And let them be*' [at the start of that verse] is in the plural, because it refers both to the [great] luminaries and to the [smaller] stars. Whoever says that the conjunction *vav* in the phrase '*and for appointed seasons*' is superfluous, since '*for a sign*' is connected to '*season*', will have to try and persuade his greatest friend to accept his doctrine, but even then it is quite uncertain that he will. [For] even if we have found two or three additional *vavs*, who can say with certainty that the one referred to here is one of the superfluous *vavs*, after [discovering that] a single *vav* [considered perhaps redundant] turns out to furnish the true meaning of [for instance] the phrase '*la-alephim*'.[18]

Moreover, the phrase '*He made the moon for seasons*' [*Psalms* 104:19] cannot be interpreted according to the words of those whose '*loins totter*'.[19] Even if it were written 'And let the moon be for a sign for the appointed seasons in the month', who would give us a sign that these [criteria] were the Lord's [own] consecrated seasons? For there are many 'seasons' in the Torah, Text and Writings.[20]

Even if [the phrase] explicitly [contained the words] 'the Lord's appointed seasons', there would still remain a great issue. [Should] a 'month' [be defined as the moment when] the moon completes its revolution around the zodiac, i.e., twenty-seven days and some hours, or when it completes its encircling of the apogee of the eccentric sphere, whose centre is not coincident with the earth's centre? Or is it, as some sages think, when the dependent cycle finishes its revolution, since the course of its epicycle is actually in the reverse direction?[21]15

However, even if we rely on knowing [the times of] the conjunctions of the luminaries, there is still [the problem of the] three conjunctions: the mean conjunction of their orbits; the true conjunction relative to the zodiac;[22] and the apparent conjunction which deviates [from these].[23] We do not know which one of these [three] is appropriate. As to those who have said that the decision depends on eyesight, '*they have been deceived*',[24]16 for '*they have eyes but see not*'.[25] Perhaps they could show us in the Torah and testimony the place where they found this '*lost object*'.[26]17 Nor did they interpret correctly when commenting on [the phrase] '*month in its month*'. This passage does not refer here to 'moon', but rather signifies that everything should be done in its [proper] time, [as in the phrases] '*on its appropriate day*' and '*on its appropriate Shabbat*'.[27]

Now it is well-known that sometimes there are six hours between the appearance of the new moon and sunset,[28] at which time the moon can be seen, though only when certain conditions pertain. Yet sometimes there are thirty hours between [these appearances] and, nevertheless, [the moon] cannot be seen even [by people standing] on hills.[29] For the moon's courses change as a result of its own orbit in combination with that of the sun, as well as being dependent on the longitude and latitude of [the respective] locations [of the observers].[30]

And if a dark cloud should dwell[31]18 on earth and the moon is not seen at the beginning of [the months of] Ellul or Tishri, should the Yom Kippur fast [last] three days [instead of one]? Moreover, who told us that the days of the month number thirty? For it was Judah the Persian [a Karaite!] who compiled a book, calculating the year and months by the sun [instead of the moon].[32]19

We also do not learn from the [Written] Torah what is entailed in 'witnessing' the month; who [constitutes] a 'witness'; whether the latter is allowed to travel a great distance on a holy day; or if the [joint] testimony of a father and son, resident alien, or woman is acceptable.[33]

Even if all these matters were clearly explained, there is another difficulty. It is not clearly explained in the Torah of Moses how to ascertain the number of months in the year. Even if [this calculation] were linked to [the definition of] Aviv, does it [refer to] wheat or barley?[34]20 Nor [does the Torah mention] when we should look,[35] nor where the barley should come from.[36]21 What happens if there is a year of drought in the Land of Israel and round about, and there is simply no seed at all, let alone new ears? should we [then] fix the year as it is,[37] or intercalate? In addition, there would be no counting of the Omer and [thus] no festival that we could [on this occasion] call Atzeret.[38]22

This is the reason why all these commandments need the received Oral Tradition [in order to be properly interpreted]. And those who say, 'But the Mishnaic writers testify by the sighting of the moon', well, the response to them is obvious. If their testimony is credible[39]23 [in the one case], let them [also] accept the [Mishnaic] testimony regarding the needs of the year,[40] as proclaimed by the *Bet Din*. For the basis of the intercalation depends on [three factors:] new ears, equinoxes and solstices and the needs of the community.[41]

Why are the laws concerning the mitzvot [surrounding] the plague of leprosy explained in great detail [in the Written Torah], seeing as it is actually a mitzvah for a single individual and [occurs only] rarely [in a community], whereas the mitzvot relevant to the appointed seasons are obligatory for all Israel at all times?[42] Therefore, why is there no firm report[43] about the latter in the Written Torah, leaving us to look for hints here and there? Why [should] such a thing [happen] in the words of such a perfectly complete Torah as this?[44]24 Surely it is a sign[45] for us that [actually] Moses relied[46] on the Oral Torah, which is '*a joy to the mind and a cure to the bone*' [based on *Psalms* 4:8 and *Proverbs* 16:24].[47] For [in reality] there is no difference between the two Torot, as both are handed down to us by our ancestors.[48]

[King] Hezekiah's Pesach will strengthen the hand of [those who have] faith.[49] For [everything Hezekiah did] was done on the authority and expert advice of the elders. He did not offer the Pesach sacrifice in its [normal] season and [even] dared[50] to eat hametz in the first month.[51] He observed the 'second Pesach' for seven days as if it were the first.[52] [Despite this] there are many proofs that the High Exalted One[53] accepted his deeds.[54] For it was [all done] through the *Bet Din*, and there was no deceit[55] in his spirit.

Commentary on Path Two

[1] *Petaltel* is a hapax legomonon. See *Deuteronomy* 32:5.

[2] Even though they are Jewish, the Karaites are heretics. In *Second Path Two*, they are termed 'deniers'. The non-Jewish 'others' may refer to Christians, discussed in the next path.

[3] *Amad al*, 'stand at', also means 'grasp', 'understand'. *Nequdah* (point) and *etzem* (itself) are both metaphors for truth, or even God.

[4] For *maqom*, 'place', as a euphemism for God, see previous *Path*.

[5] These individual Karaites and the general association of Karaism with the ancient Sadducees have been discussed above.

[6] In some editions, the term *min* is changed to *mi*, even though this spoils the rhyme. The phrase would then read 'and everyone who'. The Christian censor would have objected to *min*, which had generally come to mean 'Christian', rather than 'heretic'.

[7] See ibn Ezra's comments on *Short Exodus* 35:3.

[8] See II *Samuel* 14:19 (cited in Weiser 1977a: 2, n. 35) and *Deuteronomy* 17:11 (cited in Menorah 1988: 3, n. 13).

[9] According to ibn Ezra, an exegete may be original in non-legal passages but, for the sake of tradition and community, must follow authorised interpretations in legal passages. I have already discussed the negative Karaite attitude to traditional rabbinic authority.

[10] *Totz'aot*. A very interesting word, which signifies 'bringing forth' or 'producing'. Its verbal root is used in *Genesis* to denote the earth's yield of produce. For difficulty in translation see 'Teshuvot' in Roth 1983: 63–84, from which the following extract is taken: '... if we had not been exiled from our land, and if our language was to be found entire in our hands as in earlier days when we dwelled secure in our tranquil habitations, then we would find all the grammar of our language and all its forms (? = minei toseoteyah), and we would know its metre and understand its boundaries, for the language of every people has metre and grammar.'

[11] bn Ezra mocks Karaite 'expertise' in grammar, by suggesting that the Karaites get lost in trivial surface grammatical nit-picking, without seeing the whole semantic and pragmatic picture.

[12] *Samakh* is the root of *semikhah*, or laying-on of hands. This term was originally used for animal sacrifice on the Temple altar. It was then extended to include the ordination of judges, elders and rabbis, starting with Moses' ordination of Joshua. Ibn Ezra uses this verb in the context of upholding the spiritual heirs of these ordinands, whilst opposing the

anarchic, undisciplined tendencies of those opposed to the rabbinic tradition.

[13] Note similarity between *hafakh* here and *halaf*, as a general term for '"dissenters from the path of orthodoxy" ... a household word among polemicists on both sides of the fence, and, moreover, not necessarily derogatory.'

[14] I have already discussed how Oral Torah, as interpreted by rabbinic tradition, is essential for the comprehension of Written Torah, or scripture. Biblical interpretation alone, even when contextually aware, is insufficient for an explanation of Jewish law.

[15] The punishment of *karet*.

[16] Based on *Isaiah* 58:7, but note that here ibn Ezra emphasises ignorance rather than poverty. He could also be mocking a conflation of the sentiments in *Matthew* 5:3 and 5, in which the *'poor in spirit'* are said to inherit *'the kingdom of heaven'* (based on *Isaiah* 57:15), whereas *'the meek shall inherit the earth'* (*Psalms* 37:11). Only one letter separates the words 'poor' and 'meek' in Hebrew.

[17] *Ot* signifies letter, sign and mark.

[18] See, for example, *Deuteronomy* 5:10: *'ve-oseh hesed la-alephim le-ohavai u-leshomre-mitzvotai'* ('... *but showing mercy unto thousands, to those who love Me and to those who keep My commandments'*). The significant *vav* here is probably the first, which distinguishes God's mercy towards those who love Him from His severity towards those who serve idols rather than Him. We should probably translate this *vav* as 'but', rather than 'and'.

[19] Based on *Psalms* 69:24. Ibn Ezra puns on the letter combination *m'd*, to 'totter', also signifying 'appointed season', an anagram of *'md*, 'to stand'. Ibn Ezra implies that the Karaites cannot 'stand upright' in grammatical discussions or legal understanding, as they are devoid of the foundation which underpins the whole system. By use of anagram, ibn Ezra also demonstrates the thin line separating the concept of 'standing firm' from that of 'tottering'.

[20] These three categories probably refer to the entire Tenach: Pentateuch, Prophets and Writings.

[21] Here, ibn Ezra demonstrates his astronomical expertise. The normal lunar cycle, i.e., the visual one, does not correspond to a complete revolution of the earth, since it also depends on the sun. The correction is insignificant only because of the

much larger distance of the sun, and the length of the year. The 'dependent cycle' is known as 'Tali'. The Hebrew phrase translated as 'actually' literally means 'in truth and in perfection', an allusion to ibn Ezra's constant quest for the whole meaning.

[22] Literally 'the highest in faith'. See previous comment.

[23] Or 'relating to change in vision'. Ibn Ezra dismisses this approach in his comments on *Exodus* 12:2, as he will do below.

[24] Based on *Isaiah* 19:13.

[25] *Psalms* 115:5. In the context from which he quotes, ibn Ezra implies that the Karaite approach, based on senses alone, is akin to idolatry. Moreover Karaite 'sight' is not true sight, but self-deception.

[26] Ibn Ezra may be alluding here to *Leviticus* 5:23, which discusses types of deception needing atonement. The reference to 'Torah and testimony' may well be a sarcastic allusion to a polemical attack by the Karaite, ben Zuta.

[27] *Numbers* 28:14. *Chodesh* signifies both 'new moon' and 'month'. For ibn Ezra the context points to the second interpretation. For *yom yom* as 'daily' rather than 'two days', see *Path Four*.

[28] Ibn Ezra reverts to his previous argument against relying on eyesight.

[29] Perhaps an oblique reference to the 'lofty' Ge'onim. See *Path One*.

[30] Ibn Ezra now returns to his astronomical excursus. The periodicity of the crucial visual configuration, or 'new moon', depends on three bodies: the moon, sun and earth.

[31] *Anan*, 'the dark cloud', is the founder of Karaism. On *Exodus* 24:1, ibn Ezra states 'said Anan, may his name be blotted out like a dark cloud'. *Ke-anan* is an anagram of '*kena'an*', Canaan, the promised land. Ibn Ezra chooses this phrase deliberately in order to represent the Karaites in biblical terms as the arch-enemy of the rabbinic tradition which succeeded Moses and his followers. Just as Moses' heirs conquered the promised land, so rabbinic tradition, and ibn Ezra's own commentary, will eventually conquer the heresy of Karaism. Furthermore, just as a 'dark cloud' can obscure vision, so Karaism temporarily prevents the divine will from being realised, thus obscuring the role of the Shekhinah, or 'indwelling' presence of God on earth. However, the message

is basically optimistic. When the dark cloud passes, the Shekhinah will be revealed in all her glory.

[32] Ibn Ezra demonstrates Karaite inconsistency, by introducing the name of a Karaite exponent of a solar, rather than lunar, theory of the year. He puns on the letter combination *sfr*, which denotes verbal communication, mathematical calculation and text. It is an anagram of *prs*, 'Persian'. As in the previous remarks on *anan*, he demonstrates that a combination of factors is necessary to glean the truth, and that one-sidedness leads to error. Commenting on *Exodus* 12:2, ibn Ezra calls the solar theory 'the method of the uncircumcised', referring to the Christians. Fascinatingly, he also comments on *Leviticus* 25:9 that 'year' is a mathematical construct, whereas 'month' is a linguistic concept. He further emphasises the role of the legitimate law-makers in transmitting a workable yearly cycle by their occasional use of *ibbur*, 'intercalation'. *Ibbur* also signifies pregnancy. Ibn Ezra thus implies that by 'penetrating' the divine will, these lawmakers, i.e. the rabbis, will always adjudicate correctly.

[33] The terms *ed* (witness) and *edut* (evidence) are related to *te'udah* (testimony), mentioned above. Just as the Torah alone cannot 'testify' as to how one should obey her own laws in detail, so even the definition of a 'witness' or 'evidence' is fraught with difficulties, necessitating the 'intervention' of legal authorities. Only they can decide, firstly, whether a witness can go further than the *Shabbat* boundary in order to testify to the *Bet Din* to having seen the new moon, and, secondly, 'who' constitutes a witness.

[34] The ripening of new ears of cereals, marking the beginning of spring. However, it is necessary to ascertain exactly which cereal, wheat or barley, is meant, because the Pesach festival must always occur in Nisan, the first spring month. These two cereals ripen at different times. The biblical text does not give enough detail on these questions.

[35] For the first ears of barley. Ibn Ezra gives more details in comments on *Exodus* 12:2. There are irregularities in the comparative lengths of any two years. Cereal ears appear at different times in different locations. In Temple times people always searched physically for these ears, but if necessary the legal authorities would intercalate, taking into account other factors, as stated in the Mishnah. In philosophical terms the physical searching, exemplified by the Karaites, refers to the

sense or *Sinn* level of understanding. The rabbinic approach, based on Oral Torah, points out the right direction, giving an applied meaning or 'reference', epitomised by the term *Bedeutung* (clarification by pointing out). According to ibn Ezra, non-application equals incomprehension. He would therefore argue that the Karaites do not even understand the 'sense' of the commandments, let alone their referential meaning. Oral Torah brings Written Torah into the practical realm, which is the most important aspect of Judaism for ibn Ezra.

[36] Ibn Ezra refers to the bringing of the sheaf of barley, known as the *omer*, the waving of which symbolises the start of the seven-week period between Pesach and Shavuot, the harvest festival. A different translation is 'or perhaps the [exact] measurements [to be calculated]'.

[37] *Pshutah*. A pun on *pshat*. The 'simple' year, 'as it is', is only to be altered in cases of abnormality. Ibn Ezra is not simply commenting on definitions of 'year', but making a more profound point about the nature of *pshat*. Simple interpretations of text and law are to be commended, but need an expert to intervene when unexpected difficulties occur. Ibn Ezra sees himself as such a textual expert, just as the *Bet Din* are the legal experts. Naturally, in his eyes, the Karaites interpret as if unexpected factors never occur.

[38] Shavuot, the 'completion' of Pesach. Just as the definition of 'moon' depends on correctly understanding the nature of a 'revolution', or closing of a circle, so the true definition of Pesach entails its correct culmination in Shavuot, produced by the human *omer* ceremony. Continuity is everything, just as we, the seekers, form a circumference around the one fixed point, God.

[39] Literally 'true', 'believable', related to 'truth' and 'faith'. Ibn Ezra uses this term only of people who can be trusted as upholders of law.

[40] Ibn Ezra acknowledges that the Karaites accept Mishnaic teachings when it suits their purpose, but accuses them of inconsistency for refusing to acknowledge that the Mishnah also takes into account other factors, including the 'needs of the year'.

[41] *Tekufot* (equinoxes and solstices), stems from a root meaning 'circuit'. The three factors necessary in 'intervention' represent the earthly, the astronomical and the social respectively.

All these factors lie completely outside the purely textual sphere pursued by the Karaites.

[42] Just in case the Karaites are still not convinced by the previous arguments in favour of Oral Torah, ibn Ezra points out a biblical anomaly. Laws are not generally discussed in practical detail in Written Torah. However, in the case of leprosy, great detail is given, even though leprosy is relevant only to a few, exceptional individuals. Calendrical laws, on the other hand, are relevant to the whole community, but are not discussed in scripture.

[43] *Ad ne'eman.* This expressions alludes to both 'witness' and 'faith'.

[44] A sarcastic reference to the Karaite view of the self-sufficiency of Written Torah.

[45] Again, a pun on *ot*, as letter, sign and mark.

[46] Ibn Ezra deliberately chooses terminology which undermines the Karaite approach. *Semikhah* is used here not only in the sense of 'reliance', but also as an allusion to traditional rabbinic ordination, from which Karaites are excluded. See above.

[47] Also see *Proverbs* 16:25, which refers to people who delude themselves that they are on '*a straight path*', when their path actually leads to '*death*'. As well as 'bone', *etzem* denotes 'self' and even 'God'. See above.

[48] Ibn Ezra drives home the exclusivity of the chain of rabbinic tradition, both written and oral. He also hints at the reverence felt for these 'ancestors' by the mass of Jewish people who follow this tradition.

[49] II *Chronicles* 30. Again ibn Ezra puns, this time on Hezekiah's name, which means 'God's strength'. He refers to a Pesach which was celebrated at the 'wrong' time of year, but which was ordained by the legal authorities, who took external factors into account. In order to beat the Karaites at their own game, ibn Ezra deliberately chooses a biblical passage to prove that the Bible's own laws can, on occasion, be emended by the authorities, thus emphasising the importance of creative interpretation by legal authorities.

[50] The third use of '*yad*' in this context. The first two occurrences refer to 'strength' and 'authority' respectively. Normally one would be going *beyond authority* by infringing the Torah so blatantly. On this occasion, however, the 'infringement' was actually authorised.

[51] Instead of unleavened bread. Ibn Ezra has already stated that non-observance of *mo'ed* leads to this very sin, resulting in separation from the community through divine fiat – *karet*.

[52] In this case Pesach was celebrated a month later than 'normal'.

[53] God, euphemistically named *ram ve-nisa*. Ultimately He is the only one to whom all are answerable, including the legal authorities. Compare ibn Ezra's use of the language of elevation here to his sarcastic description of the Ge'onic path as *nisgavah* in *Path One*.

[54] See II *Kings* 18: 6, 2, as well as II *Chronicles* 30:2. In his comments on *Exodus* 12:2, ibn Ezra says of Hezekiah that 'he did not bend either to right or left in obeying the commandments of the Lord'. Contrast with his description of the Karaites as 'deviating left or right'. By obeying the legal authorities, even against all his knowledge of Written Torah, Hezekiah wins God's approval. Compare with the Karaites, who adhere solely to the text, disregarding the authority of legal experts.

[55] *Remiyah'*, related to *ram*, implies an over-elevated opinion of self. Ibn Ezra ends this path by accentuating the importance of correct motivation as well as action.

Path Three

Path Three is the path of darkness and black gloom.[1]25 It [stands] outside the circumference of the circle. [Its followers] are those who fabricate from their minds mystical explanations for every word.[2] It is their belief that the Torot[3] and laws are riddles. [Therefore] I shall not spend a long time refuting them, for '*they are a people erring in their heart*',[4]26 having interpreted the words incorrectly. However, they were right[5] in one thing, namely that every matter, however small or great, concerning a mitzvah, must be weighed in the scale of the balance of the mind.[6] For planted in the mind is knowledge [deriving] from the wisdom of the Eternal Unchanging One.[7] [However, only] in cases where this knowledge cannot support [the interpretation] of the word, or corrupts that which can be clearly perceived by the senses, should a person seek out a hidden interpretation. Weighing of knowledge is the foundation, for the Torah was not given to anyone lacking in knowledge. Moreover, the angel between Adam and his God is his intelligence.[8] Anything which knowledge does not contradict we should interpret according to its plain meaning and the normal function [of the wording],[9] leaving it in its [natural] proportions,[10] believing that this is its true [meaning].

We should not grope a wall like the blind, stretching words according to our [own selfish] requirements.[11] Why should we turn exoteric [meanings] into esoteric [ones]? If there are indeed places where they are truthfully conjoined, and both equally credible, some in bodies and some in thoughts,[12]27 as in the circumcision of the flesh[13] and the foreskin of hearts, or as in the [story of the] Tree of Knowledge [where] a hidden meaning dwells pleasantly, nevertheless the words are also true according to their obvious meaning.[14] [And] if a man [really] cannot sustain this among his ideas, he would be wise to open his eyes and also find in nature many forms,[15] like the nostrils, the tongue and the feet, which serve two purposes.[16]

Commentary on Path Three

[1]   The vocabulary implies that the allegorical Christian path is based on even more ignorance and turpitude than that of the Karaites, who are symbolised merely by the cloud named *anan*. The cloud depicted here as *hoshesh ve-afelah*, by contrast, is reminiscent of that tangible darkness encountered as one of the great plagues by the Egyptians, whilst '*the children of Israel had light in their dwellings*', a contrast not lost on ibn Ezra's readers. See *Exodus* 10:21–3. Sarna's translation of the phrase as 'benighted' is perfect.

[2]   These may be the non-Jews referred to at the beginning of the previous path, who do not even know where to start looking for God, nor the nature of exegesis. They invent explanations that are not based on any sound foundation, let alone authorised Jewish tradition.

[3]   It is not clear whether the word refers to Written and Oral Law combined, or to general religious teachings found in the Written Torah.

[4]   *Psalms* 95:10. The biblical verse ends '*and they did not know my ways*'. The Christians 'err in their hearts', or 'wander in their minds' because they do not understand traditional Jewish interpretation of scripture. See similar descriptions of Karaites, above.

[5]   The repetition of the term *tsedek* may be an allusion to Paul's anti-Jewish argument about righteousness and the Law in *Romans* 8–10.

[6]   Here it appears that ibn Ezra plays on the double meaning of *lev* as 'heart' and 'mind'. The implication is that Christians emphasise the heart at the expense of the mind, and are thus ignorant of biblical meanings based on context.

[7]   Ibn Ezra distinguishes the one, unchanging, Jewish God from the three-fold, and thus arguably polytheistic, Christian Trinity.

[8]   Intelligence is here depicted as an emissary of God, the divine portion of humanity.

[9]   *Ke-pshuto u-mishpato.* Through pun, ibn Ezra implies that the correct interpretation of Jewish law, *pshat*, is made possible only through understanding 'the normal function', *mishpat*, of biblical words and phrases.

[10] For this phrase, see II *Chronicles* 22:13: '*So the workmen wrought, and the work was perfected by them and they set the house of God in its true proportions and strengthened it*'. Ibn Ezra compares the correct interpretation of text to the correct construction of God's abode. For a similar comparison, see the section on ibn Sina, in Chapter Five.

[11] For 'wall' as a metaphor for language, see Simon 1965: 114. The image is an apt description of the crude and grotesque behaviour displayed by the Christians in making wild guesses at interpretation. The physicality of the language used by ibn Ezra contrasts with Christian idealisation and allegorisation. Compare with ibn Ezra's criticisms of Menahem ibn Saruq's approach, Chapter One.

[12] The crux of ibn Ezra's argument. In Jewish exegesis the symbolic meaning, whether allegorical or mystical, comes to enhance the more obvious meaning, not to replace it. This view is clarified in ibn Ezra's explanation of Onkelos' approach, *Path Five*, below.

[13] *Ke-milat basar.* Possibly the most brilliant pun of the whole *Introduction*. I have already discussed it in Chapter Four. The phrase does not actually appear in scripture. On the surface level ibn Ezra argues that when circumcision is mentioned in scripture it refers to the physical covenant, and should be taken at face value. On the other hand phrases such as 'foreskin of hearts' do not imply any physical circumcision of the heart, but should be interpreted symbolically as signifying

humility before God. The two phrases would therefore be a fine example of the physical and the spiritual working together within the text. However, ibn Ezra goes further. *Milah* refers to orality as well as circumcision. There are thus at least three possible interpretations of the phrase: physical circumcision; the word as flesh (a reference to Christ, the Christian God, who transcends Jewish exegesis and tradition); and Oral Torah, the true arbiter of interpretation, through exegesis working with tradition. For Jews, circumcision is a mark (*ot*: 'letter') of the covenant between God and His people. For ibn Ezra, as for other followers of Jewish tradition, adherence to Oral Torah is part of that covenant. Even today, the expression 'pound of flesh' signifies Christian contempt for all things 'Jewish', i.e., non-spiritual. Ibn Ezra wished to address this Christian misunderstanding of Judaism.

[14] Once again ibn Ezra insists that even passages that appear to demand a symbolic interpretation must also be true according to *pshat*.

[15] Ibn Ezra anticipates that some might find it hard to make sense of the idea of harmony between obvious and symbolic interpretations of the same passage. In such cases nature serves as an example. He contrasts the 'blind' Christians with the 'insightful' Jews. See *Genesis* 3:7, where Adam and Eve eat of the fruit in the Garden of Eden '*and the eyes of them both were opened and they knew that they were naked.*' Since then, humans are capable of opening their own eyes, utilising God-given initiative. The term '*notzrim*', 'forms', also designates 'Nazarenes', the followers of Christ. This further attempt to ridicule the Christian approach to life and interpretation emphasises the harmonious co-existence of the bodily and the spiritual in Judaism.

[16] The nose, tongue and feet constitute parts of the body with two functions. The nose is used for expelling air (sneezing), but also for breathing. The tongue is the organ of both taste and speech. The feet allow us to move, as well as stand in prayer. In addition, we have two nostrils and two legs. In *Second Path One*, ibn Ezra uses the nose as metaphor for not two, but four, complementary types of interpretation. See remarks on Talmage in Chapter Three. The actual status of Christian hermeneutics was no longer purely allegorical during ibn Ezra's time and has been discussed in Chapter

Four. It would appear that ibn Ezra's real concern was with forms of contemporary Jewish exegesis which tended to allegorise at the expense of the text and community. These tendencies became more evident in the thirteenth century, even leading to a ban on the study of philosophy in some circles!

Path Four

The fourth path is near to the point[1] and a [whole] bunch [of scholars] chases down this [road].[2] This is the path of the sages in the lands of the Greeks and Edomites.[3] They do not look upon the scales of balance,[4] but rely on the path of *drash*. Examples are *Lekah Tov*[5]28 and *Or-Ainayim*.[6]29 However, since these [same] midrashim can be found in the books of our forefathers, why do these later interpreters tire us by re-writing them?30

There is a *drash* [which is really] the opposite of *drash* [and] which contains a hidden inexplicable meaning. An example is the *drash* that the Torah preceded the world by two thousand years.[7] This [may be] true, [but] only [when understood] according to the secret, esoteric path, although many do not understand it thus. Nevertheless, it is impossible for us to interpret it in the way it appears.[8] For years are composed of days through number, whereas days, just like moments, are measured by [reference to] the motions of the heavenly bodies. Therefore, if there were no heavenly bodies there would be no [concept] 'day', let alone two days, a year, or number 'two thousand'.[9]

Whoever asks what the world was at the start, will surely end up ashamed for seeking 'something from nothing'.[10] [As for] the response of those who retort that the Lord created the world at a time that He knew was good,[11] it too is built on 'stones of void'.[12] Likewise, those who say that He created it to show off His power to Adam, the root [cause] of His creation,[13] have actually turned their pathetic response into a tiny part of the larger question.[14] For there are absolute proofs[15] (for those who have eyes and are not blind)[16] that the inhabited world comprises in actual fact[17]31 [only] one twelfth of the earth.[18] Moreover, the whole [of the earth's surface in proportion to the entire universe] is like a [mere] dot [in relation] to the sphere which is placed over it, how much more so [in relation to] the highest sphere.[19]

The most straightforward interpretation[20] [of the word] 'day', adhering strictly to the biblical context, [does] not [need to be] midrashic. If its meaning were 'for two thousand', it would have been written *yomaim*.[21] But [the phrase] *yom yom* should be interpreted as meaning '*on each and every day*', like [the phrase] *ish ish*.[22]32 The end of the verse proves this too: '*playing before Him at all times*', followed by '*watching daily at My gates*.'[23] If this [last quotation] is [interpreted] correctly, it surely does not mean that we should keep the true Torah for a time span of two thousand years.[24] Furthermore, [the phrase] '*for a thousand years in thy sight*' does not refer to the Lord['s sight].[25] Whoever seeks [the plain meaning of this verse] will find them in my *Commentary on Psalms*.

Drash can also be used to relieve a mind occupied by a complex [discussion of] halakhah.[26] Some *drash* [interpretations] can be explained through logical argument.[27] Some are based on a non-authoritative halakhah.[28]33 Some are good for others [than those to whom they appear to be addressed], directing beginners on the [right] path to understanding. For there is a bird that cannot see the brightness in daylight, but only at night, because its eyes are dim.[29] [Let us take,] for example, the *drash* that the world was created with [the letter] *bet* because of *brachah*.[30] If this is the case, what about [the following phrases:] '*the Lord empties the world and lays it waste*';[31] '*and I will lay it waste*';[32] '*and the grinders cease*';[33] '*they have not known them*';[34] '*from the pit of destruction*';[35] '*your clothes have not waxen old*';[36] '*the Lord destroyed*';[37] '*the Lord confounded*';[38] '*and thrust thee through*';[39] '*and cut them down*';[40] '*between the parts thereof*';[41] '*contempt and wrath*';[42] '*give birth in trouble/terror*';[43] '*I will make thee terrors*';[44] '*a man of Beli'al*';[45] '*Ba'al Peor*';[46] '*Bel bows down*';[47] '*priests of the high places*'.[48]

Similarly, the [letter] *resh*[49] in [the phrase] '*its head was of fine gold*' should be compared with '*[every] wicked and worthless man*'.[50] Anyone with a little intelligence in their heart, not to mention those with the wisdom of God within, can bring forth midrashim.[51] They are all as mere clothes to the pure naked truth.[52] Our ancient rabbis, may their name be for a blessing, said concerning such things, 'No text can be deprived of its *pshat*'.[53]

There is a *drash* on the phrase *be-reshit* in the Torah, which is interpreted as follows: '*the Lord possessed me, reshit of his ways*'.[54] Another [interpretation] is that the world was created on [account of] Leviathan, as it is said: '*He is the beginning of the paths of God.*'[55]34 Another [interpretation] is that the world was created so that God would be feared, as it is written: '*The fear of the Lord is the beginning of wisdom.*[56]35 Another is that the world was created on account of the first fruits, as it is said: '*The choicest first fruits of thy land.*'[57]

Why does [the Torah] start with [the letter] *bet*? To indicate that the Lord is One and creation dual, [representing] matter and form, or two worlds.[58] Why [does it start with] *bet*, followed by *resh*, *alef*, *shin* then *yod* and *tav*?[59] This constitutes an allegory[60] about the four hundred and ten-year existence of the First Temple (since it pre-existed heavens and earth) and its subsequent destruction.[61] This is [the meaning of the verse]: '*And the earth was formless and void, with darkness over the face of the deep.*' For darkness came to the world when the Shekhinah was removed.[62]36 [The end of this verse:] '*And the spirit of God hovered over the face of the waters*' [suggests] that the spirit of wisdom and understanding rested on the Torah commentators, the Torah being likened to water.[63]37 Finally [the phrase]: '*let there be light*', refers to the days of the Messiah.[64]38 Then the Lord '*will distinguish*' between those who hope for His salvation and those who engage in the darkest of deeds.[65]

A[nother] midrashic interpretation is that [the term] *bereshit* [comprises] two words [signifying] that everything was of fire, the foundation [of all].[66]Another [interpretation is that the word] *shit* [should be interpreted] as [in the phrase] *amin shit*.[67] These are the six directions which are found in every solid.[68]39, 40 The sum of the initial letters of the words of the [first] verse corresponds to all the letters [of the alphabet].[69] In similar vein [the verse contains] seven words, corresponding to the seven kings,[70] or to the seven planets.[71] [The verse also contains] twenty-eight letters,[72]41 which correspond both to the phases of the moon[73] and to the number of times the word 'times' occurs in [the biblical book of] *Ecclesiastes.*[74]

The book [of *Genesis*] starts with [the letter] *bet* and ends [with the letter] *mem,*[75] signifying the [number of letters in the] ineffable Name, which emerges from the mouth of the High Priest on Yom Kippur.[76] [The Lord] gave [the Name] to Moses on Sinai, and thus it is written: '*The Lord among them [bam] Sinai, in holiness.*'[77] [The Torah] starts with [the word] *bereshit* and ends [with the word] *Israel*.[78] For [Israel] entered into [divine] thought at the beginning of the world.[79] And the end of the matter is that to *drash* there is no end![80]

Commentary on Path Four

[1]   Of all paths, except his own, midrash comes closest to the truth. Nevertheless, ibn Ezra demonstrates that midrashic explanations are often irrational and ungrammatical when taken at face value. In his view, the original midrashic authors, often also legal experts, regarded their writings as rhetorical devices, supports for a more serious text, or as underlying a philosophical truth. Modern compilers of midrashic anthologies, on the other hand, are too literalistic.

[2]   *Agudah*, 'bunch' is related to the term *aggadah*, homily, which is the style under discussion here. My translation aims to depict the undisciplined, individualistic and haphazard nature of midrashic writing, as viewed by ibn Ezra.

[3]   Jews living under the aegis of Christianity, especially the Greek Orthodox form of Christianity prevalent in Byzantium.

[4]   They do not use reason in biblical exegesis.

[5]   Ibn Ezra refers to the author, Tobias ben Eliezer (died 1100), leader of the Byzantine Rabbanites at the time of the First Crusade. It appears that many contemporary Byzantine midrashic writers, the butt of ibn Ezra's criticism, were often influenced by the Karaites in their commentaries. Although Tobias' aims are very similar to those of ibn Ezra, he nevertheless attacks the Karaites for importing Muslim ideas into a Christian country. Ibn Ezra would be unlikely to approve of this downgrading of Islam in favour of Eastern Christianity.

[6]   This book was written by Tobias' pupil, Meir of Kastoria. It is lost.

[7]   For biblical sources, see *Proverbs* 8:30 and *Psalms* 90:4. For midrash, see *Genesis Rabba* I:1, VIII:2.

[8]   The idea that the Torah preceded the world by two thousand years does not make sense from the scientific point of view, and should therefore, be interpreted metaphorically. Here, ibn Ezra argues against literal interpreters of midrash. However, he will soon argue that even the biblical phraseology does not lend itself to this popular midrashic translation.

[9]   Ibn Ezra explains the contemporary scientific view of number, motion and time.

[10]   *Le-ain yesh.* This concept of creation was to become very popular in mystical circles. God is compared to the 'nothing' out of which creation, 'something', unfolds. By stating that

all attempts to find the cause of creation are nonsensical, ibn Ezra mocks midrash.

[11] Ibn Ezra now gives a list of midrashic explanations of creation with which he disagrees. See *Genesis Rabba* IX:1.

[12] See remarks on Shmuel ben Hofni, in *Path One*, above.

[13] *Yetzirah* actually means 'formation'. Ibn Ezra was one of the very few thinkers to disagree with the prevalent rabbinic view that the world had been created for the sake of humanity. Rambam was to agree with him in this respect.

[14] Humanity is just a speck in God's great scheme of things.

[15] 'Absolute' is rendered by the root *gmr*. Ibn Ezra puns on the midrashic idea, endorsed by Sa'adiah, that humanity is the 'completion' (also *gmr*), or goal, of creation. Using identical vocabulary, he takes the opposite view, that humanity is an infinitesimal dot in relation to the cosmos.

[16] The sarcastic aside contains a more serious argument in favour of using the senses, as in *Path Three*.

[17] *Emunah* denotes faith and truth.

[18] Ibn Ezra uses the findings of contemporary science.

[19] This is the nub of ibn Ezra's argument, based on mediaeval Muslim cosmology. The earth is merely the lowest in a number of spherical emanations.

[20] Literally 'and if from the straight path', i.e., the most direct route to the truth. Ibn Ezra abandons his long digression in order to return to the problem posed by the midrash. He has used scientific explanations to counter the literal interpretation of the biblical passage. He now resorts to an obviously *pshat* interpretation, based on grammatical accuracy and contextual considerations.

[21] The dual plural, signifying 'two days'.

[22] *Leviticus* 17:3: '*every man*'. *Psalms* 68:20: '*blessed be the Lord daily*'. Ibn Ezra argues that the repetition of the word *yom* does not imply 'two', but 'every'. He backs up his argument from two other biblical passages.

[23] Ibn Ezra finds parallels to the phrase *yom yom* at the end of the verse and also in verse 34, endorsing his view that the phrase cannot refer to 'two days'.

[24] In verse 34, if *yom yom* were interpreted as 'two days', rather than 'daily', it would imply, in conjunction with *Psalms* 90:4, that the *Torah* should be observed for two thousand years, rather than daily, which is the obvious sense. The whole verse is addressed to *one* person: '*Happy is the*

person who listens to Me, watching daily at My gates, guarding My door-posts'.

[25] Ibn Ezra now refers to the second part of the midrashic argument, based on *Psalms* 90:4. For God, one thousand human 'years' represents a mere day. Therefore, two thousand 'years' represents two days. Ibn Ezra does not however agree with the popular interpretation that the term *in thy eyes* refers to God, citing his *Commentary on Psalms*. This last point completely destroys the midrashic argument.

[26] Ibn Ezra now discusses further functions of *drash*, e.g., as light relief.

[27] *Sabara*. In *Second Path Four*, he groups *sabara*, tradition and reason together as equally valid components of Oral Torah. For antecedents in Islam and Sa'adiah, see Chapters Five and Seven.

[28] In these cases the midrash certainly does not even claim to be taken literally.

[29] Some midrashim are used as teaching aids for beginners, whose wiser tutors understand the true *pshat* interpretation. Ibn Ezra is sarcastically disparaging of these novices, who do not yet see the 'light'.

[30] Ibn Ezra gives a long list of words beginning with the letter *bet*, which do not have a positive connotation, unlike *brachah*, 'blessing'. He wishes to ridicule those who give 'puerile' reasons for why the Hebrew Bible commences with the word *bereshit*.

[31] *Isaiah* 24:1.

[32] *Isaiah* 5:6.

[33] *Ecclesiastes* 12:3.

[34] *Psalms* 147:20.

[35] *Isaiah* 38:17.

[36] *Deuteronomy* 29:4.

[37] *Lamentations* 2:2.

[38] *Genesis* 11:7.

[39] *Ezekiel* 16:40.

[40] *Ezekiel* 23:47.

[41] *Jeremiah* 34:18.

[42] *Esther* 1:18.

[43] *Isaiah* 65:23.

[44] *Ezekiel* 26:21.

[45] *Proverbs* 16:27: depicting worthlessness.

[46] *Deuteronomy* 4:3: worshipping false gods.

[47] *Isaiah* 46:1: a pagan idol.

[48] I *Kings* 13:33: illegitimate cultic installations.

[49] Ibn Ezra now refers to the second letter of the first word of the Hebrew Bible.

[50] *Daniel* 2:32 and I *Samuel* 30:22. Ibn Ezra contrasts a positive connotation of the letter *resh* in the word *r'sh* with a negative connotation, *ra*, to emphasise the futility of ascribing such attributes to letters.

[51] Compare with *Path Three*, where intelligence is depicted as the go-between (angel) between God and humanity.

[52] This is the nub of *Path Four*. Ibn Ezra suggests that anyone can produce rhetoric, which is mere 'window-dressing' for *ha-guf ha-pshut*, 'the body laid bare'. Note the connection between *pshat* and nudity in this phrase.

[53] *Ain mikra yotse midai pshuto*. Talmud *Yevamot* 11b, 24a and *Shabbat* 63a. In case there is any doubt, ibn Ezra cites a Talmudic dictum in his defence of *pshat*. In *Path Five* he cites another dictum to make a contrasting point!

[54] There is a midrashic interpretation of the phrase '*In the beginning*' (*Genesis* 1:1) which involves the verse: '*The Lord possesses me beginning of His path*' (*Proverbs* 8:22). This 'beginning' is generally taken to refer to the Torah, personified as female wisdom. It appears in the chapter dealing with the pre-existence of Torah, which ibn Ezra has already dismissed as scientifically and exegetically impossible.

[55] *Job* 40:19. The biblical passage actually refers to the creature, Behemot. Leviathan is mentioned later in v. 25. The commentator Rashi conflates the idea of the *tanninim* (great sea creatures) of *Genesis* 1:21 with this creature, and it is possible that ibn Ezra is following him here. Ibn Ezra would disagree with the idea that the world was created on, or on account of, any creature, be it Leviathan or Behemot!

[56] *Psalms* 111:10. For this midrash see *Numbers Rabbah* XI:1, *Deuteronomy Rabbah* XI:6, *Song of Songs Rabbah* I:9.

[57] *Exodus* 23:19. Here the word *reshit* is translated as 'choice', meaning 'first' in excellence. See *Genesis Rabba* I:4,8.

[58] The letter *bet* is not only the second letter of the Hebrew alphabet, but also represents the number two, the start of duality. *Aleph*, the first letter, is not pronounced and represents the one, unique God, or pure form. For more on ibn Ezra's use of the terms *etzem* and *tzurah*, see Chapter Two.

[59] These are the letters which form the word *bereshit*, the first word of the Torah.

[60] *Remez*: hint or allegory; one of the four interpretative methods.

[61] This calculation is based on a midrash in which the first letter of *bereshit*, *bet*, signifies 'Temple' (house). The following three letters form *r'sh*, signifying the idea of 'precedence'. These initial four letters are therefore interpreted as referring to the First Temple. By gematria, a rabbinic formula in which each letter has a corresponding numerical value, the last two letters, *yod* and *tav*, add up to four hundred and ten. Thus, the first word of the Torah can be considered as an allegory on the number of years that the First Temple existed before its destruction. The midrash therefore concludes that the world was created on account of the Temple which, like the Torah, is deemed to have pre-existed creation. See Talmud *Pesachim* 54a.

[62] *Genesis* 1:2. Continuing the parallelism between the creation of the world and the building of the First Temple, the midrashist links the second verse of *Genesis* to the destruction of the Temple, at which time the Shekhinah, or divine presence, was thought to have departed the earth.

[63] For this midrash see *Pirke de Rabbi Eliezer* 1981: 18.

[64] See *Genesis* 1:3.

[65] See *Genesis* 1:4, where the Lord '*distinguished*' between light and dark. For a midrash based on this verse and which incorporates most of the ideas criticised by ibn Ezra in the whole passage, see *Genesis Rabba*, II 5. In his own commentary on the passage *ad loc*, ibn Ezra emphasises divine 'thought', whereas the midrash stresses ethical behaviour.

[66] The term *bereshit* can be formed into two words, *esh* and *brit*, denoting 'fire' and 'foundation' respectively. Alternatively, the word *shit* also means 'foundation'. See Talmud *Succah* 49a.

[67] See *Daniel* 3:1. The phrase is Aramaic for 'six cubits'.

[68] Literally 'the six extremities found in every body'. For midrashim on the number six, see *Genesis Rabba* I:4,8. The idea of 'six directions' is prevalent in the *Sefer Yetzirah*. Ibn Ezra's commentary on the work is not extant. Both this and the previous midrash try to explain creation using contemporary scientific views. The idea is that the Hebrew word

connoting 'creation' provides the reason for its own existence in its very letter composition. Just as the world is composed of elements and directions, so the Hebrew word 'creation', when deciphered, reveals the secrets of its own composition. The *Sefer Yetzirah* depicts the Hebrew letters as the blue-print of creation.

[69] Just as there are twenty-two letters in the Hebrew alphabet so, by gematria, the sum of the first letters of every word in *Genesis* 1:1 totals twenty-two.

[70] There are seven words in the verse, representing the seven Hebrew vowels, known as 'kings'.

[71] See *Sefer Zahot* 2:2, where ibn Ezra points out a similar correspondence between the seven Hebrew vowels and the seven known planets.

[72] The names of the known planets also comprise twenty-eight letters.

[73] Literally 'camps of the moon'.

[74] Commenting on *Ecclesiastes* 3:1, ibn Ezra states: 'Some say that these twenty-eight 'times' correspond to the twenty-eight phases of the zodiac in whose orbit the moon appears each month.' It therefore appears that ibn Ezra *does* approve of correspondences based on number symbolism.

[75] The Book of *Genesis* ends with the word *Mitzraim*, 'Egypt', the last letter of which is letter *mem*.

[76] By gematria the two letters *bet* and *mem* add up to the number forty-two. See Talmud *Kiddushin* 71a. It was generally believed that there existed an ineffable forty-two-letter name of God, which was known only to the High Priest, who enunciated it on Yom Kippur, the holiest day of the year.

[77] *Psalm* 68:18. The Hebrew for the phrase *'among them'* is '*bam*'. This proves to the midrashists that the ineffable name, interpreted as being synonymous with the name 'Lord', was originally given to Moses at Sinai and passed down through the chain of tradition to the High Priest.

[78] This sentence can be construed as a pun on the meanings of 'start' and 'end'. The Torah as Pentateuch starts with the word meaning *'start'* (*reshit*), and ends in *Deuteronomy*, with the word '*Israel*': For many midrashic writers Israel, the Jewish people, is the 'end' or 'goal' of 'creation'. The structure of the Pentateuch is supposed to underline this fact by its choice of first and last words.

[79] Together with the Temple and the Torah, the Jewish people, Israel, is often considered as one of the seven entities which pre-dated creation. See Midrash *Psalms* 93:2 and *Bereshit Rabba* 1:4.

[80] Ibn Ezra finishes *Path Four* with an ironic flourish! He states that midrash has 'no end', meaning that it is limitless, unstructured and purposeless. This is why, despite its ingenious and amusing qualities, it does not ultimately succeed in reaching the centre of the circle of knowledge.

Path Five

The fifth path [is the one] upon which I shall base my commentary. It is right in my eyes in the sight of the Lord, who is the only One I fear.[1] I shall be no respecter of persons when I explore the Torah text, but shall thoroughly, and to the best of my ability, seek the grammatical [form] of every word.[2] Then I shall do my utmost to explain it. You will find [an explanation of] every word whose [meaning] you seek, the first time it appears in the commentary.[3]42, 43

For example, the explanation of [the word] *shamayim*[4]; will be found in [my commentary on] the first verse [of *Genesis*, where it appears], and likewise with all [other] linguistic terminology. I shall not discuss massoretic reasons for why one [word] is sometimes [written] in full, and another defectively, for all their explanations follow the path of *drash*. In the text a word is sometimes written in full, completely clearly, whilst at other times, a silent letter is omitted as a short cut. Since [the massoretes] give midrashic reasons for full and defective [spellings], let's see if they can explain how [the scribes] could have written the books. For Moses wrote [the phrase], '*the Lord will reign*' without a *vav*, whereas the copyist of *Proverbs* wrote '*because of a servant when he reigns*' with a *vav*. [The actual reason for the discrepancy is that] many years [elapsed] between the two [writers].[5] The [massoretic] explanations [on the other hand] are totally puerile.[6] Moreover, *pshat* interpretations preclude the need for [the excuse of] scribal emendation.

However, the Aramaic translator of the Targum translated truly[7] and clarified all the silent [letters] for us.[8] Now if, in places, he drew on midrashim, we know that he knew the root [meanings] better than we.[9]44 He simply wished to add further interpretations, because even the uneducated could understand its *pshat*. An example is [the word] *iroh*, which [Onkelos] did not translate as *'son of a she-ass'* [the obvious interpretation, but as *iro*, *'his city'*]. He also translated *bni* as *'they will build'* [instead of the normal *'colt of'*. Finally, he interpreted] *atono* [as *itano*,] *'the gate of the [Temple] entrance'*, [instead of *'his she-ass'*].[10]45 Despite all this, the path of *pshat* does not deviate on account of *drash*,[11] since [according to the midrash] 'there are seventy faces to Torah'.[12]46

However, concerning [verses dealing with] laws, statutes and regulations [in contrast to non-legal texts], if we find two [possible] meanings to a verse, one of which follows the exegesis of the official interpreters [of Oral Torah], *zaddikim*, every one of them, we must, without a doubt, lean with all our might on their true [interpretation].[13] Heaven forbid that we should get mixed up[14] with the Sadducees who say that the tradition[al interpretation of the official interpreters] contradicts the written biblical text and grammatical rules.[15] In fact, our esteemed forefathers were true, all their words are true, and [now], may the Lord God of truth lead His servant on the path of truth.[16]

Commentary on Path Five

[1]   Ibn Ezra now defines his own path. He starts by advocating total exegetical freedom, based on linguistic norms associated with the Spanish–Muslim tradition. He clearly differentiates between etymology and interpretation. He disassociates himself from midrashic interpretations of discrepancies in spellings, replacing these with historical and common-sense explanations. He also sees no need to ascribe changes in orthography to scribal emendations. He then cites the author of one of the first Bible commentaries, *Targum Onkelos*, as an example of someone who used midrash knowingly, but only in addition to grammatical explanations. As in *Path Three*, ibn Ezra advocates the co-existence of different types of interpretation, rather than the replacement of one by the other. However, ibn Ezra ends by limiting the total exegetical freedom pronounced at the outset of this path. He maintains that, in all verses of a legal nature, one should follow the authorised interpreters of the day, rather than, for example, the Karaites, who criticise the latter for their deviations from the text and ignorance of etymology. Even if it appears that the Karaites understand the structure of the biblical verse better than the rabbinic authorities, ibn Ezra holds that the

latter and their interpretations can be compared in veracity to God Himself, and therefore must be obeyed in halakhic exegesis. In *Second Path Five*, he even offers to teach grammatical structure to these rabbis, in order to assist them in correct interpretation! It is obvious that ibn Ezra considers the unity of the community as paramount, outweighing even grammatical precision. This is why he is so keen to sow the seeds of his own expertise on the stony ground of Askenazi Europe. He hopes that the whole Jewish people, *klal Israel*, will learn to become exegetical experts and so safeguard their very survival!

[2] For the biblical style of his vow, see *Deuteronomy 6:5*, which forms part of the *Shema*, the most important prayer in the Jewish liturgy: '*Hear, oh Israel: the Lord our God; the Lord is One. And thou shalt love the Lord thy God with all thy heart and with all thy soul and with all thy might.*' For ibn Ezra, love of God's uniqueness (oneness) involves a total and undivided devotion to the text. The biblical passage goes on to advocate the continuous teaching of God's words to ones children. As implied previously, ibn Ezra regards the Jews of Ashkenazi lands as spiritual children who must be instructed in grammatical exegesis.

[3] Sarna states that ibn Ezra 'abandoned' this method in his *Commentary*, 'perhaps because it was too innovative and not favorably received'. Weiser points out, that in the *Second Commentary*, ibn Ezra sets out all the grammatical problems of each verse in advance and then explains the details.

[4] 'Heavens'. See *Genesis 1:1*.

[5] Ibn Ezra discusses two spellings of the phrase: '*he will reign*'. The first appears in the Pentateuch, *Exodus 15:18*, without a *vav*. The second appears in *Proverbs 30:22* with *vav*. Ibn Ezra uses an argument based on common sense, acknowledging that different parts of scripture were written down at different times.

[6] Compare with his reference to 'beginners', given in *Path Four*.

[7] Note that ibn Ezra does not say 'factually', or 'correctly'.

[8] *Ne'elmot* can also refer to 'hidden meanings'.

[9] Knowledge of the 'roots' is an essential part of ibn Ezra's philosophy. It is permissible to use midrash if, like Onkelos, you are also an acknowledged expert in *pshat*. However, there were occasions when ibn Ezra criticised Onkelos' translations.

[10] See *Genesis* 49:11. The passage's context is vital for an understanding of Onkelos' interpretation. The patriarch, Jacob, prophesies on his death-bed regarding his sons, the twelve tribes of Israel. Jacob here addresses Judah, the son from whom the Davidic line, and ultimately the Messiah, will arise. This is how the phrase '... *until Shiloh come*' is interpreted by most Jewish commentators, including Onkelos. Onkelos chooses to interpret the subsequent phrase: '... *binding his foal to the vine and the son of his she-ass to the vine branch*', in a manner appropriate to the solemnity of the occasion. The *vine* becomes a symbol of Israel (see *Psalms* 80:9). Through pun, '*his foal*', becomes '*His city*', Jerusalem. '*The vine branch*' also refers to Israel (see *Jeremiah* 2:21). Through pun again, '*his she-ass*' becomes '*His Temple*'. A connection is thus made with the expression *sha'ar ha-iton*, or '*the Temple's gate of the entrance*' (see *Ezekiel* 40:15), which David's *son*, Solomon, '*will build*' (pun on '*son of*'). However, ibn Ezra does not mention Onkelos' second interpretation, in which the phrase *bni-itono* symbolises peripatetic Torah teachers, riding on asses in order to spread the divine word (see *Judges* 5:10 and also Talmud *Eruvin* 54b). Most of the above can be found in Rashi's commentary *ad loc*, which ibn Ezra would have read. Weiss Halivni describes Onkelos' first interpretation, stemming from Talmud *Ketuvot* 111b, as 'context and continuation', i.e., *pshat*, rather than *drash*.

[11] No doubt an allusion to the previous verse, *Genesis* 49:10, which starts with the words: '*A sceptre shall not depart from Judah*', using the same verb, *sar*. Ibn Ezra compares his *drash* model to the sceptre of Judah, a symbol of the chain of political and legal tradition which continued even after the demise of the monarchy in Judah, through the heads of the Babylonian academies, descendants (whether actually or spiritually) of the house of David. At once politics, law and exegesis are merged in ibn Ezra's schema.

[12] See *Numbers Rabbah* 13:15 for the famous midrashic dictum that there are many and varied facets or aspects to exegesis. Naturally, this dictum appears to contradict that in *Path Four*: '*no text can be deprived of its pshat*'! Ibn Ezra side-steps this potential problem by actually interpreting the midrashic dictum as inclusive of *pshat*, rather than allowing for 'seventy' different midrashic interpretations!

[13] Ibn Ezra immediately details the occasions when rabbinic authority must be followed: in all cases relevant to community and appropriate legal behaviour. In *Second Path Five*, he states that, concerning legal passages, he will deliberately ignore his knowledge of linguistic rulings in order to follow the rabbinic leadership. However, he offers to give contemporary sages grammar lessons, in order to help them interpret correctly, thus vividly portraying his tension.

[14] The Hebrew is a pun with the alternate meaning '*to become an Arab*' (*arav*). Although expertise in Arabic philology is extremely important, loyalty to the Jewish community is paramount.

[15] Ibn Ezra's last dart is aimed at the Karaites, originally from Muslim lands, who obviously remained a thorn in ibn Ezra's flesh until the end.

[16] Ibn Ezra finishes by re-emphasising his view that the early rabbinic commentators and their words were divinely inspired, even if we, who come later, do not always understand their interpretations. Because of their direct link with the divine, however, we should always follow their approach in matters of law and society.

9

IBN EZRA'S PHILOSOPHICAL GRAMMAR

So, take and use Thy work:
Amend what flaws may lurk,
What strain o' the stuff, what warpings past the aim!
Perfect the cup as planned!
Let age approve of youth, and death complete the same!
(Robert Browning, 'Rabbi Ben Ezra': XXXII)

In this book I have attempted to present ibn Ezra's approach to exegesis in as holistic a way as possible, viewing him from different angles and relating his exegesis to his philosophy. Ibn Ezra has long been in need of this more sympathetic approach. Few commentators have included ibn Ezra among the great philosophers of the Middle Ages. Most of the major twentieth-century anthologies of mediaeval Jewish philosophy have barely mentioned him.[1] By emphasising the philosophical flavour of ibn Ezra's exegesis, I hope to demonstrate that he was more than just a very talented, although not especially original, bridge-builder.[2]

In this final chapter I suggest why ibn Ezra should be regarded as a great universalist thinker, as well as a unique expositor of the Jewish exegetical tradition. The relationship between his grammatical, philosophical and traditional approaches generates a synthesis which creates a novel and highly sophisticated hermeneutic. This hermeneutic is important not only for the history of Jewish thought, but may also serve as a guide for the future of interpretation.

As I have demonstrated in the previous chapters, ibn Ezra was not only a product of his age, but also an innovator. To the extent that he drew on the latest scholarship in philosophy, science, grammar and religion, he can be regarded as typical of the highly educated mediaeval Spanish Jewish elite. He combined a thorough knowledge of Jewish, Muslim and Christian thought, and utilised the positive elements of each, discarding the rest by sarcasm and innuendo. However, in his approach to *pshat*, he broke completely new ground. It is this aspect of his work, however, which has been misread by most modern rabbinic scholars and postmodernists alike, who conclude that he is a mere 'grammarian' in the narrow sense, and therefore irrelevant to their respective aims.

The key to ibn Ezra's approach is his unusual insistence on the exclusive use of Hebrew in his oeuvre. It could be argued that, since he was writing for the Jews of Christian Europe, who did not know Arabic, it is not surprising that he chose Hebrew as the language in which to express himself to them. The new environment was, after all, sympathetic to an exegetical approach in which the understanding and use of Hebrew was of paramount importance.

However, there were also internal reasons for ibn Ezra's choice of Hebrew in exegesis, namely his understanding of the potentialities of the language. In his view, the correct *pshat* interpretation represents a deepening understanding on the part of the reading audience, enabling them to grasp the symbolic meaning of a text without sacrificing the surface meaning. In this way, the ordinary becomes the symbolic: *pshat* becomes *sod*. To reach this level of textual understanding, the exegete has to combine knowledge of contemporary grammar, science and philosophy (the domain of the Jews living in Muslim cultures) with a sophisticated understanding of the role, as well as content, of Jewish tradition.

Unlike some exegetes, for instance his contemporary, Rashbam, ibn Ezra did not separate the literary and exegetical from the legal and halakhic, but aimed to combine them all into a 'philosophical grammar'.[3] Ibn Ezra did not believe in pure philosophy *per se*. Nowadays he would be regarded as an applied philosopher. He believed that philosophical speculation which aimed to transcend language in order to reach the concepts themselves was neither possible nor desirable within the Jewish community. He was aware of how the double faith theory, first outlined by Sa'adiah Gaon, was, in his own day, splitting Jewish communities resident in Muslim lands.

Ibn Ezra also believed that a true understanding of Hebrew grammar was impossible without the concomitant desire for supernal knowledge. In both cases an exact understanding of the potentialities of the Hebrew language was a vital element in the attainment of greater wisdom and the elucidation of the symbolic from the surface meaning of the text. This is beautifully expressed by the poet Coleridge: '... by a symbol I mean, not a metaphor or allegory or any other figure of speech or form of fancy, but an actual and essential part of that, the whole of which it represents.'[4]

It is noteworthy that despite the above, ibn Ezra extols the midrashic Jews of Christian Europe for approaching more closely to the centre of the circle of knowledge than any other group, including the Ge'onim. It is hardly surprising that ibn Ezra rejected the approaches of the Karaites and Christian allegorists, but it might be expected that his awe of the Ge'onim would have mitigated against his decision to award the highest accolade to the Jews of Christian Europe. After all, the Ge'onim were not only experts in Muslim culture, from which he himself had learned an enormous amount, but they were also the key figures in the chain of Jewish tradition, both Sephardi and Ashkenazi.

The Ge'onim had been the transmitters and interpreters of Jewish Law, the purveyors of the Oral Torah. For ibn Ezra, this was especially true of Sa'adiah, whom he respected more than any other of his predecessors. Why, then, in *Path One*, does he dismiss the adherents of this group as mere dabblers in 'gentile wisdoms', capable only of attaining the outer perimeter of the circle of knowledge? The answer may lie in the fact that all these Ge'onim wrote in Arabic, and most of their legal and linguistic examples, not to mention their philosophical explanations, used Arabic terminology. In addition, they were more interested in systematisation than in engaging with the text itself.

This tendency in the Ge'onim does not, however, fully explain ibn Ezra's preference for the purveyors of the midrashic approach. On the positive side, it is probable that despite ibn Ezra's dislike of the literal interpretation of midrash, he appreciated its 'playful', experimental qualities and philosophical possibilities. Ibn Ezra's criticism of midrash is therefore aimed at literal, surface level interpretations, which do not delve into the 'esoteric' level of philosophical allegory and symbolic mysticism.

Ibn Ezra knew that the original authors of the first midrashim were also associated with the legal side of Jewish tradition, i.e., the Mishnah and the Talmud. According to him, they knew the 'secret', or philosophical, meaning of the midrashim. To ibn Ezra, their expertise lay not only in an intuitive understanding of the Greek philosophy mediated through Islam, but also in their synthesis of this philosophy and traditional Jewish exegesis. He therefore attributed to these rabbis an approach similar to his own, one which combined the three pillars of grammar, philosophy and tradition.

It appears that between 1139 and 1140 ibn Ezra was faced by a dilemma. On the one hand, he could stay in Spain and attempt to reverse the 'arabisation' of Judaism, which was threatening to divide the Jewish people into two intellectual classes. On the other hand, he could leave for an environment in which the Hebrew element was prominent, but which, as yet, lacked the requisite scientific, philosophical and language skills for a successful continuation of the Jewish exegetical tradition. Ibn Ezra chose the second course, which proved a wise decision. With ibn Ezra, exegesis in Ashkenazi domains was to involve 'recreation', in the double sense of engaging with language playfully and producing something new with it. One important repercussion of his emphasis on Hebrew in this enterprise was his recognition as a precursor of Hebrew language mysticism.[5]

However, the thirteenth century also saw a waning of Jewish interest in grammar and philosophy, not least because the spiritual centre of Judaism moved to Christian domains. Here, these subjects were regarded in some Jewish circles with mistrust, largely because of their Muslim, i.e., 'alien', antecedents. It seems clear that ibn Ezra anticipated these developments and returned philosophy to what he considered its Jewish framework. He pointed out the dangers of the Graeco–Muslim approach espoused by the Ge'onim and their Spanish successors, emphasising instead the advantages of *all* the tools of Jewish exegesis, including a disciplined used of midrash.

What is ibn Ezra's *pshat* approach? I have outlined the development of the term's definition up to ibn Ezra's day. Ibn Ezra appears to be the only important mediaeval Jewish exegete not to have regarded *pshat* as the 'literal' approach to the text, a stance first suggested by the Babylonian Ge'onim. Neither did he regard *pshat* solely as the 'authoritative' or 'contextual' interpretation, suggested by the earlier rabbis of the Mishnah and Talmud periods, although this definition came closer to his own. Because *pshat* is linked directly to *sod* in ibn Ezra's system, it is no longer merely an interpretative device, but is imbued with divinity. One could even argue that just as engaging in midrashic interpretations had been a religious act for the rabbis of the Mishnah and Talmud, so engaging in *pshat* interpretations became a religious act for ibn Ezra.

When ibn Ezra does use *pshat* as a device for historical and contextual interpretations, it is usually in response to literal interpretations of midrash. Ibn Ezra's actual evaluation of *pshat*, however, is that it represents the essence of the text, its *pshut*, 'the pure naked truth', as he states in *Path Four*. For ibn Ezra, this essence lies in certain philosophical or symbolic interpretations. The role played by *pshat* in surface interpretation is merely the first step *en route* to the meaning as '*pshut*', 'meta-meaning', depicted by the hermeneutic modes of *remez* and *sod*.

We can understand this idea more clearly by comparing it to ibn Ezra's view that one needs to understand the body in order to train the soul to unite with her Creator. In similar fashion, he advocates mastery of the basics of grammar, science and philosophy, the roots, or 'body' of secular knowledge, in order fully to understand the sacred text. His arguments concerning *pshat* follow the same train of thought. Knowing when to interpret the text at surface level is essential in judging correctly when a more esoteric interpretation is necessary. *Remez* and *sod* depend on *pshat*. The role of *drash* thus becomes that of rhetoric, window dressing. Alternatively, it can be used as a philosophical hermeneutic device, in which case its role approaches that of *remez*.

Knowledge of Hebrew and judicious use of intellect play an important role in ibn Ezra's definition of *pshat*. Ibn Ezra refers to both as innate human faculties. Hebrew is the archetypal language. Intellect is humanity's bridge to the divine, for 'the angel between Adam and his God is his intelligence'. By thus extending and deepening their understanding of *pshat* and *drash*, ibn Ezra provided the Jews of Christian Europe with the tools to develop their own exegesis. In this way he hoped to save the Jewish tradition from what he regarded as its impending physical and spiritual destruction in the Muslim environment.

Ibn Ezra's choice of new ground on which to sow his seeds of knowledge proved prescient. Despite the political, religious, and sociological disadvantages for Jews in Christian Europe, ibn Ezra's death paralleled the end of the 'Golden Age' for the Jews in Muslim Spain. However, Jewish exegesis continued to flourish in Christian Europe. Ibn Ezra was made part of the official interpretative canon by his inclusion in *Mikra'ot Gedolot*, largely through the efforts of Ramban, whom he greatly influenced both exegetically and philosophically. He was also widely translated by Christian scholars, thereby finding a general, European audience.

Gradually, Spain itself declined as a European centre, its place being taken by Italy, France and the Protestant north. Italy, France and England would experience and benefit from ibn Ezra's presence during the last quarter of his life. However, as we have seen, his glowing reputation among some of the more radical thinkers of early modern times led to a rejection of his ideas in some parts of the traditional Jewish community, which extends to our own day.

If we turn to the current era, we find that ibn Ezra's major achievement, his novel and unique philosophy of Torah, has been misunderstood by most sections of the Jewish community. He is still largely regarded as a pure grammarian who rejected midrash. His reformulation of the four key hermeneutic methods has largely been ignored. Segments of the contemporary traditionalist Jewish community have become increasingly 'literalistic' in their own approach to the text, and can rightly be accused of 'peshatism' in the negative sense coined by Rawidowicz. This approach to midrash lacks both the creative playfulness of the early rabbis and the philosophical re-formulations of the mediaeval period.

On the other hand, postmodernists, often university academics, do not necessarily work within the parameters of Jewish tradition and are thus often ignorant of the early rabbinic and mediaeval approaches to midrash. Some have equated *pshat* with a boring, western, or 'Greek–Christian' approach, which would destroy the inherent possibilities of the 'word', by encouraging the search for the 'real meaning' of the text. Both sides could learn much from ibn Ezra's exegetical approach. The modern 'peshatists' need to lose their rigidity and fear of 'secularity'. The postmodernists must recognise that the roots of their imaginative skills lie in a specific, unashamedly Jewish, linguistic and legal interpretative tradition.

The texts of the great Jewish exegetes, including ibn Ezra, tended to attract two main types of reader within the traditional Jewish community. The first type of reader would study the commentaries on the Pentateuch in order to understand biblical exegesis as interpreted through the religious canon. They would read ibn Ezra primarily to elucidate points of etymological or linguistic interest, even though these explanations often contradicted the midrashic explanations of the more popular Rashi. The second type of reader was more interested in symbolic interpretations. They would read ibn Ezra, often through first having seen him discussed in Ramban, for his philosophical or mystical interpretations. These two types of reader and their respective modes of interpretation, whether etymological–linguistic or philosophical–mystical, have been strongly differentiated in the last three hundred years. This is most unfortunate, for ibn Ezra suits both type of reader, and gives both types of textual interpretation, sometimes even in the same verse.

The post-modern approach, on the other hand, is largely a reaction to the rational, literal and historical hermeneutic approaches of the nineteenth and early twentieth centuries. Postmodernists emphasise the value of language in its own right, highlighting its fragmentary quality and capacity for elusive, open-ended and fluid interpretation. They have dismissed the goal-oriented type of interpretation, which construes the sacred text as having relevance only in its own time and context. They stress the playful and multi-faceted nature of the 'word', and demonstrate a sophisticated literary awareness of language. Even those with no obvious training in Hebrew or early rabbinic thought are aware of the importance of the terms 'midrash' and 'canon', and have adopted them into their own literary vocabulary. Most importantly, there has been a growing awareness among postmodernists of the unique import of Hebrew as a vehicle for polysemous interpretation.

A rare example of a postmodernist who *is* aware of the Jewish roots of midrash is Susan Handelman. She attacks the idea of the 'incarnate' word, which she attributes to thinkers grounded in the 'Greek–Christian' tradition. Instead, she links both rabbinic and post-modernist hermeneutic approaches to the Freudian interpretation of dreams as 'holy writ', in which 'meaning' lies 'hidden in the most trivial and inconsequential details'.[6] Handelman contrasts the holy early rabbinic enterprise of interpretation with the 'dogma' and abstraction of Christian theology. According to her, Christian, and thus western, hermeneutics 'disregard[ed] the "letter", that play of equivocalness and multiplicity of interpretation in which the Rabbis delighted'.[7]

Handelman emphasises the dialogical and subjective quality of the biblical text by stressing its orientation towards 'truth', rather than 'realism'. She also prefers interpretation to doctrine as a devotional device, stating that the rabbinical dictum: 'no text ever loses its plain meaning' does not invalidate a polysemous approach.[8] However, in her zeal for the amorphous and the fragmented, Handelman underestimates the danger of anarchy in interpretation and the significance of halakhah in Jewish tradition.[9] As we have seen, the tendency towards undisciplined interpretation and the marginalisation of Jewish Law is criticised by ibn Ezra in his *Introductions*.

Boyarin criticises Handelman's assumption that midrash has played a universal role in Jewish exegesis. He asserts, on the contrary, that midrash has actually been marginalised in Jewish tradition by the 'allegorical-Aristotelian tradition ... best represented by Maimonides'.[10] It is therefore all the more surprising that he does not mention ibn Ezra's language-based philosophical exegesis as a possible antidote to the Maimonidean 'logocentric' approach.

Boyarin is right to emphasise the importance of the 'interpretative community' in 'correctness of interpretation'.[11] Ibn Ezra was fully aware that the future of Judaism lay in those communities in which interpretation was as accessible to as many people as possible. The midrashic approach was thus a key factor in this enterprise, but not in the unsophisticated, even puerile, guise it had assumed under the contemporary writers of midrashic anthologies. He appears to have anticipated Boyarin in wishing to redefine midrash as a 'generating force' rather than a 'proof-text',[12] but in its philosophical, rather than rhetorical guise.

Notwithstanding the above, Boyarin does appear to be aware of ibn Ezra's dual role of grammarian and symbolist, mentioned above. On the one hand he describes him as 'the great champion of the plain sense' of the text but, on the other hand, he also cites one of ibn Ezra's highly sophisticated symbolic interpretations, in which midrash plays its due part.[13] However, Boyarin does not appear to appreciate the reasons for ibn Ezra's use of varying hermeneutic tools in different contexts. Neither does he explore further his own reformulation of Kermode's definition of midrash as a 'reading of the "plain sense"' which 'grows and changes throughout history'.[14] A further exploration of this reformulation would surely acknowledge ibn Ezra's magisterial role in the development of the role of *pshat* in the history of interpretation.

I have already mentioned the reverence in which in Ezra was held by the fourteenth-century mystical schools. For the mystics, the letters of the Hebrew alphabet were manipulated in a type of meditative practice which led to higher states of consciousness and even to experiences of the divine. Through these practices, the mystics felt better able to fulfil the mitzvot and thereby realise Jewish Law in as meaningful a way as possible.

These types of activity should interest those for whom the aim of exegesis goes beyond mere word-play or theorising. It is possible to see in ibn Ezra's enterprise a sincere attempt to 'wrestle' with the text, in order to gain an insight into the nature of God. Ibn Ezra shares with postmodernists a view of language as *potentially* open-ended. However, his sense of responsibility to the Jewish community and his own spiritual nature prevented him from regarding this factor as a goal in itself. As he himself says, 'And the end of the matter is that to *drash* there is no end.' His aim was to reach the centre of the circle, not to keep going round in circles. Bearing his goal in mind, it took intellectual courage for him not to dismiss midrash completely, but to accommodate it within his four-fold framework.

In contrast to some sections of the contemporary traditionalist community, ibn Ezra recognised the validity of all the hermeneutic tools lying at the disposal of the Jewish tradition. His re-interpretation of *pshat* includes the view that polysemy is possible only when based on a thorough understanding of the text through scientific, historic and contextual data. These achievements of the nineteenth century should therefore not be dismissed out of hand as irrelevant to a contemporary hermeneutic.

The current desire in some quarters to 'safeguard' the Jewish community and tradition against the inroads of 'secularism', and the post-modern wish to explore the text *ad infinitum* are not necessarily mutually exclusive activities. A contemporary hermeneutic might benefit from a reassessment of ibn Ezra's definition of *pshat*. It is surely time to recognise that *pshat* and *drash* both have a place in exegesis. The key factor now is innovation, based on past discoveries, not merely on rejection and self-indulgence.

I conclude by summarising the key points made in this chapter. Firstly, many modern supporters of the midrashic approach demonstrate a surprising ignorance of definitions of *pshat* up to the time of ibn Ezra. Secondly, there has been a reaction in some quarters against the 'scientific' and 'objective' historicism of the nineteenth century, which is generally associated with *pshat* interpretations. Thirdly, in order to counter the accusation of 'legalism' made by commentators inimical to the Jewish herme-neutic tradition, emphasis is nowadays often placed on the more imaginative side of exegesis, without due consideration of context.

Whilst the 'preserving' side of ibn Ezra has been adequately acknowledged, it is time to emphasise his creativity. Ibn Ezra was:

the first major biblical exegete in Spain and in his thought Aristotelian, Neoplatonic, Hermetic and Pythagorean elements were together molded into a highly influential form of Judaism. This stressed the importance of the commandments as the ideal type of behavior, designed to protect the Jews from pernicious influences and to draw the supernal efflux from above. This talismanic reading of Judaism includes some astral magic and allowed a more "scientific" interpretation of the commandments. Abraham ibn Ezra was also a well-known astronomer, whose writings ... contributed to the transmission of Arabic science to Christian Europe.[15]

Here we see ibn Ezra as 'Renaissance Man' before his time. It is often forgotten that he was actually the first Spanish biblical exegete, a fact that itself demanded innovation, the drastic step of moving abroad to a completely different type of Jewish environment.

It is thus clear that ibn Ezra was not only determined to forge some 'middle way' for his exegesis. He was a passionate genius, who used the work of his predecessors, as well as that of his contemporaries, to create a system which, through an exquisite and unequalled use of the Hebrew language, formed a backdrop to later mystical currents. Not only that but, through translations into Latin, his work in the 'secular sciences' also influenced the wider European community. Ibn Ezra acknowledged that Sa'adiah had forged the relevant tools for reinterpretation in his own era, thereby safeguarding the two Torot at a time when Rabbanite Judaism was under threat. Ibn Ezra saw his task in a similar light, but realised that additional tools were necessary in his own day. Ibn Ezra was willing to sacrifice his physical life, abroad, in order to safeguard the future of the Jewish hermeneutic tradition as an ever-present, vibrant continuity. As Beinart says: 'He was ... an extremely courageous man ... a spiritual giant for whom the only thing that ultimately mattered was the fate of his own people'.[16]

Ibn Ezra did not live to see all his ideas bear fruit. One of his most important bequests to posterity, however, is the idea that in exegesis the physical and spiritual must be 'truthfully conjoined'. He discards all paths to the 'truth' which ignore contemporary learning. However, he is equally censorious of approaches which downplay the importance of Jewish Law. For him, those who are willing to combine a traditional religious and halakhic approach with a sophisticated understanding of contemporary hermeneutics will sow the seeds of their own reward. They will understand the secret of 'the Tree of Knowledge, [where] a hidden meaning dwells pleasantly' within the heart of *pshat*.

NOTES

1 THE BIOGRAPHY OF ABRAHAM IBN EZRA

1 Rashi is the acronym for the northern French biblical exegete and Talmud commentator, Rabbi Solomon ben Isaac (1040–1105). See E. I. J. Rosenthal, 'The Exposition and Exegesis of Scripture', in 'The Study of the Bible in Medieval Judaism', in Lampe (ed.) 1969: 267. For the role of Ramban (Rabbi Moshe ben Nahman, or Nahmanides: 1194–1270) in ibn Ezra's inclusion as part of the authorised Jewish interpretative canon, see Twersky, 'Introduction', in Twersky (ed.) 1983: 4.

2 This concept, usually attributed to Rambam (Rabbi Moses ben Maimon, or Maimonides: 1135–1204), will be discussed below.

3 The Second Commentary was written in 'Rodus', probably Rouen, Normandy, in 1153.

4 For controversy surrounding ibn Ezra's exact birthplace, see Abramson 1970: 397–8. For the arguments about his birth and death dates, see Fleischer, below, although as recently as 1993 Sarna reiterated the alternative dates of 1092 and 1167 respectively. See Sarna, 'Abraham ibn Ezra as an Exegete', in Twersky and Harris (eds) 1993: 1. For his death date, see H. Beinart, 'España y el Occidente en los Dias de Abraham ibn Ezra', in Días Esteban (ed.) 1990: 38.

5 *Ibid.*: 28–9. For ibn Ezra's reaction to this transfer of political power, see Levin 1969: 13–14.

6 Comparisons are often made between Halevi's departure, together with ibn Ezra's son, Isaac, from Spain for Palestine in 1140, and ibn Ezra's departure for Rome in the same year. See Levin 1969: 17. E. Silver, 'New Light on Abraham ibn Ezra's Early Life from Analysis of his Exegesis and other Prose Works', in Díaz Esteban (ed.) 1990: 317.

7 See Levin 1969: 23. Beinart, 'España', *op. cit.*: 1990: 25–38. Silver, 'Early Life', *ibid.*: 319.

8 Fleischer 1929/30: 353.

9 *Be-nefesh nibhelet*. See Silver, citing Levin, 'Early Life', *op. cit.*, 1990: 320.

10 For Hebrew, see Levin 1969: 23. Silver, 'Early Life', *op. cit.*, 1990: 319.

11 See Baron 1952–83 (iv): 10–12. For the comparative tolerance of the popes towards the Jews, see Roth 1948: 193.

12 Benjamin visited between 1160 and 1165, when the demography would have been similar to that thirty years earlier. 'Edom' is the general term used in Jewish tradition for both ancient Rome and Christendom, which is seen, negatively, as Rome's immediate spiritual successor. For ibn Ezra's description of his findings in Rome, see Levin 1969: 343, n. 76, 24, 345, n. 79.

13 Simon 1991: 149–151. S. Reif, 'Abraham ibn Ezra on Canticles', in Díaz Esteban (ed.) 1990: 243–4. Compare with Friedlaender 1877b: 143–4, 165.

14 Jewish Law and Jewish lore, respectively.

15 I discuss the influence of the Ge'onim on ibn Ezra in Chapter Seven.

16 See H. Shai, 'Abraham ibn Ezra's Hebrew Commentary to the Bible and Medieval Judaeo-Arabic Commentaries and Grammaries', in Díaz Esteban (ed.) 1990: 309.

17 Roth 1948: 245.

18 Levin 1969: 24.

19 The word means 'comfort' in Hebrew.

20 An acronym of the title, *Moznai-Lashon Ha-Kodesh* (*Balance of the Holy Tongue*).

21 See Levin, 1969: 25. Sarna, 'Exegete', *op. cit.*, 1993: 7.

22 Cited in Levin 1969: 25, 346, n. 82. Original in German, translated into Hebrew.

23 Levin 1969: 346, n. 82. Also see n. 83.

24 See Shai, 'Hebrew Commentaries to Commentaries', *op. cit.*, 1990: 309.

25 See Carmi 1981: 14–15, 89.

26 *Ibid*: 16, 24, 33.

27 *Ibid*: 34. Levin 1969: 25, 346, n. 87. J. Yahalom, 'The Poetics of Spanish Piyyut in Light of Abraham ibn Ezra's Critique of its Pre-Spanish Precedents', in Díaz Esteban (ed.) 1990: 390–1.

28 For Sa'adiah's attitude to poetry, see Carmi 1981: 21–3.

29 See Levin 1969: 25, 346, n. 88.

30 Levin 1969: 25. Ibn Ezra makes similar remarks about the Karaite, ben Zuta. Also see Fleischer 1929/30: 222. Friedlaender 1877b: 33ff, 168, n. 1.

31 *Al dikduk ha-lashon*. Normally translated as 'etymology', but in my opinion the phrase implies a whole structure, based on sound grammatical roots.

32 *Ikar-ha-inyan*. See Levin 1969: 26.

33 See Fleischer 1933/4: 79. The five *Megillot* are the biblical books: *Song of Songs, Ecclesiastes, Esther, Lamentations* and *Ruth*.

34 See Levin 1969: 26, 346, n. 92.

35 See Fleischer 1933/4: 78.

36 Levin 1969: 346, n. 96, citing Roth.

37 See Baron 1952–83 (iv): 26.

38 Levin 1969: 26.

39 This is the Hebrew version of the Bible, printed together with all those commentaries acknowledged as belonging to the 'canon' of biblical exegesis in Jewish tradition.

40 Levin 1969: 27.

41 Commentaries on the biblical books: *Joshua*, *Judges*, *Samuel*, *Kings*, *Ezekiel*, *Proverbs*, *Ezra*, *Nehemiah* and *Chronicles* are mentioned in various parts of his *Commentary on the Torah*, but are not extant. See Sarna, 'Exegete', *op. cit.*, 1993: 4, 22, ns 8–16.

42 See Levin 1969: 27, 347, n. 100 for the following examples. In the *Commentary on Isaiah*, ibn Ezra refers to his previous commentaries on the *Minor Prophets* (Rome), *Ezekiel* (no longer extant) and *Psalms*. Simon 1991: 145–9, 260, n. 18, supports Fleischer's suggestion that the latter was written in either Rome or Lucca before the commentaries on the *Torah* and *Isaiah*.

43 Probably written in 1145. See Simon 1985: 270.

44 Friedlaender 1877b: 51–7. *Idem* 1877a: 62, 66. *Idem* 1873: 164, 177. For Rambam's view of prophecy, see Leaman 1990: 39–64.

45 Levin 1969: 347, n. 101.

46 Free translation of Levin 1969: 27. Simon 1985: 270 describes ibn Ezra' s similar attitude to Muslims.

47 Eg. *Isaiah* 48–65. See Levin 1969: 347, n. 103. Simon 1985: 269.

48 Levin 1969: 28, 347, n. 104. Simon 1985: 271.

49 See Fleischer 1933/4: 79–81. *Sefer ha-Yesod* is no longer extant.

50 See Fleischer 1933/4: 82. Sirat 1985: 352–5. For discussion, see Simon 1991: 149, 264, n. 39. Also see Fleischer 1925/6: 165–8.

51 For text, see Allony 1984: 85, lines 10–11.

52 For biblical allusion, see *Isaiah* 59:10. The verb actually means 'to grope'.

53 *Ain mikra yotze midai-pshuto*. This idea is discussed in more detail in later chapters.

54 See Fleischer 1933/4: 83–4. L. Glinert, 'The Unknown Grammar of Abraham ibn Ezra. Syntactic Feature of Yesod Diqduq', in Díaz Esteban (ed.) 1990: 129–36.

55 Discovered only in the twentieth century by J. M. Millás. See Levin 1969: 347, n. 107, 348, n. 127; Baron 1952–83 (viii): 362–3, n. 38. Sarna, 'Exegete', *op. cit.*, 1993: 26, n. 120.

56 For ibn Ezra's possible stay in Pisa, see Fleischer 1933/4: 79. Levin 1969: 28. Also see Baron 1952–83 (iv): 26.

57 Levin 1969: 28; Yahalom, 'Poetics', *op. cit.*, 1990: 392.

58 Ibn Ezra discusses this subject as part of his attack on the Karaites in *Path Two* of the *Introduction*. Also see Sarna, 'Exegete', *op. cit.*, 1993: 26, n. 117.

59 *Ibid*: n. 119. Fleischer 1931/2: 290; Baron 1952–83 (viii): 352, n. 12.

60 Levin 1969: 29–30. Simon 1985: 270. Beinart, 'España', *op. cit.*, 1990: 35.

61 Fleischer 1929/30: 353–4.

62 *Ibid.*: 356.

63 Rabbi Abraham, Rabbi Isaac ben Judah and Rabbi Jonathan ben David respectively. See Fleischer 1929/30: 356–7. Levin 1969: 30, 347, n. 118.

64 See Baron 1952–83 (iv): 55–6. By 1160, this practice was replaced by a cash payment to the bishop and an annual tax. It is likely that ibn Ezra would have witnessed the stoning.

65 See Levin 1969: 348, n. 122. Baron 1952–83 (iv): 177, 365–6, n. 43.

66 See Levin 1969: 31. For the importance of cosmology in *Sefer ha-Shem*, see Y. Z. Langermann, 'Some Astrological Themes in the Thought of Abraham Ibn Ezra', in Twersky and Harris (eds) 1993: 61–5.

67 Translation of extract quoted in Fleischer 1929/30: 356. Also see Levin 1969: 31.

68 Translation of Fleischer 1929/30: 298. See Sirat 1985: 274–7. Beinart, 'España', *op. cit.* 1990: 35.

69 See Fleischer 1929/30: 38–43. Simon 1985: 147.

70 This is known as the *Long* or *Alternative Commentary* and was written in about 1153. See Simon 1985: 148.

71 See Friedlaender 1877b: 146.

72 See Fleischer 1930/32: 218.

73 Correct, legally sanctioned, therefore religious, behaviour. See Levin 1969: 32.

74 *Hitbodedut* means 'act of isolating oneself', 'meditation' and 'intense concentration'. The concept was already used in the Hekhalot mysteries practised by the Merkabah mystics in the first centuries CE. For *hitbodedut* in ibn Ezra see Idel 1988a: 105ff, 128, 142, n. 8, 161, n. 119. For the influence of ibn Ezra's interpretation of *hitbodedut* on Geronese Kabbalah, see Wolfson 1994: 296.

75 See Levin 1969: 33. Fleischer 1930/32: 291–2.

76 Simon 1985: 146.

77 See Levin 1969: 33, 349, n. 142. Friedlaender 1877b: 189.

78 See Levin 1969: 349, n. 143. Friedlaender 1877b: 102.

79 Levin 1969: 33–4. The phrase in the *Second Introduction, Path Four*, 'as a book laid down and abandoned', refers to a hidden wisdom known only to the early rabbis, and may also relate to this idea.

80 See Langermann, 'Astrological Themes', *op. cit.*, 1993: 38–9.

81 Fleischer thinks it may have been written later, in England. See 1930/32: 222.

82 See Rosenthal, 'Exposition', *op. cit.*, 1969: 267–8. Fleischer 1930/32: 223. Simon 1985: 146. Reif, 'Abraham ibn Ezra on Canticles', in Díaz Esteban (ed.) 1990: 243.

83 For date, see Simon 1985: 146. The second recension has also been discovered and published by Simon, together with this standard version. *Idem* 1985: 259, n. 7, 300.

84 Friedlaender 1877b: 167. It is possible that ibn Ezra also wrote *Sefer Yesod-ha-Mispar* and *Sefer Ha-Ehad* in Rouen. The first is a grammatical work. See Fleischer 1930/32: 290. Baron 1952–83 (viii): 352, n. 12. Simon 1965: 113. The second is a mathematical work, which Fleischer thinks may have been written in Italy.

85 Fleischer 1930/32: 294–5.

86 *Ibid.*: 295–6. Japhet and Salters 1985: 12.

87 See Levin 1969: 37. Simon 1965: 130–8. Japhet and Salters 1985: 48, n. 124.

88 See Weiss Halivni 1991: 26–8, 48, 81–2, 169, although in our view he is biased in favour of Rashbam's *pshat* approach, to the detriment of ibn Ezra.

89 1120–90. See Sirat: 1985: 69, 81, 113, 213.

90 See Fleischer 1930/32: 297–8. I have discussed ibn Ezra's negative view of ibn Saruq above.

91 See *Deuteronomy* 28:64. The view that the phrase *ketze ha-aretz* was an allusion to England was based on a mistranslation of the word 'Angleterre' as 'angle (or edge) of the earth'. This phrase was used to good effect by Menasseh ben Israel in his appeal to Oliver Cromwell in 1650 to allow the Jews back to England, and thus hasten the advent of the Messiah. See Méchoulan and Nahon 1987: 84, 139, 143, 151.

92 See Baron 1952–83 (iv): 135–6.

93 *Ibid.*: 75–8.

94 *Ibid.*: 80. Margolis and Marx 1927: 384–6.

95 See Simon 1991: 200–11. For date of composition see Fleischer 1928/9: 256.

96 For instance, here he concedes that the Karaites know the Bible extremely well.

97 The verse reads: '*And God called to the light day and to the dark He called night. And the evening and the morning: day one.*'

98 See Chapter Six on the Karaites and also ibn Ezra's *Introduction*, Path Two.

99 See Levin 1969: 40. For the seriousness with which ibn Ezra regarded the Rashbam's 'misinterpretation', see Simon, 'Ibn Ezra's Harsh Language and Biting Humor: Real Denunciation or Hispanic Mannerism', in Díaz Esteban (ed.) 1990: 325–34.

100 For Rashbam's exegetical approach and ibn Ezra's changing opinion regarding the correct definition of 'day', see Simon 1965: 106, 110ff.

101 For correct date of ibn Ezra's death, in 1164, see Friedlaender 1877b: 201–2. Fleischer 1928/9: 250, 256. As ibn Ezra was seventy-five at the time of his death, he must have been born in 1089.

102 See Levin: 1969: 41–2. Beinart, 'España', *op. cit.*: 1990: 38.

2 A HISTORY OF THE SCHOLARLY WORK ON IBN EZRA

1 Simon, 'Interpreting the Interpreter: Supercommentaries on Ibn Ezra's Commentaries', in Twersky and Harris (eds) 1993: 86.

2 Friedlaender 1877b: 213. Sirat 1985: 344, 477. Simon, 'Interpreting', *op. cit.*, 1993: 98, 119, 124, n. 18.

3 Simon regards ibn Tibbon as the most important and influential thirteenth-century supercommentator. Ibn Tibbon also translated al-Batalyawsi's *Arabic Book of Intellectual Circles*, which has many similarities with the work of ibn Ezra.

4 Simon, 'Interpreting', *op. cit.*, 1993: 111. For a fascinating account of the nineteenth century's unfairly negative reaction to this stance, epitomised particularly by Graetz, see *idem* 126–7, n. 43.

5 Simon, 'Interpreting', *op. cit.*, 1993: 119–21.

6 For Krinsky and Netter, see Simon 1976a: 646–7.

7 See Harris, 'Ibn Ezra in Modern Jewish Perspective', in Twersky and Harris (eds) 1993: 130. Spinoza's view was based on ibn Ezra's contention that Moses could not have written parts of the *Torah* (*Pentateuch*).

8 *Ibid.*: 134–6, 162, ns 18–20. Weiss Halivni 1991: 29–30 describes Mendelssohn as 'paraphras[ing]' ibn Ezra's *Paths Four* and *Five*. He concludes that Mendelssohn preferred ibn Ezra's exegesis to that of Rashbam precisely because the latter's 'love of peshat has caused him occasionally to deviate from the truth'.

9 Harris, 'Modern Jewish Perspective', *op. cit.*, 1993: 136.

10 *Ibid.*: 131: '... Ibn Ezra ... emerged as the darling Jewish exegete of various modern Gentile Bible critics.'

11 See Weiss Halivni 1991: 20, 31, 152.

12 *Ibid.*: 32, 187, ns 26, 29.

13 See Harris, *op. cit.*: 130, 160, n. 6, 140, 163, n. 26.

14 See Weiss Halivni, *op. cit.*: 178, n. 25.

15 Harris, 'Modern Jewish Perspective', *op. cit.*, 1993: 139.

16 *Ibid.*: 140, 162–3, n. 25. Weiss Halivni 1991: 32–3.

17 Harris, 'Modern Jewish Perspective', *op. cit.*, 1993: 140–3, 164–5, ns 29–36.

18 According to Weis Halivni, Sofer was 'attracted to peshat but suppressed it', because of his fear of Hellenism. Also see Harris, 'Modern Jewish Perspective', *op. cit.*, 1993: 141: '[T]o Sofer a natural, monosemic exegesis deprives the biblical reader of the ability to discern the uniqueness of the biblical language, which is capable of bearing many meanings'.

19 For differing approaches to biblical research, see Simon, 'Interpreting' *op. cit.*, 1993: 126–7, n. 43. *Idem* 1965: 138. P. Morris, 'A Walk in the Garden: Images of Eden' and 'Exiled from Eden: Jewish Interpretations of Genesis', in Morris and Sawyer (eds) 1992: 23–7, 118–22.

20 Graetz' work was published in 1874 and popularised in ten editions up to 1930, the date of the English translation, *History of the Jews*. See Silver, 'New Light on Abraham ibn Ezra's Early Life from Analysis of his Exegesis and other Prose Works', in Díaz Esteban (ed.) 1990: 319–20.

21 Fleischer has been quoted extensively in Chapter One. According to Silver, 'Early Life', *op. cit.*, 1990: 318: '... Fleischer ... single-handedly turned a new leaf in our overall view of Abraham ibn Ezra', initiating study of his prose works in order to discover reasons for his travels.

22 Prijs and Simon have rectified the errors based on Bacher's suppositions.

23 For details, see Prijs 1973: vii, n. 6. Baron 1952–83 (**viii**): 362–3, ns 38–9.

24 See Sirat 1985: 11–12. Langermann, 'Some Astrological Themes in the Thought of Abraham Ibn Ezra', in Twersky and Harris (eds) 1993: 28–85.

25 Prijs 1973: vii, n. 2.

26 Olitzky 1890: 99–106. Also see Sirat 1985: 426.

27 Ibn Ezra's commentary on this work is unfortunately not extant.

28 Harris, 'Modern Jewish Perspective', *op. cit.*, 1993: 144, 165, ns 39–41.

29 See Guttmann 1964: 327. Harris, 'Modern Jewish Perspective', *op. cit.*, 1993: 144–5, 150.

30 Harris, *ibid.*: 158.

31 Guttmann 1964: 329–33. Kreisel: 1994.

32 Guttmann 1964: 338–41.
33 Harris, 'Modern Jewish Perspective', *op. cit.*, 1993: 165, n. 41.
34 Langermann, 'Astrological Themes', *op. cit.*, 1993: 33.
35 For lack of Muslim sources, see Greive 1973, who examines ibn Ezra almost exclusively from the philosophical view-point, neglecting exegetical, religious and sociological factors. For arguments on matter/substance and form, and their relation to 'subject' and 'object' in ibn Ezra, see *idem* 22–5. Kreisel 1994.

3 CLASSICAL AND MEDIAEVAL JEWISH APPROACHES TO TEXT

1 See F. Talmage, 'Apples of Gold: The Inner Meaning of Sacred Texts in Medieval Judaism', in Green (ed.) 1986: 319–21, 349, n. 47. According to Idel, this is '... one of the best if not the best article that has ever been written on medieval Jewish exegesis.' See 'Frank Ephraim Talmage: in Memoriam', in Walfish (ed.) 1993: 23.
2 It is traditionally thought that the *Mishnah* was edited in Palestine by ca. 200 CE, the *Palestinian Talmud* by ca. 400 and the *Babylonian Talmud* by ca. 500. However see Neusner 1991.
3 Daube 1989: 2.
4 The main nineteenth-century proponents of this approach were Graf and Wellhausen. More recently, Gadamer 1979, Ricoeur 1981, Fishbane 1988 and Boyarin 1990 have demonstrated its drawbacks.
5 Loewe 1964: 167. Italics added.
6 *Ibid.*: 183. Also see Weiss Halivni 1991: 25. He suggests that originally *pshat* meant 'context' and took on its 'simple, plain meaning' later, in the mediaeval period. In other words, the early rabbis took deliberate account of the context in interpretation.
7 See *Joshua* 10:13 and II *Samuel* 1:18.
8 Handelman 1982. For an opposing view, see Daube 1949, Neusner 1991, Stern 1984: 193–213.
9 Rawidowicz 1974: 46.
10 *Ibid*: 79.
11 Boyarin 1990: 18. Also see F. Kermode, 'The Plain Sense of Things', in Hartman and Budick (eds) 1986: 179–94. The phrase comes from a poem by Wallace Stevens.
12 Fishbane 1988: 15. Also *idem* 1998: 9–21.
13 Faur 1986: 132–3. Also see ibn Ezra's final remarks on midrash in *Path Four*: '... to *drash* there is no end'.
14 Faur 1986: 84–147.
15 Bowker 1969: 25, 35–6. He refers to the Septuagint, the Greek translation of the Hebrew Bible.
16 Fishbane 1988: 53–70.
17 Vermes, 'Bible and Midrash: Early Old Testament Exegesis', in Ackroyd and Evans (eds) 1970: 199–221. Neusner would disagree with this assessment. Vermes later defined pure exegesis as '"rendering the message of the text intelligible, coherent, and acceptable"'. Cited in G. Brooke: 'Reading the Plain Meaning of Scripture in the Dead Sea Scrolls', in Brooke (ed.) 2000: 78.

18 Vermes, 'Early Old Testament Exegesis', *op. cit.*, 1970: 228–9.
19 For an alternate view on the redaction of the Mishnah, see Neusner 1991: 22ff. Aggadah derives from the Hebrew verb 'announce' or 'tell'.
20 See Weiss Halivni 1991: 8, 13. He claims that the mediaeval scholars recognised that the Talmudic rabbis were aware that extra-scriptural factors affected interpretation.
21 Faur 1986: 95.
22 Newman 1969: 23–4.
23 Weiss Halivni 1991: 15.
24 *Ibid.*: 27–8.
25 See Fishbane 1988: 53, 69, n. 12. Boyarin 1990: 50–1, 123.
26 Wolfson 1929: 24–5.
27 *Ibid.*: 26–7. For a comparison with ibn Ezra, see *Path Three*.
28 Jacobs 1961: vii, 13. This comparison between nature and religious interpretation also owes something to Hellenistic influences.
29 See *Path Three*.
30 Jacobs 1961: 37. The term is related to the final level of halakhic study, *sabir*, discussed above, with reference to Faur 1986.
31 For the interesting statement that the Talmud is 'a literary work but different from every other literary work in that its verbal exposition by those who study the work is indispensable to the form itself', see Jacobs 1984: 213. Compare with Goldenberg, 'Talmud', in Holtz (ed.) 1984: 158.
32 Faur 1986: 120–1. Faur replaces the term *'interpretatio'* 'by 'semantic'. For the development of this idea from the Muslim concept of *ta'wil*, see Chapter Five. Also see Boyarin 1990: 152. Simon, 'The Spanish School of Biblical Interpretation', in Beinart (ed.) 1992: 130–1.
33 Goldenberg, 'Talmud', *op. cit.*, 1984: 159.
34 Faur 1986: 121.
35 Weiss Halivni 1991: 162, 53, 191, n. 3. Here he cites Kamin 1980 as holding that *pshat* refers to both the text and to its semantic meaning. This definition contradicts Faur 1986: 122. Faur interprets pshat as 'semiotic' interpretations, which expound the mind of the author. For him, only drash interpretations are 'semantic' and context-bound.
36 Weiss Halivni 1991: 54–61. See *Babylonian Talmud Yevamot* 11b, 24a and *Shabbat* 63a.
37 See Fakhry 1983: 280–1. For the political reasons behind some of the figurative exegeses, see Saperstein 1980.

4 EARLY CHRISTIAN HERMENEUTICS

1 See Lampe, 'The Reasonableness of Typology', in Lampe and Woollcombe (eds) 1957: 15, 32. Lampe is not averse to using such phrases as 'misleading' and 'sheer rubbish', when he refers to approaches with which he disagrees. He is particularly scathing of the first-century Jewish Alexandrian philosopher, Philo. For a more sympathetic view of Philo, see Handelman 1982. However, also see Boyarin 1995: 4–5, 37–9, 78–82. For Talmage's views of Lampe, see 'Apples of Gold', in Green (ed.) 1986: 341–2 and 353, n. 130.

2 Woollcombe, 'The Biblical Origins and Patristic Development of Typology', in Lampe and Woollcombe (eds) 1957: 54.

3 Talmage, 'Apples of Gold', *op. cit.*, 1986: 353, n. 129, citing Danielou.

4 For more on these type of connections in Jewish thought, see Lancaster 1993. Wolfson 1990, 1994, 1995a, 1995b. Also see discussion on *Path Three* in Chapter Eight.

5 Lampe, 'To Gregory the Great', in 'The Exposition and Exegesis of Scripture', in Lampe (ed.) 1969: 163–4.

6 See II *Corinthians* iii.6. For discussion see Jackson 1979: 8–9. Handelman 1982: 83.

7 See Smalley 1983: 14. For positive Christian influence on Jewish exegesis in ibn Ezra's period, see M. Signer, '*Peshat, Sensus Litteralis, and Sequential Narrative*', in Walfish (ed.) 1993: 203–16.

8 Sutcliffe, 'Jerome', in Lampe (ed.) 1969: 89. This terminology is in marked contrast to ibn Ezra's desire to 'conjoin' matter and spirit. See *Path Three*.

9 Sutcliffe, *ibid.*: 99.

10 *Ibid.*: 96.

11 Loewe, 'The Medieval History of the Latin Vulgate', in Lampe (ed.) 1969: 109.

12 *Ibid.*: 140.

13 For the famous conversion of Petrus Alfonsi in 1106, his subsequent verbal and written attacks on Judaism and the Jews of Aragon, his position as royal doctor, and his eventual transfer to the English court of Henry I, see H. Beinart, 'España ye el Occidente en los Dias de Abraham ibn Ezra', in Díaz Esteban (ed.) 1990: 31–2. Beinart describes Alfonsi's writings as 'one of the first anti-Jewish works written in Aragon, in which the author ridiculed Judaism and everything sacred to it.' Beinart is sure that ibn Ezra knew both the writings and the 'travelling doctor' himself. Also see links with the Karaite, Salmon ben Jeroham, Chapter Six.

14 Smalley 1983: 13. Ibn Ezra regards reason or 'balance of the mind' as a useful tool in solving difficult exegetical problems.

15 For negative Jewish approaches to Augustine, see Handelman 1982: 117. Faur: 1986 118–23. Boyarin 1995: 1, 8. For a more positive approach, see Talmage, 'Apples of Gold', *op. cit.*, 1986: 342, 353, n. 132. Stern 1988: 145 regards Augustine as the Church Father whose approach most closely resembles 'midrashic polysemy' and rates his approach as 'one of the most inspired exegeses in the entire history of Scriptural interpretation'.

16 Smalley 1983: 26.

17 *Ibid.*: 36. See I *Samuel* 1:2. However, for a similar, twelfth-century example, by Andrew of St. Victor in defence of the 'literal' approach, see Signer, '*Peshat*', *op. cit.*, 1993: 208, 214, n. 43.

18 Smalley 1983: 38.

19 *Ibid.*: 39, with reference to John the Scot.

20 *Ibid.*: 45–6. For parallels in Muslim exegesis, see following chapter.

5 MUSLIM HERMENEUTICS

1 For Muslim influence, see Langermann, 'Some Astrological Themes in the Thought of Abraham ibn Ezra', in Twersky and Harris 1993: 28–85. For ibn Sina's influence, see Greive 1973 who, however, fails to acknowledge the Jewish background to ibn Ezra's oeuvre.
2 Fakhry 1983: 68.
3 *Ibid.*: 71.
4 *Ibid.*: 70.
5 See *Second Path Four.* The Karaites shared this view.
6 Fakhry 1983: 91. F. Klein-Franke, 'Al-Kindi', in Nasr and Leaman (eds) 1996: 171.
7 Fakhry 1983: 92.
8 *Ibid.*: 96. See also L. Goodman, 'Muhammad ibn Zakariyya' al-Razi', in Nasr and Leaman (eds) 1996: 202–3.
9 Fakhry 1983: 101.
10 See A. Tanenbaum, 'Beholding the Splendor of the Creator', in Díaz Esteban (ed.) 1990: 337. Also see Vajda 1947: 48.
11 Fakhry 1983: 31.
12 See *Second Path Four*, in which 'creation' is compared to 'cutting'. See I. Lancaster, 'Abraham ibn Ezra's Definitions of Creation', in Díaz Esteban (ed.) 1990: 175–80. Also see *Second Commentary on Exodus* 25:40. Altmann 1969: 25–6. Greive 1973. Tanenbaum, 'Splendour', *op. cit.*, 1990: 48.
13 See D. Black, 'Al-Farabi', in Nasr and Leaman (eds) 1996: 189.
14 Guttmann 1964: 119–20.
15 Leaman 1985: 92. Also see Black, 'Al-Farabi', *op. cit.*, 1996: 185–7.
16 Goodman 1992a: 37. He regards al-Farabi's interest in grammar, translation and the philosophy of language as motivated by the fact that he was not a native speaker of Greek. Similarly, ibn Ezra was not a native speaker of Hebrew.
17 R. Loewe, 'The Influence of Solomon Ibn Gabirol on Abraham Ibn Ezra', in Díaz Esteban (ed.) 1990: 207. Also see M. Idel, 'Reification of Language in Jewish Mysticism', in Katz (ed.) 1992: 43.
18 Goodman 1992a: 38.
19 *Ibid.*: 39. I shall discuss al-Ghazali later in the chapter. For a Jewish appraisal of the world as a semiotic system, see Faur 1986, mentioned above.
20 Goodman 1992a: 40.
21 *Ibid.*: 41.
22 *Ibid.*: 43.
23 *Ibid.*: 44.
24 See Black, 'Al-Farabi', in Nasr and Leaman, *op. cit.*, 1996: 180.
25 Goodman 1992a: 46. According to ibn Ezra, this was the mistake of the allegorists and midrashists.
26 Leaman 1985: 8.
27 *Ibid.*: 9.
28 See Chapter Nine.
29 Faur 1986: xvii, 123–4, xxii, 152.
30 Sirat 1985: 16.

NOTES

31 Greive 1973.
32 Fakhry 1983: 134. For similar views in ibn Ezra, see *Second Path Four.*
33 Fakhry 1983: 139–40.
34 Wolfson 1973: 251.
35 Erigena, however, placed it below ratio (logos) and intellectus (nous), but above the five external senses and imagination. In Muslim and Jewish philosophy it became 'a generic term', based on Aristotle, divided into imagination, cogitation and memory. Galen, on the other hand, placed 'common sense' either with the external senses or with imagination, which was sometimes considered a function of common sense. Some thinkers localised these faculties in the three ventricles of the brain. See ibn Ezra's *Commentary on Exodus.* Also see Kemp 1996: 32, 45–6.
36 Wolfson 1973: 255–7. For ibn Ezra's view of intellectual 'investigation' see *Second Path Four.* For the development of theories of memory from Augustine to ibn Sina, see Kemp 1996: 20–4, 40–60, 74–6, 91–7, 115–17.
37 Wolfson 1973: 257. See ibn Ezra's *Commentary on Exodus* 31:3 and 20:1ff. Ibn Ezra relates the retentive aspect of memory to 'keeping' (i.e. both remembering and preserving) the Sabbath.
38 See *Path Three.*
39 For the double meaning of *milah* in Hebrew, and thence the relationship between the oral and sexual in Jewish tradition, see Wolfson 1987: 189–215. Lancaster 1993: 71ff.
40 See Wolfson 1973: 505–8.
41 See *Exodus* 25:9, 40.
42 See *Exodus* 25:12. For some of the above translations of ibn Ezra's grammatical terminology, see Prijs 1950: 35–8, 58, 78–9, 69, 102–3. For more on *inyan*, see Wolfson 1973: 320, n. 29. Israeli applies this term to the fourth mode of knowledge, 'writing'. Compare *Second Path Three*, in which ibn Ezra exhorts us to gain 'understanding' (*binah*) of the words of Torah, to Israeli's suggestion that we should 'grasp' (*amad al*) the truth of the 'little things' (*inyanim*). For more on the creative symbolism of the Tabernacle, see Lancaster 1993: 33–53. Fishbane's remarks on the thirteenth-century *Zohar*, which depicts a similar, but midrashically-based, 'tree' motif as symbol of a multi-levelled hermeneutic system, fail to acknowledge ibn Ezra's earlier precedent. See Fishbane 1998: 105–6, 110.
43 Fakhry 1983: 168. Compare to ibn Ezra, *Path Three.*
44 See M. Idel, 'Jewish thought in Medieval Spain', in Beinart (ed.) 1992: 266. Sirat 1985: 110–12.
45 Goodman 1992a: 35.
46 *Ibid.*: 37. As stated above, Handelman finds Plato incompatible with Jewish multi-levelled hermeneutics, but this is because of her rather rigid view of *pshat*. Compare with Loewe 1964 and Weiss Halivni 1991.
47 Fakhry 1983: 178.
48 *Ibid.*: 181.
49 Goodman 1992a: 35–6.

50 Greenstein, 'Medieval Bible Commentaries', in Holtz (ed.) 1984: 253. For ibn Ezra's balanced attitude to the letter *vav* ('and'), contrast *Paths Four* and *Five*.
51 Greenstein, 'Medieval Bible Commentaries', *op. cit.*, 1984: 255.
52 Goodman 1992a: 35.
53 See *Second Path Five*.
54 Altmann 1969: 46.
55 *Ibid*: 47. Fishbane's depiction of the thirteenth-century Zoharic gloss, which links the term *kav* to *Genesis* 1: 9 (*yikavu*: '*let* the waters *be gathered together*'), fails to mention ibn Ezra, or Muslim precedents. This is particularly surprising as Fishbane also links the idea of *middah* (measure), 'place' and 'oneness' to the 'line' motif, all themes discussed by ibn Ezra. See *Long Commentary on Exodus*: 33:23. Altmann 1969: 53–7, 205–6. Fishbane 1998: 114–22.
56 Compare his awareness of the deceptive powers of the eye when looking at a planet: Fakhry 1983: 219, with ibn Ezra's ridiculing of Karaite testimony regarding the sighting of the new moon, *Path Two*.
57 Fakhry 1983: 221.
58 Leaman 1985: 40. M. Campanini, 'Al-Ghazzali', in Nasr and Leaman (eds) 1996: 262.
59 Leaman 1985: 76.
60 *Ibid*.: 83–6.
61 For example Altmann, Idel, Talmage and E. Wolfson, as well as many fourteenth-century commentators: 'The fascination which Ibn Ezra held for the fourteenth century may have been partly due to the rising interest in astrology. It may also reflect the then growing impact of Kabbala, since Ibn Ezra appeared to be closer to the mystical approach than any other Jewish philosopher.' Altmann 1969: 197.
62 Fakhry 1983: 239.
63 *Ibid*.: 247–8.
64 For Sirat's identification of this concept in Halevi with Andalusian Aristotelian philosophy, see section on ibn Bajjah.
65 Fakhry 1983: 248.
66 *Ibid*.: 249. For a similar view in ibn Ezra, see Altmann 1969: 47. He refers to the *Commentary on Exodus* 33:22, where the intellect is equated with the 'Prince of the Presence', a euphemism for 'face'.
67 Fakhry 1983: 250–1.
68 *Ibid*.: 257.
69 *Ibid*.: 261. Also see L. Goodman, 'Ibn Bajjah', in Nasr and Leaman (eds) 1996: 298.
70 Fakhry 1983: 262–3.
71 Sirat 1985: 115–6.
72 Pines 1980.
73 Goodman, 'Ibn Bajjah', *op. cit.*, 1996: 302.
74 Fakhry 1983: 264.
75 *Ibid*.: 265.
76 *Ibid*.: 267.
77 Goodman, 'Ibn Tufayl', in Nasr and Leaman (eds) 1996: 316.
78 Goodman 1992a: 50.
79 Fakhry 1983: 279.

80 *Ibid.*: 283.
81 *Ibid.*: 280. Italics added. The phrase bears an uncanny resemblance to the Talmudic dictum: 'no text can be deprived of its *pshat*'. I have discussed Hebrew 'usages' above and shall do so again.
82 Fakhri 1983: 281.
83 *Ibid.*: 282. This had been al-Ghazali's view, in contrast to ibn Sina.
84 *Ibid.*: 286. See his similar criticism of ibn Sina: 290.
85 *Ibid.*: 287.
86 *Ibid.*: 288.
87 *Ibid.*: 289. These views were similar to those of ibn Gabirol.
88 For ibn Rushd's views on the relationships between the different types of intellects, see Kemp 1996: 69–76.

6 THE KARAITES

1 See *Path Five*.
2 Nemoy 1952: xv.
3 The name first appeared in the ninth century. The Hebrew 'qara' means 'read', as well as 'call', or 'missionarise'. This is reminiscent of the Shi'ite 'callers', or 'propagandists on behalf of Ali'. A third interpretation connects the name with the Arabic *karra*, 'expert reader in Scripture'. All these derivations are conjectural.
4 As transmitted by Jafet ben Ali, an aristocratic Iraqi Karaite. Although Anan's teaching attracted few adherents and aroused strong criticism, he was elevated by later Karaism as the originator of the group. See Simon 1991.
5 Nemoy 1952: xx–xxi. For further discussion of Sa'adiah's views on philology and tradition, see following chapter.
6 Nemoy 1952: 8.
7 *Ibid.*: 21–2.
8 See D. Frank, 'Ibn Ezra and the Karaite Exegetes Aaron Ben Joseph and Aaron ben Elijah', in Díaz Esteban (ed.) 1990: 103.
9 An anagram on the phrase 'champion sage': *rosh ha-kesilim* for *rosh ha-sekhelim*. See Nemoy 1952: 30.
10 Simon 1991: 212–3. For al-Kumisi's strong anti-scientific and anti-traditional influence on Salmon ben Jeroham and Jafet ben Ali, see *idem*: 214.
11 Nemoy 1952: 43.
12 *Ibid.*: 44. Al-Kirkisani 'wielded too little practical influence among his fellow-Karaites to be regarded by Sa'adia as a formidable opponent.' This may also explain why he is not mentioned by name by ibn Ezra in either the *Introductions* or the *Commentaries*.
13 Sirat 1985: 42.
14 'Ve-ha-maskil yavin'. See *Commentary on Genesis* 1:1.
15 Nemoy 1952: 61.
16 Sirat 1985: 38. For a more detailed investigation of Karaite and Rabbanite attitudes to the holy script, see Sirat, La Bible hébraïque et les livres qui la portent', in Walfish (ed.) 1993: 239.
17 Nemoy 1952: 63. For a similar, far earlier, rabbinic view, see *Babylonian Talmud Berakhot* 31b.

NOTES

18 For Muslim influences on al-Kirkisani, see Sirat 1985: 44. For al-Kirkisani's influence on ben Hofni concerning astrology and magic, see Vajda 1947: 64, n. 1.
19 Nemoy 1952: 69. He describes 'Salmon's extraordinary hatred of Sa'adiah, and the violent language he used in referring to him'. Sa'adiah may have insulted him personally.
20 *Ibid*: 71, 341–3.
21 For biblical antecedents, see *Joshua* 10:13, where the '*Book of Yashar*' is said to record that the sun miraculously stood still. *Psalms* 118:27, '*God is the Lord who has enlightened us. Bind the sacrifice with cords up to the corners of the altar.*' *Ezekiel* 3: 1–4, where the son of man ingests God's words and then prophesies them through 'regurgitation' to the people. *Proverbs* 3:18, in which the Torah is compared to the Tree of Life. Those who 'grasp' it gain true understanding.
22 Sirat 1985: 38. Salman's 'opposition to every object of study other than religion extended to Euclid, to Hebrew grammar, and to foreign languages, although he himself also wrote in Arabic'. He also introduced the idea of 'roots' to describe knowledge of scripture, just as, in another context, ibn Ezra describes the superior scriptural and interpretative knowledge of the ancient rabbis, like Onkelos, as akin to 'knowing the roots'. See *Path Five*.
23 Simon 1991: 215. For a possible anti-Rabbanite link between Salmon and the Spanish Jewish convert to Christianity, Petrus Alfonsi of Huesca, see Fishbane 1998: 30–2.
24 Following Weiser 1977a, Frank states that Jafet is mentioned explicitly twenty eight times, although I have found only twenty seven. He features mainly in the *Commentary on Exodus*. See 'Karaite Exegetes', *op. cit.*, 1990: 103, n. 16.
25 Sirat 1985: 42, 43, 47, 100.
26 *Ibid.*: 77.
27 Simon 1991: 214–5. Also see the quotation from *Path Two*, mentioned above with reference to Benjamin, citing Karaite deviators and meanderers.
28 Nemoy 1952: 233.
29 For this and previous quotations, see *ibid.*: 109–22.
30 Both words stem from the same root: 'rise up'.
31 Simon 1991: 331.
32 But see Weiser 1977a: 63.
33 Ibn Ezra is ambivalent about the relative primacy of reason and revelation. However, it is probably true to say that he regarded the preservation of tradition as the end–goal of exegesis. The rationalist Gaon, Shmuel ben Hofni, was highly regarded by Joseph and shared his disdain for the unashamedly anthropomorphic *Shi'ur Qoma*, whilst Ibn Ezra defended it.
34 Nemoy 1952: 124. Jeshua's *Shorter Commentary on the Torah* dates from 1054, and was thus current in ibn Ezra's time.
35 Husik 1916: 55–8.
36 Guttman 1964: 81. There were definite kalamic influences on ibn Ezra's work, too, one of which appears in *Path Four*. See Levin 1969: 197–8.

37 He is the only Karaite to be addressed as 'Rabbi' in ibn Ezra's commentaries. Contrast with ibn Ezra's negative attitude towards him in *Path Two*.
38 For further discussion of the letter *vav*, see *Path Two*.
39 See the far more extreme anti-Karaite polemic on this subject in *Path Two*.

7 THE GE'ONIM

1 Jacobs 1984: 210–11.
2 Steinsaltz 1976: 33–4.
3 Unless otherwise stated, all references are to the *Babylonian*, rather than the *Palestinian Talmud*.
4 Faur 1986: 318. Groner 1985: 4–5.
5 Newman 1969: 35.
6 Groner 1985: 7–8.
7 *Ibid.*: 9.
8 Saperstein 1980: 14–15.
9 For an earlier date, see J. Heinemann, 'The Nature of the Aggadah', in Hartman and Budick (eds) 1986: 52.
10 Saperstein 1980: 3–5. For example: 'the words of your sages seem to be nothing other than the words of jesters in schools for children'. Compare with ibn Ezra in *Path Four* and *Path Five* respectively. Midrashim 'are good for others, directing beginners on the path to understanding', whilst massoretic 'explanations are totally puerile'.
11 Saperstein 1980: 7.
12 *Ibid*: 8. Also see Chapter Six.
13 J. Goldin, 'The Freedom and Restraint of Haggadah', in Hartman and Budick (eds) 1986: 61, 65–6.
14 For a similar development in Christianity, see Chapter Four.
15 Greenstein, 'Medieval Bible Commentaries', in Holtz (ed.) 1984: 216.
16 Taken from *Talmud Yevamot* 11b, 24a, *Shabbat* 63a; *Midrash Numbers Rabbah* 13:15, respectively.
17 For the debate on the subject see Friedlaender 1877b: 130, ns 1, 2. Weiser 1977a: 1, n. 13, 54–5. Simon, 'Ibn Ezra's Harsh Language and Biting Humor: Real Denunciation or Hispanic Mannerism?', in Díaz Esteban (ed.) 1990: 325–34. *Idem*, 'The Spanish School of Biblical Interpretation', in Beinart (ed.) 1992: 117–28. *Idem*, 'Who was the Proponent of Lexical Substitution whom Ibn Ezra Denounced as a Prater and a Madman?', in Walfish (ed.) 1993: 217–32. Weiss Halivni 1991: 142, 219–20, n. 31.
18 Guttman 1964: 88–9. Husik 1916: 16. In Chapter Six the 'glory' was mentioned with reference to the Karaite, Benjamin.
19 Husik 1916: 2.
20 *Ibid.*: 5–6; Vajda 1947: 69.
21 In ibn Ezra, the book is entitled *Sefer-ha-Rof'aim*, but its actual name is *Musar-ha-Rof'aim*. This is the only book by Israeli which refers to the Bible. See Sirat 1985: 59.
22 Guttmann 1964: 84. Husik: 14.

23 Sirat 1985: 21. Vajda 1947: 45 translates the Hebrew phrase 'rosh ha-medabrim be-kol makom' as 'l'initiateur universel', implying originality as well as importance. Also see Malter 1941: 273.

24 Malter 1941: 160.

25 See commentary on *Ecclesiastes* 5:1 and comments by Malter 1941: 153–4.

26 In this context, 'purity' refers to grammatically accurate language.

27 Goodman 1992a: 47.

28 Sirat 1985: 21.

29 Ibn Ezra's stricture was not extended to Sa'adiah's translations of the Bible into Arabic, including Arabic script. Ibn Ezra justifies these translations as demonstrating to the majority Muslim population that Arabic-speaking Jews were not ignorant of legal parts of the Torah. See Weiser 1977a: 22.

30 Simon, 'Harsh Language', *op. cit.*, 1990: 329.

31 Husik 1916: 27–8, 35. For a different emphasis see Vajda 1947: 50. For a compromise position, see Guttmann 1964: 62–5.

32 Wolfson 1973: 564–5.

33 Sirat 1985: 22.

34 Despite Simon's view that ibn Ezra follows Sa'adiah in denying any incompatibility between the text, the senses and reason. See Simon, *op. cit.*, 1992: 130.

35 Malter 1941: 195–6.

36 Simon 1991: 24.

37 Simon, 'Spanish School', *op. cit.*, 1992: 131.

38 Malter 1941: 175–6.

39 Weiss Halivni 1991: 80–1. Italics added. Ibn Ganach, otherwise known as ibn Janah, died in 1040.

40 Saperstein 1980: 10, 217, n. 40.

41 Groner 1985: 169.

42 See Weiser 1977a: 68–9.

43 Kasher 1928/9: 268, n. 89.

44 Saperstein 1980: 10–12; 217, n. 42. Also see Heinemann, 'Aggadah', *op. cit.*, 1986: 52–3 and, for parallel with ibn Ezra, Goldin, 'Haggadah', *op. cit.*, 1986: 58–61.

45 Saperstein 1980: 12–13.

46 Groner 1985: 133, n. 1.

47 For the meaning of 'deposited' and 'transmitted', see Faur 1986: 102. Groner 1985: 133, n. 3.

48 Groner 1985: 16–17.

49 Faur 1986: 124.

50 See Sarna, 'Abraham ibn Ezra as an Exegete', in Twersky and Harris (eds) 1993: 19–20.

8 INTRODUCTION TO THE TORAH: TRANSLATION AND COMMENTARY

1 For criticisms of the Weiser edition, see Simon 1976a: 647–54.

2 *Ibid.*: 646.

3 For more on the role of the *modern* interpreter, see Fishbane 1998: 4–5.

4 Also see Weiser 1977a 1, n. 3.

5 For ibn Ezra's phrase: 'wisdom is to the soul as food is to the body', see Friedlaender 1877a: 95 and *idem* 1873: 252–3.

6 For a modern psychological approach to the concept of the 'eyes of the soul', see Wilber 1979: 4ff. He is unaware of Jewish precedents.

7 See *Torat Haim* I 1986: 10.

8 For more on the circle motif, see J. Harris, 'Ibn Ezra in Modern Perspective', in Twersky and Harris 1993: 152. For midrashic allusions to *Tohu* (*Genesis* 1:2: often translated as 'formless' and interpreted as 'confusion'), representing the thread or green line surrounding the world at the beginning of creation, see Urbach 1979, p. 195 and p. 774. I am indebted to mediaeval mathematics expert, Jonathan Broido, for suggesting that the phrase *keqav ha-rakhav hu ha-khut ha-sovev be-tkhilah* could also be translated as 'the line that generates it by revolution', thereby depicting a spiral motion. The 'circumference' would then be a 'sweeping line'.

9 However, for an alternative interpretation involving the concept of *Tohu* as the circumference of the world, which produces darkness, in contrast to *Bohu* (void), which produces light, see Urbach 1979: 195, 774.

10 Also see Friedlaender 1877a: 95 and *idem* 1873: 253.

11 For an overview of *midrashic* definitions of the term *middah*, see Fishbane 1998: 56–72.

12 Also see Weiser 1977a: 2, n. 27.

13 For Karaite definition of *ha'atakah*, see Z. Ankori, 'Some Aspects of Karaite–Rabbanite Relations in Byzantium on the Eve of the First Crusade', in Chazan (ed.) 1976: 177ff, 228ff.

14 Ankori, 'Relations', *op. cit.*, 1976: 201–2, n. 73.

15 See Schlüter 1982.

16 Weiser 1977a translates as 'led astray'. See 4, f. 67.

17 See Nemoy 1952: 118, n. 17.

18 However, for terminological antecedents, see Ankori, 'Relations', *op. cit.*, 1976: 168. He cites Tobias ben Eliezer, the author of the midrashic anthology, *Lekakh Tov*, whom ibn Ezra criticises in *Path Four*!

19 See Schachter 1986: 147. Z. Langermann, 'Some Astrological Themes in the Thought of Abraham Ibn Ezra', in Twersky and Harris (eds) 1993: 38.

20 For Karaite views on the definition of Aviv, see Ankori, 'Relations', *op. cit.*, 1976: 195ff. For political ramifications, see *idem*: 203–4.

21 For possible similarities between Byzantine Karaites and their Greek Orthodox compatriots with regard to Pentecost, see Ankori, 'Relations', *op. cit.*, 1976: 190.

22 See Schachter 1986: 135–6.

23 For Karaite lunar observance, see Ankori, 'Relations', *op. cit.*, 1976: 193 ff.

24 For precedent see Tobias ben Eliezer, cited by Ankori, *op. cit.*, 1976: 221.

25 See 'Abraham ibn Ezra as an Exegete', in Twersky and Harris (eds) 1993: 5.

26 For use of verb *ta'ah* with reference to the Karaites, see Ankori, 'Relations', *op. cit.*, 1976: 192.
27 However, also see Boyarin 1995, 31ff.
28 For relations between traditionalists and Karaites in this area, see Ankori, 'Relations', *op. cit.*, 1976: For Tobias' exegetical approach see *idem*: 186. Also see N. de Lange, 'Abraham ibn Ezra and Byzantium', in Díaz Esteban (ed.) 1990: 182–3. De Lange depicts a culture far more scientifically and grammatically aware than that conceded by ibn Ezra.
29 See de Lange, *ibid*: 182.
30 See Ankori, 'Relations', *op. cit.*, 1976: 188–9.
31 For more on this concept in philosophical circles, see C. Manekin, 'Hebrew philosophy in the fourteenth and fifteenth centuries: an overview', in Frank and Leaman (eds) 1997: 353–8.
32 See Simon 1965: 92–138.
33 For examples, see Urbach 1979: 586–90, 600, 616–7.
34 Also see Fishbane 1998: 22–3, 41–55 and especially 196, n. 31, where ibn Ezra's interpretation is specifically mentioned.
35 Also see Urbach 1979: 93–4.
36 See Urbach 1979: 50–7, 306, 537, 578–9, 592, 611–2.
37 Also see J. Goldin, 'The Freedom and Restraint of Haggadah', in Hartman and Budick (eds) 1986: 62. Urbach 1979: 684–5.
38 For the link between the destruction of the Temple and the advent of the Messiah, see Urbach 1979: 655, 665–6. For the link between 'the days of the Messiah' and the fulfilment of Torah study, see *idem*: 313, 671. For the link between light and the Messiah, see Fishbane 1998: 74–5.
39 See Gruenwald 1971: 146.
40 For an interesting example of an eleventh-century meditative practice, stemming from Barcelona and Narbonne and based on recitating the *Shema*, whilst moving the head in the six directions, see Fishbane 1998: 119–20.
41 See Weiser 1977a: 9.
42 See 'Exegete', *op. cit.*, 1993: 7.
43 Weiser 1977a: 10, n. 184.
44 See Simon 1965: 114.
45 See Weiss Halivni 1991: 63–4. Also see Simon 1965: 111–39.
46 For the earlier tradition regarding the multiplication of each divine word into seventy languages, see Babylonian Talmud *Shabbat* 88b. For Muslim parallels to the concept of *panim*, see Talmage 'Apples of Gold', in Green (ed.) 1986: 319.

9 IBN EZRA'S PHILOSOPHICAL GRAMMAR

1 Compare the brevity of treatment in Guttmann 1964, Vajda 1947 and Frank and Leaman (eds) 1997 with the extended treatment in Sirat 1985.
2 See Simon, 'The Spanish School of Biblical Interpretation', in Beinart (ed.) 1992: 135–6.
3 For term, see Wittgenstein 1969.
4 Abrams 1993: 399.

5 See B. Septimus, '"Open Rebuke and Concealed Love": Nahmanides and the Andalusian Tradition', in Twersky (ed.) 1983: 23–4.
6 Handelman 1982: xiv–xv.
7 *Ibid.*: 14.
8 *Ibid.*: 30–1, 52, 55. For debate, see Handelman 1985 and Stern 1984, 1985 and 1988.
9 For a critical attitude to Handelman, see Boyarin 1995: 27.
10 Boyarin 1990: xii.
11 *Ibid.*: 36–7.
12 *Ibid.*: 22.
13 *Ibid.*: 50, 123.
14 See Chapter Three.
15 Idel, 'Jewish Thought in Medieval Spain', in Beinart (ed.) 1992: 266.
16 'Fue ... un gigante del espíritu para quien sólo lo que concernía a su pueblo tenía valor trascendental.' H. Beinart, 'España y el Occidente en los Dias de Abraham ibn Ezra', in Díaz Esteban (ed.) 1990: 38.

BIBLIOGRAPHY AND FURTHER READING

Texts by ibn Ezra in chronological order

Perushe ha-Torah le-Rabbenu Avraham ibn Ezra 1: *Bereshit* (1977a). A. Weiser (ed.). Jerusalem: Mossad ha-Rav Kook.

Abraham Ibn Esra's Kommentar Zu Genesis Kapitel 1 (1973). L. Prijs (ed.). Wiesbaden: Franz Steiner GMBH.

Perushe ha-Torah le-Rabbenu Avraham ibn Ezra 2: *Shemot* (1977b). A. Weiser (ed.). Jerusalem: Mossad ha-Rav Kook.

The Commentary of Ibn Ezra on Isaiah 3 (1877a). M. Friedlaender (ed.). London: Trübner.

Yesod Dikduk hu Sfat Yeter (1984). N. Allony (ed.). Jerusalem: Mossad ha-Rav Kook.

Safah Berurah (1839). G. H. Lippmann (ed.). Fürth: D. I. Zürndorff.

'He'tek Perush ha-Rav A. ibn Ezra al ha-Torah' (1877b). In M. Friedlaender (ed.). *Essays on the Writings of Abraham ibn Ezra* 4. London: Trübner: 1–68.

Yesod Mora (1840). J. Baer (ed.). Frankfurt am Main.

Translations of ibn Ezra texts

Cantera, F. and Levy, R. (1939). *The Beginning of Wisdom: An Astrological Treatise by Abraham ibn Ezra*. Baltimore: Johns Hopkins University Press.

Egers, J. (ed. and tr.) (1886). *Divan des Abraham ibn Esra mit seiner Allegorie Hai Ben Mekiz*. Berlin: Itskawsky.

Nutt, J. W. (ed. and tr.) (1870). *Two Treatises on Verbs Containing Feeble and Double Letters*. London and Berlin: Asher.

Oles, M. A. (1958). 'A Translation of the Commentary of Abraham Ibn Ezra on Genesis with a Critical Introduction'. Cincinnati, Ohio: Hebrew Union College. Unpublished PhD Dissertation.

Rosin, D. (1885). 'Gereimte Einleitung zum unvollständig vorliegenden Pentateuch-Commentar', in *Reime und Gedichte des Abraham Ibn Ezra* 1 (34). Breslau: 56–73.

Schachter, J. F. (1986). *Commentary of Abraham ibn Ezra on the Pentateuch* **3**: *Leviticus*. Hoboken, N.J.: Ktav.
Strickman, N. M. and Silver, A. M. (1988–99). *Ibn Ezra's Commentary on the Pentateuch*. New York: Menorah.

Jewish textual sources

Authorised Daily Prayer Book of the United Hebrew Congregations of the Commonwealth. (1992). S. Singer (tr.) I. Jakobovits and J. Sacks (centenary eds). Cambridge: Press Syndicate of the University of Cambridge.
Daily Prayer Book: Ha-Siddur Ha-Shalem. (1949). P. Birnbaum (tr.) New York: Hebrew Publishing Company.
Encyclopedia of Biblical Interpretation **1**. (1953). M. M. Kasher. New York: American Biblical Encyclopedia Society.
Jerusalem Bible. (1992). Jerusalem: Koren.
Midrash Bereshit Rabbah **1**. (1965). J. Theodor and Ch. Albeck (eds). Jerusalem: Wahrmann.
Midrash on Psalms. (2 vols) (1959). W. G. Braude (tr.). New Haven: Yale University Press.
Midrash Rabbah. (10 vols) (1939). H. Freedman and M. Simon (eds). London: Soncino.
Midrash Tanhuma **1**. (1963/4). S. Buber (ed.). Jerusalem: Ortsel.
Midrash Tanhuma **1**: *Genesis*. (1989). J. T. Townsend (ed. and tr.). Hoboken, N.J.: Ktav.
Mikra'ot Gedolot. (1975/6). Jerusalem: Eshkol.
Pirke de R. Eliezer. (1981). G. Friedlander (ed. and tr.). 4th ed. New York: Sepher-Hermon.
Ramban: Commentary on the Torah (1, 2: *Genesis* and *Exodus*). (1971–3). C. B. Chavel (tr. and annot.). New York: Shilo Publishing House.
Sefer Yetzira 'A Preliminary Critical Edition of Sefer Yezira' (1971). I. Gruenwald (tr.). *Israel Oriental Studies* **1** (**38**) Tel Aviv: 132–77.
Torah Shelemah **1, 2** (1926/7–1928/9). M. M. Kasher (ed.). Jerusalem: Weiss.
Torat-Haim. (1986). Jerusalem: Mossad ha-Rav Kook.
Talmud Bavli. (34 vols) (1935–52). I. Epstein (ed.). M. Simon (tr.). London: Soncino.
Talmud Bavli. (20 vols) (1981). Ramat Gan: Ortsel.

General bibliography

Abrams, M. H. (1993). *The Norton Anthology of English Literature* **2**. New York: W. W. Norton.
Abramson, S. (1970). 'Iggeret Rav Yehudah ha-Levi le-Rav Moshe ben Ezra', in S. Abramson and A. Mirsky (eds). *Sefer Haim Shirmann*. Jerusalem: Schocken: 397–403.

Abrahamov, B. (1993). 'Necessary Knowledge in Islamic Theology'. *British Journal of Middle Eastern Studies.* **20** (1): 20–32.

Ackroyd, P. R. and Evans, C. F. (eds). (1970). *The Cambridge History of the Bible* 1. Cambridge: Cambridge University Press.

Alexander, P. S. (1992). 'Pre-emptive Exegesis: Genesis Rabba's Reading of the Story of Creation'. *Journal of Jewish Studies* 43: 230–45.

Altmann, A. (1969). *Studies in Religious Philosophy and Mysticism.* London: Routledge and Kegan Paul.

——. (1972). 'Maimonides' Four Perfections'. *Israel Oriental Studies* 2. Tel Aviv: University of Tel Aviv: 15–24.

Altmann, A. and Stern, S. (1958). *Isaac Israeli: A Neoplatonic Philosopher of the Early Tenth Century.* Oxford: Clarendon Press.

Anderson, G. (1989). 'Celibacy or Consummation in the Garden? Reflections on Early Jewish and Christian Interpretations of the Garden of Eden'. *Harvard Theological Review* 82: 121–48.

Ashtor, E. (1973–84). *The Jews in Muslim Spain.* (3 vols). Philadelphia: Jewish Publication Society of America.

Bacher, W. (1876). *Abraham ibn Esra's Einleitung zu seinem Pentateuch-Commentar.* Vienna: Karl Gerold's Sohn.

Baer, I. (1961). *A History of the Jews in Christian Spain* 1. Philadelphia: Jewish Publication Society of America.

Baron. S. W. (18 vols). (1952–83). *A Social and Religious History of the Jews.* New York: Columbia University Press.

Bazak, J. (ed.). (1977–8). *Jewish Law and Jewish Life: Selected Rabbinical Responses* 1–8. New York: Union of American Hebrew Congregations.

Beinart, H. (ed.). (1992). *Moreshet Sepharad: The Sephardi Legacy* 1. Jerusalem: Magnes Press.

Ben-Menahem, N. (1978). *Inyanei-ibn Ezra.* Jerusalem: Mossad ha-Rav Kook.

Ben Sasson, H. H. (ed.). (1976). *A History of the Jewish People.* London. Weidenfeld and Nicolson.

Ben-Shammai, H. (1983). 'Simon, Uriel: *Arba Gisot le-Sefer-Tehillim me-R. Sa'adiah Gaon ad R. Avraham ibn Ezra'. Kiryat Sefer* 58: 400–6.

Berlin, A. (1991). 'The Medieval Jewish Reading of Psalms'. *Prooftexts* 11: 303–7.

——. (1992). 'Azariah de' Rossi on Biblical Poetry'. *Prooftexts* 12: 175–83.

Berrichon-Sedeyn, O. (tr.). (1989). 'LEO STRAUSS: Remarques sur Le Livre de La Connaissance de Maimonide'. *Revue de Métaphysique et de Morale* 3: 293–308.

Bohm, D. (1980). *Wholeness and the implicate order.* London: Routledge & Kegan Paul.

Boorstin, D. J. (1986). *The Discoverers.* Harmondsworth, Middlesex: Penguin.

Bowker, J. (1969). *Targums and Rabbinic Literature.* Cambridge: Cambridge University Press.

Boyarin, D. (1990). *Intertextuality and the Reading of Midrash*. Bloomington: Indiana University Press.
——. (1995). *Carnal Israel: Reading Sex in Talmudic Culture*. Berkeley: University of California Press.
Brague, R. (1989). 'Athènes, Jérusalem, La Mecque: L'interprétation "musulmane" de la philosophie grecque chez Leo Strauss'. *Revue de Métaphysique et de Morale* **3**: 309–36.
Brion, F. (1989). 'Le temps, l'espace et la genèse du monde selon Abû Bakr al-Râzî'. *Revue Philosophique de Louvain*. **87** (4): 139–64.
Brooke, G. (ed.). (2000). *Jewish Ways of Reading the Bible*. (Journal of Semitic Studies Supplement 11). Oxford: Oxford University Press.
Carmi, T. (ed. and tr.). (1981). *The Penguin Book of Hebrew Verse*. Harmondsworth, Middlesex: Penguin.
Chazan, R. (ed.). (1976). *Medieval Jewish Life*. New York: Ktav.
Chittick, W. C. (1992). 'The Circle of Spiritual Ascent According to Al-Qunawi'. In P. Morwedge (ed.). *Neoplatonism and Islamic Thought*. Albany: State University of New York Press: 179–209.
Daube, D. (1949). 'Rabbinic Methods of Interpretation and Hellenistic Rhetoric'. *Hebrew Union College Annual* **22**: 239–64.
Davidson, H. A. (1972). 'The Active Intellect in the *CUZARI* and Hallevi's Theory of Causality'. *Revue des Études Juives* **131**: 351–96.
——. (1987). *Proofs for Eternity, Creation and the Existence of God in Medieval Islamic and Jewish Philosophy*. New York: Oxford University Press.
De Lange, N. R. M. (1976). *Origen and the Jews: Studies in Jewish–Christian Relations in Third-Century Palestine*. Cambridge: Cambridge University Press.
Díaz Esteban, F. (ed.) (1990). *Abraham ibn Ezra y su Tiempo: Actas del Simposio Internacional 1989*. Madrid: Asociación Española de Orientalistas.
Dillon, J. M. and Long, A. A. (eds) (1988). *The Question of 'Eclecticism': Studies in Later Greek Philosophy*. Berkeley: University of California Press.
Dotan, A. (ed.) 1992. *Proceedings of the Ninth Congress of the International Organisation for Masoretic Studies: 1989*. Chico, CA. Scholars Press.
Fakhry, M. (1983). *History of Islamic Philosophy*. 2nd ed. New York: Columbia University Press.
Faur, J. (1986). *Golden Doves with Silver Dots: Semiotics and Textuality in Rabbinic Tradition*. Bloomington: Indiana University Press.
Fishbane, M. (1988). *Biblical Interpretation in Ancient Israel*. 2nd ed. New York: Oxford University Press.
——. (1998). *The Exegetical Imagination: On Jewish Thought and Theology*. Cambridge, Mass.: Harvard University Press.
Fleischer, J. L. (1925/6). 'Al D'var *Sefer ha-Yesod* u-*Sfat Yeter* le-R. A. ibn Ezra'. *Kiryat Sefer* **3**: 165–8.

——. (1928). 'Aifo met Rabbenu Avraham ibn Ezra z"l?'. *Kiryat Sefer* 5: 126–41.

——. (1928/9). 'Be-aizu Shanah met Rabbi Avraham ibn Ezra?'. *Mizrach u-Ma'arav* 2: 245–56.

——. (1929/30). 'Rabbenu Avraham ibn Ezra be-Tzarfat'. *Mizrach u-Ma'arav* 4: 352–60.

——. (1930–2). 'Rabbenu Avraham ibn Ezra be-Tzarfat'. *Mizrach u-Ma'arav* 5: 38–46, 217–24, 289–300.

——. (1932). 'Rabbenu Avraham ibn Ezra va-Avodato ha-Sifrutit be-Ir-Roma'. *Otzer-ha-Haim* 8: 97–100, 129–31, 148–50.

——. (1933). 'Rabbenu Avraham ibn Ezra va-Avodato ha-Sifrutit be-Ir-Roma'. *Otzer-ha-Haim* 9: 18–22, 85–6, 96–9, 134–6, 151–5.

——. (1933/4). 'Rabbenu Avraham ibn Ezra va-Avodato ha-Sifrutit be-Ir-Lucca she-be-Italiah'. *Ha-Soker* 2: 77–85.

——. (1935–7). 'Rabbenu Avraham ibn Ezra va-Avodato ha-Sifrutit be-Ir-Lucca she-be-Italiah'. *Ha-Soker* 4: 186–94.

Frank, D.H. and Leaman, O. (eds) (1997). *History of Jewish Philosophy*. London and New York: Routledge.

Friedlaender, M. (1877b). *Essays on the Writings of Abraham ibn Ezra* 4. London: Trübner.

Gadamer, H-G. (1979). *Truth and Method*. London: Sheed and Ward.

Gertner, M. (1978). 'The Hebrew concept of "Independence"'. In A. H. Friedlander and F. S. Worms (eds). *Meir Gertner: An Anthology*. London: B'nai Brith and The Jewish Book Council: 184–197.

Goitein, S. D. (1959). 'The Biography of Rabbi Judah Ha Levi in the Light of the Cairo Geniza Documents'. *Proceedings of the American Academy for Jewish Research*: 41–56.

——. (1968–88). *A Mediterranean Society: The Jewish Communities of the Arab World as Portrayed in the Documents of the Cairo Genizah*. (5 vols). Berkeley: University of California Press.

——. (1974). *Jews and Arabs: Their Contacts Through the Ages*. 3rd ed. New York: Schocken.

Goldenberg, R. (1992). 'The Workings of the Talmudic Mind'. *Prooftexts* 12: 185–7.

Goodman, L.E. (1990). 'Three Meanings of the Idea of Creation'. In D. B. Burrell and B. McGinn (eds). *God and Creation: An Ecumenical Symposium*. Notre Dame, Indiana: University of Notre Dame Press: 85–113.

——. (1992a). 'Jewish and Islamic Philosophy of Language'. *Sprachphilosophie* 1: Berlin and New York: Walter de Gruyter: 34–55.

——. (ed.) (1992b). *Neoplatonism and Jewish Thought*. Albany: State University of New York Press.

Green, A. (ed.) (1986). *Jewish Spirituality 1: From the Bible through the Middle Ages*. London: Routledge & Kegan Paul.

——. (1989). *Jewish Spirituality II: From the Sixteenth-Century Revival to the Present*. New York: Crossroad.

Greive, H. (1973). *Studien zum Jüdischen Neoplatonismus: Die Religionsphilosophie des Abraham Ibn Ezra.* Berlin and New York: Walter de Gruyter.

Groner, Z. (1985). *The Legal Methodology of Hai Gaon.* Chico, CA: Scholars Press.

Guttmann, J. (1964). *Philosophies of Judaism.* London: Routledge & Kegan Paul.

Halevi J. (1946). *Sefer ha-Kuzari: Book of Kuzari by Judah Hallevi.* (tr. H. Hirschfeld). New York: Pardes.

Hand, S. (ed.). (1989). *The Levinas Reader.* Oxford: Basil Blackwell.

Handelman, S. A. (1981). 'Interpretation as Devotion: Freud's Relation to Rabbinic Hermeneutics'. *Psychoanalytic Review* 68: 201–18.

——. (1982). *The Slayers of Moses: The Emergence of Rabbinic Interpretation in Modern Literary Theory.* Albany: State University of New York Press.

——. (1985). 'Fragments of the Rock: Contemporary Literary Theory and the Study of Rabbinic Texts – A Response to David Stern'. *Prooftexts* 5: 75–93.

——. (1991). *Fragments of Redemption: Jewish Thought and Literary Theory in Benjamin, Scholem, and Levinas.* Bloomington: Indiana University Press.

Harris, J. M. (1991). *Nachman Krochmal: Guiding the Perplexed of the Modern Age.* New York: New York University Press.

Hartman, G. H. and Budick, S. (eds) (1986). *Midrash and Literature.* New Haven: Yale University Press.

Holdcroft, D. (1991). *Signs, Systems and Arbitrariness.* Cambridge: Cambridge University Press.

Holtz, B. W. (ed.) (1984). *Back to the Sources: Reading the Classic Jewish Texts.* New York: Summit Books.

Husik, I. (1916). *A History of Mediaeval Jewish Philosophy.* New York: Macmillan.

Idel, M. (1979). 'The Ladder of Ascension – The Reverberations of a Medieval Motif in the Renaissance'. In I. Twersky (ed.). *Studies in Medieval Jewish History and Literature.* Cambridge, Mass.: Harvard University Press: 83–93.

——. (1988a). *Studies in Ecstatic Kabbalah.* Albany: State University of New York Press.

——. (1988b). *Kabbalah: New Perspectives.* New Haven: Yale University Press.

——. (1988c). *The Mystical Experience in Abraham Abulafia.* (tr. J. Chipman). Albany: State University of New York Press.

——. (1989). *Language, Torah and Hermeneutics in Abraham Abulafia.* (tr. M. Kallus). Albany: State University of New York Press.

——. (1990). *Golem: Jewish Magical and Mystical Traditions of the Artificial Anthropoid.* Albany: State University of New York Press.

Jackson, B. S. (1979). 'Legalism'. *Journal of Jewish Studies* 30:1–22.

———. (1984). 'The Ceremonial and the Judicial: Biblical Law as Sign and Symbol'. *Journal for the Study of the Old Testament* 30: 25–50.

———. (1985). 'Law'. In P. J. Achtemeier (ed.) *Harper's Bible Dictionary*. San Francisco: Harper and Row: 548–51.

———. (1989). 'Ideas of Law and Legal Administration: A Semiotic Approach'. In R. E. Clements (ed.). *The World of Ancient Israel: Sociological, Anthropological and Political Perspectives*. Cambridge: Cambridge University Press: 185–202.

———. (1993). 'Culture juridique juive'. In A. J. Arnaud (ed.). *Dictionnaire Encyclopédique de Théorie et de Sociologie du Droit*. Paris and Brussels: Librairie Générale de Droit et de Jurisprudence: 159–61.

———. (ed.) (1978–94). *The Jewish Law Annual*. (11 vols). Leiden: Brill.

Jacobs, L. (1961). *Studies in Talmudic Logic and Methodology*. London: Vallentine, Mitchell.

———. (1984). *The Talmudic Argument: A Study in Talmudic Reasoning and Methodology*. Cambridge: Cambridge University Press.

Jaffee, M. S. (1991). 'The Hermeneutical Model of Midrashic Studies: What it Reveals and What it Conceals'. *Prooftexts* 11: 67–76.

Japhet, S. and Salters, R. B. (eds and trs) (1985). *The Commentary of R. Samuel Ben Meir (Rashbam) on Qoheleth*. Jerusalem: Magnes Press.

Katz, S. T. (ed.). (1992). *Mysticism and Language*. New York: Oxford University Press.

Kaufmann, D. (1884). ''Muammar al-Sulami und der unbekannte Gaon in ibn Ezra's Yesod Mora'. *Monatsschrift für die Geschichte und Wissenschaft des Judentums* 33: 327–32.

Kemp, S. (1996). *Cognitive Psychology in the Middle Ages*. Westport, CT: Greenwood.

Kreisel, H. (1994). 'On the Term *Kol* in Abraham ibn Ezra: A Reappraisal. *Revue des Études Juives* 153 (1–2): 29–66.

Lampe, G. W. H. (ed.). (1969). *The Cambridge History of the Bible* 2. Cambridge: Cambridge University Press.

Lampe, G. W. H. and Woollcombe, K. J. (eds) (1957). *Essays on Typology*. London: SCM Press.

Lancaster, B. L. (1991). *Mind Brain & Human Potential: The Quest for an Understanding of Self*. Shaftesbury: Element Books.

———. (1993). *The Elements of Judaism*: Shaftesbury: Element Books.

Lauterbach, J. Z. (1910–11). 'The Ancient Jewish Allegorists in Talmud and Midrash'. *Jewish Quarterly Review* (N. S. i): 291–333, 503–31.

Leaman, O. (1985). *An Introduction to Medieval Islamic Philosophy*. Cambridge: Cambridge University Press.

———. (1988a). *Averroes and his Philosophy*. Oxford: Clarendon Press.

———. (1988b). 'Maimonides, Imagination and the Objectivity of Prophecy'. *Religion* 18: 69–80.

211

——. (1990). *Moses Maimonides*. London and New York: Routledge.
Lerner, R., Mahdi M. and Fortin, E. L. (eds) (1963). *Medieval Political Philosophy: A Sourcebook*. New York: Free Press.
Levin, I. (1969). *Avraham ibn Ezra: Hayav ve-Shirato*. Tel Aviv: ha-Kibbutz ha-Me'ukhad.
Lévinas. E. (1990). *Nine Talmudic Readings*. (tr. A. Aronowicz). Bloomington: Indiana University Press.
Lewy, H., Altmann, A. and Heinemann, I. (eds) (1969). *Three Jewish Philosophers*. New York: Atheneum.
Lifshitz, A. (1979). 'Le-Torat ha-Beri'ah shel R. Abraham ibn Ezra'. *Sinai* 84: 105–25.
——. (1982). *Pirke-Iyun be-Mishnat ha-R. ibn Ezra*. Jerusalem: Mossad ha- Rav Kook.
Loewe, R. (1964). 'The 'Plain' Meaning of Scripture in Early Jewish Exegesis'. In J. G. Weiss (ed.). *Papers of the Institute of Jewish Studies* 1: 140–85.
——. (1989). *Ibn Gabirol*. London: Peter Halban.
Maimonides, M. (1948). *The Code of Maimonides: Sanctification of the New Moon*. (tr. S. Gandz). New Haven: Yale University Press.
——. (1963). *The Guide of the Perplexed*. (ed. and tr. Sh. Pines). Chicago: University of Chicago Press.
Malter, H. (1941). *Life and Works of Saadia Gaon*. Philadelphia: Jewish Publication Society of America.
Morewedge, P. (1979). *Islamic Philosophical Theology*. Albany: State University of New York Press.
——. (ed.). (1981). *Islamic Philosophy and Mysticism*. Delmar: Caravan Books.
Morris, P. and Sawyer, D. (eds) (1992). *A Walk in the Garden: Biblical, Iconographical and Literary Images of Eden*. Sheffield: Sheffield Academic Press.
Morris, T. V. and Menzel, C. (1986). 'Absolute Creation'. *American Philosophical Quarterly* 23 (4): 353–62.
Nasr, S. H. and Leaman, O. (eds) (1996). *History of Islamic Philosophy*. London and New York: Routledge.
Nemoy, L. (1952). *Karaite Anthology*. New Haven: Yale University Press.
Netton, I. R. (1982). *Muslim Neoplatonists: An Introduction to the Thought of the Brethren of Purity*. London: George Allen and Unwin.
——. (1989). *Allah Transcendent: Studies in the Structure and Semiotics of Islamic Philosophy, Theology and Cosmology*. London: Routledge.
Neuman, A. A. (1942). *The Jews in Spain: Their Social, Political and Cultural Life during the Middle Ages*. (2 vols). Philadelphia: Jewish Publication Society of America.
Neusner, J. (1991) *The Twentieth Century Construction of "Judaism": Essays on the Religion of Torah in the History of Religion*. Atlanta: Scholars Press.

Newman, J. H. (1955). *An Essay in Aid of a Grammar of Assent*. New York: Image Books.

Newman, J. H. S. (1969). *Halachic Sources: From the Beginning to the Ninth Century*. Leiden: Brill.

Novak, D. and Samuelson, N. (eds) (1986). *Creation and the End of Days: Judaism and Scientific Cosmology* (Proceedings of the 1984 Meeting of the Academy for Jewish Philosophy). Lanham: University Press of America.

Olitzky, M. (1890). 'Die Zahlensymbolik des Abraham Ibn Esra'. *Jubelschrift für Israel Hildesheimer*. Berlin: H. Engel: 99–106.

Orschansky, G. (1900). *Abraham ibn Ezra als Philosoph*. Breslau: Th. Schatzky.

Pagels, E. (1988). *Adam, Eve and the Serpent*. New York: Random House.

Pearl, Ch. (1988). *Rashi*. London: Peter Halban.

Pines, Sh. (1980). 'Shi'ite Terms and Conceptions in Judah Halevi's *Kuzari*'. *Jerusalem Studies in Arabic and Islam* 2: 165–251.

Prijs, L. (1950). *Die Grammatikalische Terminologie Abraham ibn Esras*. Basle: Sefer.

Rawidowicz, S. (1974). 'On Interpretation'. In N. Glatzer (ed.). *Studies in Jewish Thought*. Philadelphia: Jewish Publication Society of America: 45–80.

Rojtman, B. (1998), *Black Fire on White Fire: An Essay on Jewish Hermeneutics, from Midrash to Kabbalah*. (tr. S. Rendall). Berkeley: University of California Press.

Rosen, S. (1988). *The Quarrel between Philosophy and Poetry*. New York and London: Routledge, Chapman and Hall.

Rosenberg, J. (1991). 'Grammar with a Small "g". *Prooftexts* **11**: 183–97.

Rosin, D. (1898–9). 'Die Religionsphilosophie Abraham Ibn Ezra'. *Monatsschrift für die Geschichte und Wissenschaft des Judentums* **42**: 17–33, 58–73, 108–15, 154–61, 200–14, 241–52, 305–15, 345–62, 394–407, 444–57; **43**: 22–31, 75–91, 125–33, 168–84, 231–40.

Rotenstreich, N. (1963). *The Recurring Pattern: Studies in Anti-Judaism in Modern Thought*. London: Weidenfeld and Nicolson.

Roth, C. (1948). *A Short History of the Jewish People*. 3rd ed. London: Horovitz.

Roth, N. (1983). 'Jewish Reactions to the Arabiyya and the Renaissance of Hebrew in Spain'. *Journal of Semitic Studies* 28: 63–84.

Sa'adiah Gaon. (1967). *Saadia Gaon: The Book of Beliefs and Opinions*. (tr. S. Rosenblatt). New Haven: Yale University Press.

Sacks, J. (1993). *One People: Tradition, Modernity and Jewish Unity*. London: Littman.

Saperstein, M. (1980). *Decoding the Rabbis: A Thirteenth Century Commentary on the Aggadah*. Cambridge, Mass.: Harvard University Press.

Scheindlin, R. P. (1990). 'Redemption of the Soul in Golden Age Religious Poetry'. *Prooftexts* **10**: 49–67.

Schlüter, M. (1982). *"Deraqon und Gotzendienst": Studien zur antiken jüdischen Religionsgeschichte, ausgehend von einem griechischen Lehnwort in mAZ 1113*. Frankfurt am Main: Peter Lang.

Scholem, G. (1961). *Major Trends in Jewish Mysticism*. 3rd ed. New York: Schocken.

———. (1987). *Origins of the Kabbala*. (ed. R. J. Z. Werblowsky). (tr. A. Arkush). Princeton: Jewish Publication Society of America and Princeton University Press.

Schwartz, R. (ed.) (1990). *The Book and the Text: The Bible and Literary Theory*. Cambridge, Mass.: Basil Blackwell.

Segal, E. (1991). 'Midrash and Literature: Some Medieval Views'. *Prooftexts* **11**: 57–65.

———. (1992). 'Interpreting Midrash 3: Midrash and the Tannaitic Aggada'. *Prooftexts* **12**: 188–92.

Septimus, B. (1982). *Hispano–Jewish Culture in Transition*. Cambridge, Mass.: Harvard University Press.

Shields, C. (1990). 'The Generation of Form in Aristotle'. *History of Philosophy Quarterly* **7**: 367–90.

Simon, H. and Simon, M. (1984). 'Abraham ibn Ezra', in *Geschichte der jüdischen Philosophie*. Munich: Beck: 103–8.

Simon, U. (1965). 'Le-darkho ha-parshanit shel ha-R. A. ibn Ezra al-pi sheloshet be'urav le-pasuk echad'. *Bar Ilan* **3**: 92–138.

———. (1976a). 'Perushe-ha-Torah le-rabbenu ibn Ezra al-pi kitvei-yad u-defusim rishonim ... me-et Asher Weiser'. *Kiryat Sefer* **51**: 646–54.

———. (1976b). 'Prijs, L., ed., Abraham ibn Esra's Kommentar zu Genesis Kapitel 1'. *Kiryat Sefer* **51**: 654–8.

———. (1985). 'Ibn Ezra Between Medievalism And Modernism: The Case Of Isaiah XL–LXVI'. *Studien Vetus Testamentum* **36**: 257–71.

———. (1991). *Four Approaches to the Book of Psalms: From Saadiah to Abraham Ibn Ezra*. (tr. L. J. Schramm). Albany: State University of New York Press.

Sirat, C. (1985). *A History of Jewish Philosophy in the Middle Ages*. Cambridge: Cambridge University Press.

Smalley, B. (1981). *Studies in Medieval Thought and Learning*. London: Hambledon Press.

———. (1983). *The Study of the Bible in the Middle Ages*. 3rd ed. Oxford: Basil Blackwell.

Soloveitchik, J. B. (1983). *Halakhic Man*. Philadelphia: Jewish Publication Society of America.

———. (1986). *The Halakhic Mind: An Essay on Jewish Tradition and Modern Thought*. New York: Free Press.

Staley, K. (1989). 'Al-Kindi on Creation: Aristotle's Challenge to Islam'. *Journal of the History of Ideas* **50**: 355–70.

Steiner, G. (1975). *After Babel: Aspects of Language and Translation*. New York: Oxford University Press.

Steinsaltz, A. (1976). *The Essential Talmud*. London: Weidenfeld and Nicolson.

———. (1989). *The Talmud: The Steinsaltz Edition, A Reference Guide*. (ed. and tr. I. V. Berman). New York: Random House.

Stern, D. (1984). 'Moses-cide: Midrash and Contemporary Literary Criticism'. *Prooftexts* **4**: 193–213.

———. (1985). 'Literary Criticism or Literary Homilies? Susan Handelman and the Contemporary Study of Midrash'. *Prooftexts* **5**: 96–103.

———. (1988). 'Midrash and Indeterminacy'. *Critical Inquiry* **15**: 132–61.

———. (1996). *Midrash and Theory: Ancient Jewish Exegesis and Contemporary Literary Studies*. Evanason, IL: Northwestern University Press.

Strauss, L. (1987). *Philosophy and Law: Essays Toward the Understanding of Maimonides and His Predecessors*. Philadelphia: Jewish Publication Society of America.

Twersky, I. (1982). *Studies in Jewish Law and Philosophy*. New York: Ktav.

———. (ed.) (1983). *Rabbi Moses Nahmanides (Ramban): Explorations in His Religious and Literary Virtuosity*. Cambridge, Mass.: Harvard University Press.

Twersky, I. and Harris, J. M. (eds) (1993). *Rabbi Abraham Ibn Ezra: Studies in the Writings of a Twelfth-Century Jewish Polymath*. Cambridge, Mass.: Harvard University Press.

Urbach, E. E. (1979). *The Sages: Their Concepts and Beliefs*. (2 vols). 2nd ed. (tr. I. Abrahams). Jerusalem: Magnes Press.

Vajda, G. (1947). *Introduction à la Pensée Juive du Moyen Âge*. Paris: Vrin.

Walfish, B. (1989). 'The Two Commentaries of Abraham ibn Ezra on the Book of Esther'. *Jewish Quarterly Review* **79** (4): 323–43.

Warner, M. (ed.) (1990). *The Bible as Rhetoric: Studies in Biblical Persuasion and Credibility*. London and New York: Routledge.

Watt, W. (1962). *Islamic Philosophy and Theology*. Edinburgh: Edinburgh University Press.

Wegner, J. R. (1982). 'Islamic and Talmudic Jurisprudence: The Four Roots of Islamic Law and their Talmudic Counterparts'. *American Journal of Legal History* **26**: 25–71.

Weingreen, J. (1976). *From Bible to Mishna: The Continuity of Tradition*. Manchester: Manchester University Press.

Weiss Halivni, D. (1991). *Peshat and Derash: Plain and Applied Meaning in Rabbinic Exegesis*. New York: Oxford University Press.

Whorf, B. L. (1956). *Language, Thought and Reality*. Cambridge, Mass.: MIT.

Wilber, K. (1979). 'Eye to Eye'. *Revision* (Winter/Spring): 3–25.

Wittgenstein, L. (1969). *Philosophische Grammatik*. Oxford: Basil Blackwell.

——. (1974). *Philosophical Grammar*. (tr. A. Kenny). Oxford: Basil Blackwell.

——. (1980). *Remarks on the Philosophy of Psychology* 1. (eds G. E. M. Anscombe and G. H. von Wright) (tr. G. E. M. Anscombe). Oxford: Basil Blackwell.

Wolfson, E. R. (1987). 'Circumcision, Vision of God, and Textual Interpretation: From Midrashic Trope to Mystical Symbol'. *History of Religions* 27: 189–215.

——. (1990). 'God, the Demiurge and the Intellect: On the Usage of the Word *Kol* in Abraham ibn Ezra'. *Revue des Études Juives* 149 (1–3): 77–111.

——. (1994). *Through a Speculum that Shines: Vision and Imagination in Medieval Jewish Mysticism*. Princeton, N.J.: Princeton University Press.

——. (1995a). *Along the Path: Studies in Kabbalistic Myth, Symbolism and Hermeneutics*. New York: State University of New York Press.

——. (1995b). *Circle in the Square: Studies in the Use of Gender in Kabbalistic Symbolism*. New York: State University of New York Press.

Wolfson, H. A. (1929). *Crescas' Critique of Aristotle*. Cambridge, Mass.: Harvard University Press.

——. (1973). *Studies in the History of Philosophy and Religion* 1 Cambridge, Mass.: Harvard University Press.

Yovel, Y. (1989). *Spinoza and Other Heretics: The Marrano of Reason*. Princeton N.J.: Princeton University Press.

INDEX OF WORKS CITED

NAME INDEX

Abelard, Peter 60
Abishai of Sagori 23
al-Balkhi, Hivi 20
al-Batalyawsi, ibn al-Sid 87
Alcuin (Albinus Flaccus) 59
Alexander of Aphrodisias 99
al-Farabi, abu Nasr 67, 69–74, 77,
   78, 80, 92, 95, 98, 128
Alfonsi, Petrus 194n13, 199n23
al-Ghazali, abu Hamid
   Muhammad 71, 72, 75, 80,
   88–98, 195n19, 198n83
al-Kindi, abu Yusuf Ya'qub ibn
   Ishaq 65–8, 69, 70, 78, 96,
   110, 126
al-Kirkisani, Jacob 103–14,
   198n12, 199n18
al-Kumisi, Daniel 104, 106–8, 113,
   198n10
Almosnino, Moses of Salonika
   25
al-Nahawandi, Benjamin 104–6,
   148, 199n27, 200n18
al-Razi, Muhammad 68–9
al-Sirafi, Said 74–7
Antiochenes 58, 60
Aristotle 64, 66–7, 69, 71, 72,
   80–1, 95–9, 130
Ash'arites 77–9, 88–9, 97, 98
Augustine 60–1, 194n15, 196n36

Bacher, Wilhelm 4, 32, 191n22
Bede, Venerable 60–1
ben Ali, Jafet 104, 112–15, 118,
   120, 198n4, n10, 199n24

ben David, Anan 20, 103–7, 148,
   154, 198n4
ben Eliezer, Joseph, the Spaniard
   (Bonfils Tov Elem) 9, 23, 24
ben Eliezer, Tobias 165, 202n18,
   n24, 203n28
ben Hisdai, Moshe 21
ben Hofni, Shmuel 68, 110, 124–5,
   134–8, 140–1, 146, 148,
   199n33
Benjamin of Tudela xv, 11, 13,
   187n12
ben Jeroham, Salmon 104, 110–12,
   128, 144, 194n13, 198n10,
   199n19, n22, n23
ben Judah, Jeshua, abu al-Farag
   Furkan ibn 'Asad 104, 114,
   119–21, 148, 200n37
ben Kallir, Eleazar 4–5, 127–8
ben Mashiach, Hasan 104, 115,
   148
ben Mattiya, Eleazar 23
ben Meir, Moshe 14
ben Moses, Aaron 76
ben Samuel, Jacob 115
ben Zuta (Sahl ben Masliah, abu al
   Surri Sahl) 104, 114–19, 154,
   187n30
Berlin, Naftali (the Neziv) 29, 30
Brothers of Purity 71, 73, 80, 84–8,
   94
Browning, Robert v, 1, 22, 36, 55,
   64, 101, 122, 142, 176

Coleridge, Samuel Taylor 177

221

Mu'tazilites 66, 77, 78, 110

Narboni, Moses 24
Nathan of Jehiel 3–4
Netter, Solomon Zalman 25, 190n6

Olitzky, M. 32, 191n26
Onkelos 51, 173–4, 199n22
Origen 57, 58, 59

Paul 82
Philo 57, 193n1
Plato 64, 68, 70–1, 85, 98, 196n46
Plotinus 64
Proclus 64–5, 126
Ptolemy 12, 69

Radak (David Kimhi) 23
Rambam (Moses ben Maimon;
    Maimonides) 71, 81–2, 92,
    94, 98, 126, 183, 188n44
  and ibn Ezra 8, 23–4, 33–5, 166,
    186n2
Ramban (Moses ben Nachman;
    Nachmanides) 23, 31, 180–1,
    186n1
Rashba (Solomon ben Adret) 13
Rashbam (Samuel ben Meir) 27,
    29, 41, 52, 189n88, 191n8
  and ibn Ezra 17, 20, 25, 127,
    177, 190n99, n100
Rashi (Solomon ben Isaac) 1, 17,
    23, 112, 120, 135, 168, 174,
    181, 186n1

'Rav Isaac' 125–6, 145, 147
Rosin, David 32–4

Sa'adiah Gaon 97, 124, 127–34,
    166–7, 177, 187n28
  and Ge'onim 125–6, 129, 135,
    138, 140, 178
  and ibn Ezra 5, 20, 67, 79, 97,
    104, 117–8, 120, 127–9, 133,
    137–8, 146, 185, 201n29, n34
  Islamic influences on 65, 84,
    129–30, 132
  and Karaites 75, 101, 103, 105,
    107–8, 110, 112–3, 115–16,
    119, 198n12, 199n19
Schelling, Friedrich 33
Schick, Moses 30
Schlesinger, Akiva Joseph 30
Sherira Gaon 125, 138–9, 141
Shmuel ha-Nagid 136, 139
Sofer, Moses 30, 191n18
Spinoza, Baruch, 25, 26, 190n7
Steinschneider, Moritz 23, 31–2

Tam, Jacob (Rabbenu) 16–17

Victorines 61–2, 194n17

Wessely, Naftali Herz 27
Whorf, Benjamin Lee 71
Wittgenstein, Ludwig xvii, 203n3

Yediah ha-Penini ben Abraham of
    Béziers xv, 13

SUBJECT INDEX

Academies 3, 6, 13, 30, 101–2, 123, 140, 145, 174
  see also Babylon
Acquired Intellect 74, 84, 92–3
Active Intellect 69–70, 74, 80, 84, 92–3, 99
  see also Mind
Adam 91
  in ibn Ezra 49, 51, 109–10, 113, 158, 162, 166, 180
  see also Language; Microcosm
Agent 66, 89, 120, 136
  see also Angel
Aggadah 30, 34, 47, 48, 53, 124, 128, 139, 193n19
  and ibn Ezra 8, 16
  see also Hermeneutics
Allegory 57, 183
  in Christianity xviii, 7, 9, 37, 50–1, 55–7, 61
  in ibn Ezra 16, 19, 37, 41, 57, 82, 84, 94, 120, 158–62, 164, 178, 180
  in Islam 64, 99
  in Sa'adiah 118, 133
  see also Christianity; Hermeneutics; Philosophy
Almohads 2, 13, 15, 93–4
  see also Spain
Amoraim 41, 123
  see also Mishnah
Analogy 74, 99, 116
  see also Middot
Ancient Sages 19, 41–2, 47, 51, 68, 163, 175

  see also Forefathers
Angel 46, 66, 87, 137, 140, 158, 168
  in ibn Ezra 50–1, 89, 136, 147, 180
  see also Dreams; Intellect; Prophecy
'Angleterre' xv, 17, 190n91
  see also 'End'; England
Anthropomorphisms 124
  in Ge'onim 138–9
  in ibn Ezra 79, 109, 138
  in Islam 79, 85, 94, 96
  in Karaites 109, 110, 113, 119
  see also Bible; God; Hermeneutics; Shi'ur Qoma
Anti-semitism 8, 11, 15, 30, 161, 194n13
  see also Christianity
Arabic xiv, 48, 53, 64, 77
  in Ge'onim 127, 129, 138–41, 201n29
  in ibn Ezra xv, 1, 3, 4, 8–10, 14–15, 177–80
  in Karaites 76, 102, 107, 109, 112, 115, 119, 175
  in Muslims 65, 70–4
  see also Grammar, Philosophy; Translations
Aristotelianism 8, 32, 33, 38, 66–7, 70, 75, 80, 95, 96, 120, 130, 183, 184
  see also Aristotle; Hermeneutics; Philosophy

Witness 116, 150–1, 155, 157
  see also Sign; Testimony
Word 42, 85–6, 93, 105, 181–2,
    203n46
  in ibn Ezra 82, 85–6, 158–62,
    196n39
  see also Christianity; Letter; *Milah*
Writing 42, 44, 58, 73, 76–7, 82,
    195n30
  see also Hermeneutics; Letter;
    Text
Written Torah xiii, 25, 30, 39,
    50–1, 181

in classical and mediaeval
    traditional Judaism 42, 52,
    98, 118, 122, 172
  in ibn Ezra 7, 83, 98, 133–4,
    143, 149–51, 153, 156,
    158–62, 163–4, 168
  in Karaites 101, 111, 112, 116,
    120
  see also Bible; Hermeneutics;
    Scripture; Text; Tradition

Yeshivah, *see* Academies